GUSTAVE DORÉ

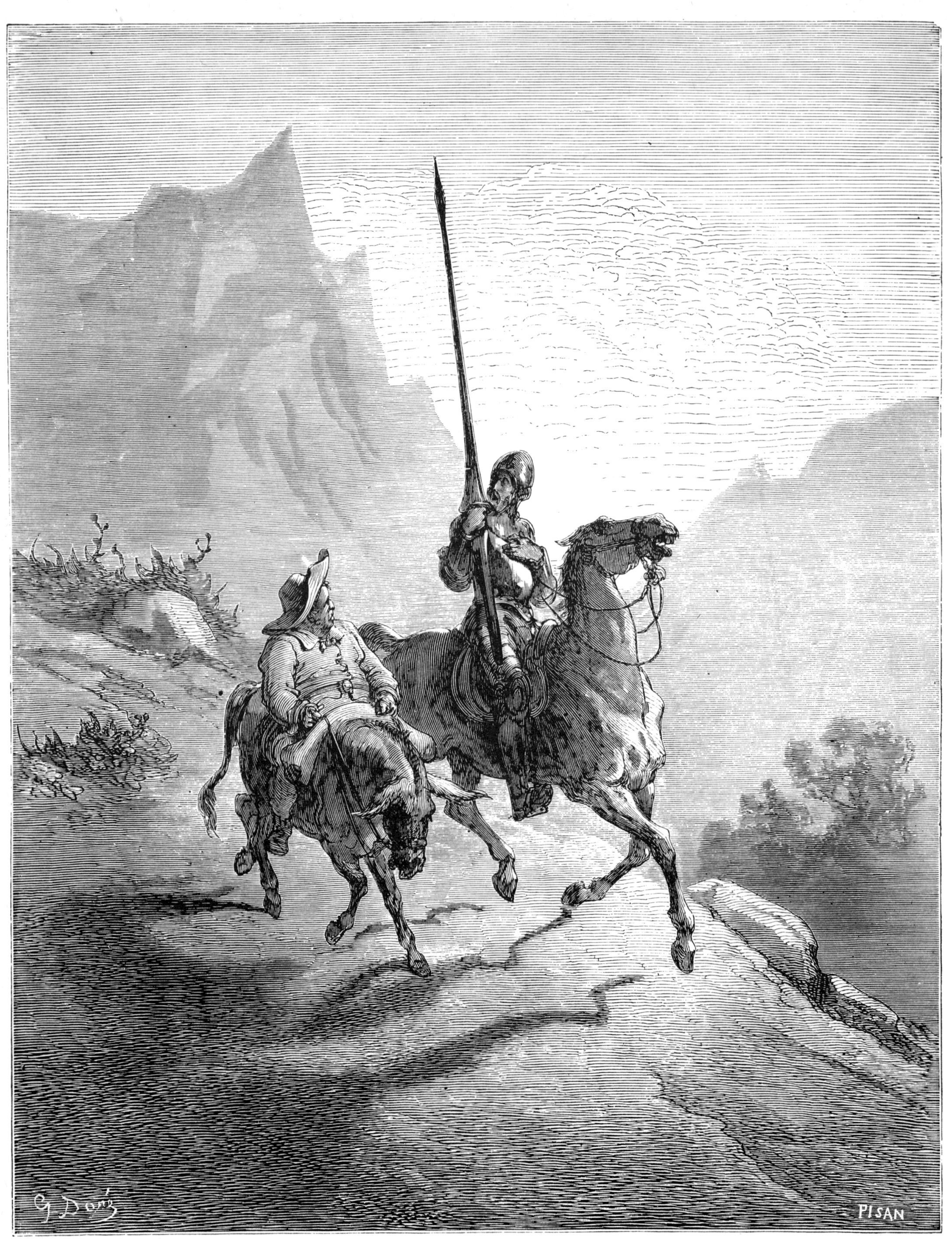

'It was yet early in the morning, at which time the sunbeams did not prove so offensive.'

GUSTAVE DORÉ

ILLUSTRATIONS to DON QUIXOTE

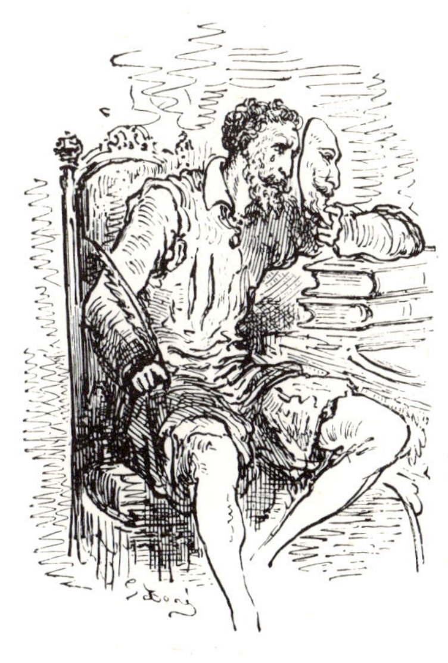

Jeannie Ruzicka

academy editions · london / st martin's press · new york

The illustrations on pages 5, 6, 7 and 8, and on the back cover appeared as chapter headings in J. W. Clark's 1880 edition of the Doré *Don Quixote.* The illustration on the title page was used originally as a tailpiece for the same edition, while those on the front cover and on page 9 are details from the full page engravings reproduced on pages 47 and 111, respectively, in the current volume.

This edition first published in Great Britain in 1974 by
Academy Editions 7 Holland Street London W8

This edition first published in the U.S.A. in 1974 by
St. Martin's Press Inc. 175 Fifth Avenue New York N.Y. 10010

Library of Congress Catalog Card Number 74-80991

Printed and bound in Great Britain at the University Printing
House, Cambridge.

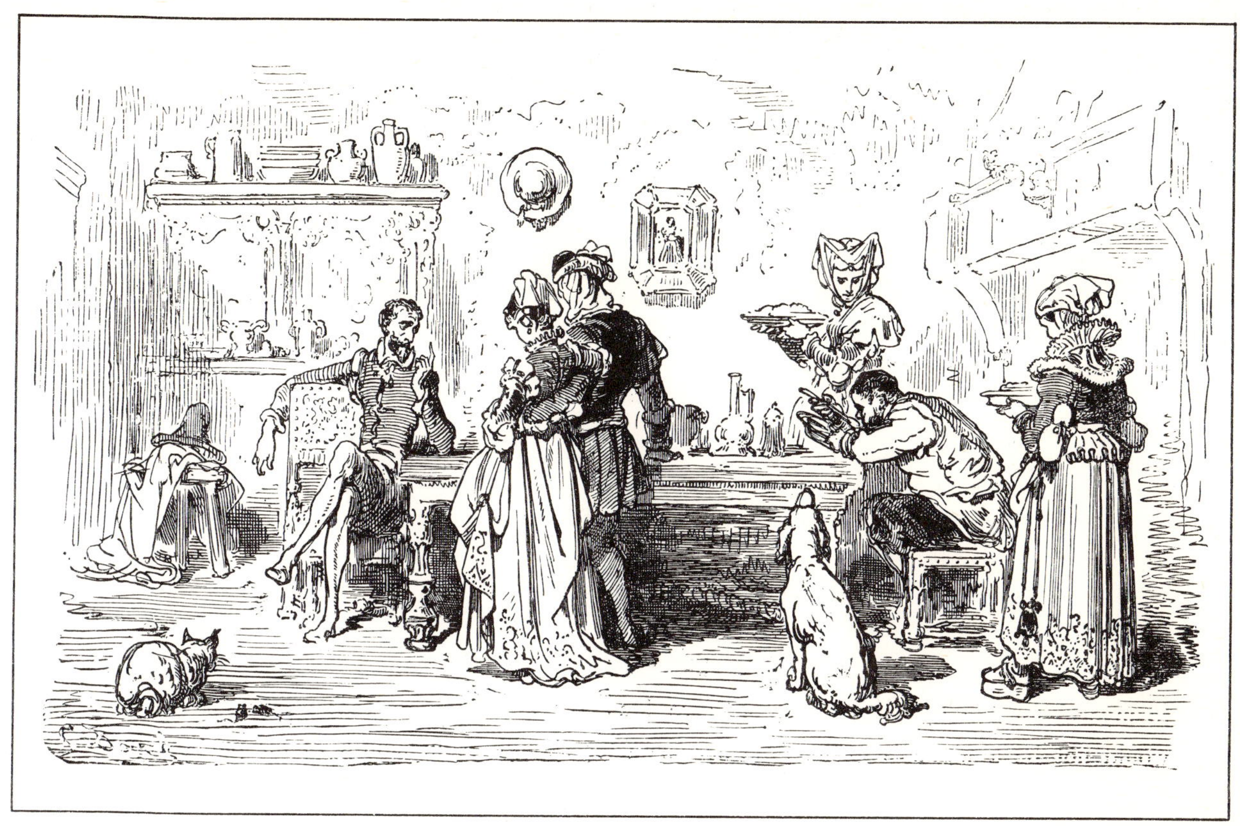

INTRODUCTION

Gustave Doré was perhaps the last of the great nineteenth century illustrators and certainly was the era's most prolific graphic artist. He worked quickly and with great facility, often undertaking four or five projects simultaneously and employing a virtual assembly line of engravers. The result of this process was a vast number of lithographs, wood cuts and sketches, many of which were ephemeral or second-rate but some of which were also the masterly illustrations to The Bible, *Don Quixote* and the *Divine Comedy.* Doré's oeuvre is an almost bewilderingly varied body of work, one that combines both unsurpassed draughtsmanship and staggering invention. He excelled at portraying the remote and the weird, at suggesting scenes of horror and awe, drawn with elaborate detail and an often morbid extravagance. As with other artists and illustrators of the period in both England and France, Doré was possessed by a Romantic attraction to the sublime and the monumental. This consciousness of the violence and immensity of nature is most apparent in the unearthly surrealist, forbidding landscapes and in the tumultuous spaces, which marked the work of Doré as much as it did that of such artists of similar vision as John Martin. But in addition to his melodramatic Romanticism and often wilful perversity, Doré was initially, perhaps even fundamentally, a satirist, and the satirical exaggeration of the grotesque, combined with his occasionally humorous approach to subjects, remains the most significant element in all of his work.

Born in Strasbourg in 1833, Doré began to draw as a young child, exhibiting the same dexterity and imagination which characterized his mature work. By the age of sixteen his career as a professional artist was under way, and he was contributing a weekly cartoon to M. Phillipon's satirical *Journal pour rire.* Greatly influenced by Grandville, Doré's drawings were, on the one hand, broadly humorous and good-natured, while being at the same time less politically biting than Daumier's,

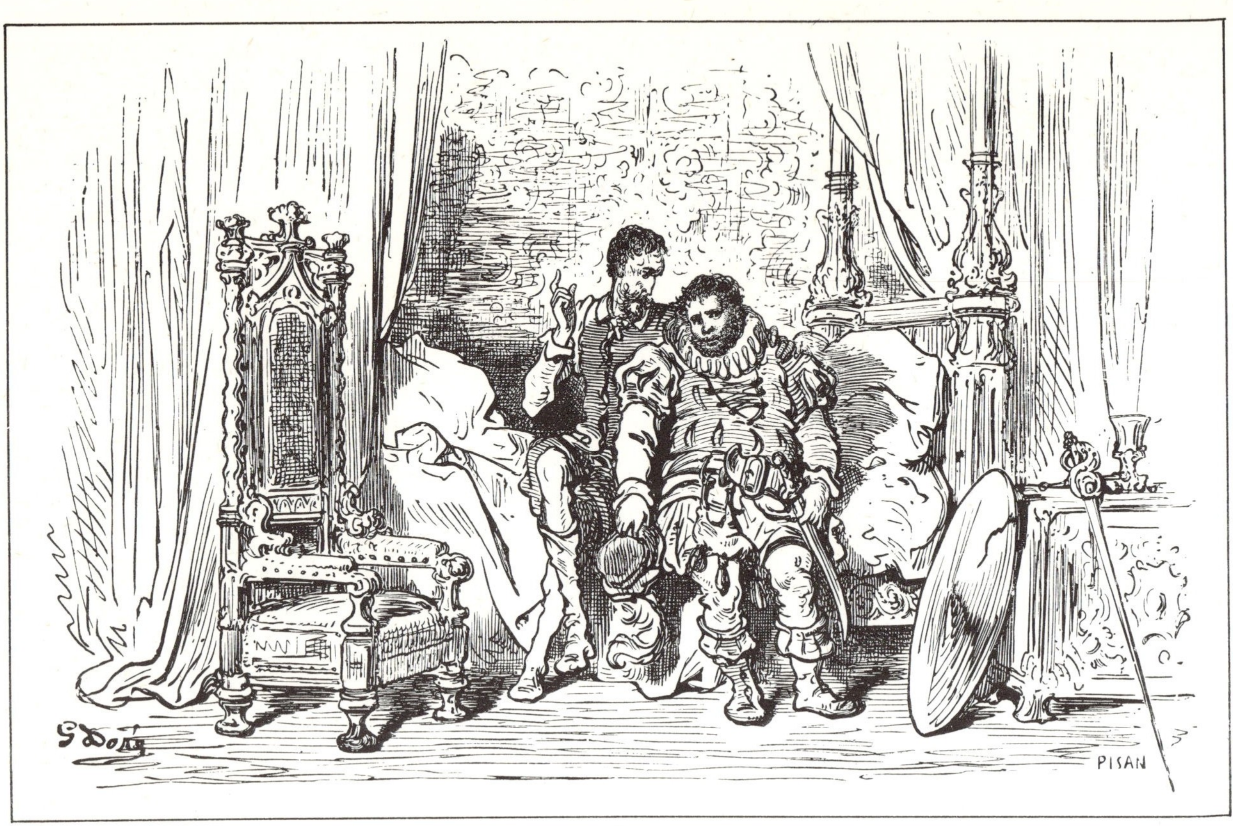

who, as a former contributor, had involved the magazine in censorship problems. Not surprisingly, Phillipon encouraged Doré, and for the next few years his work appeared frequently in Parisian journals. In 1854, Doré published an illustrated edition of Rabelais, a work which, with its combination of boisterous humour and the picaresque, anticipated the more accomplished designs for *Don Quixote*. This book established Doré's reputation as an illustrator, and its success brought numerous commissions. Doré's graphic interpretation of the classics was so remarkable that he planned to illustrate and to bring out in uniform format an extensive series of literary masterpieces. He was, as his contemporaries attested, irrepressibly, albeit amiably, ambitious, and although the vast project was not completed, it did result in the famous designs for works by Coleridge, Milton, Perrault, Balzac and Dante, some two hundred books in all including quasi-realistic travel accounts and pure fantasy. Doré's glittering success in France was matched by the acclaim which greeted his work across the Channel, and in England he is still best known, perhaps, for his vision of mid-nineteenth century *London*. While depicting all sections of society in High Victorian London, Doré produced some of his most remarkable work in his staggeringly detailed and evocative treatment of the London poor, a series of almost Dantesque scenes which document the hard and grinding existence of the slums more tellingly than any passage in Dickens. The qualities of realistic observation, totally divorced from his accustomed concoction of the Gothic, the sublime and the fantastic, marks *London* as unique in the canon of Doré's work and serves to underline the variety of his style. Yet despite the critical and popular success of his work, Doré denigrated his achievement and contemptuously dismissed it as journalism. Afraid of being type-cast, he experimented with different media, and as early as 1853 he decided to devote himself to painting and sculpture.

He produced paintings of vast size with appropriately edifying subjects, but although these were entered regularly at the Salon, they were, with equal regularity, ignored. These works did achieve some commercial, if not critical, success in England, where the Doré gallery was created to maintain a permanent collection of his work. But the indifference of the Parisian artistic community, summed up in one newspaper's New Year's prediction that 'in the next year M. Doré will continue to make more crazy paintings and boring sculpture', proved to be the major disappointment in what was

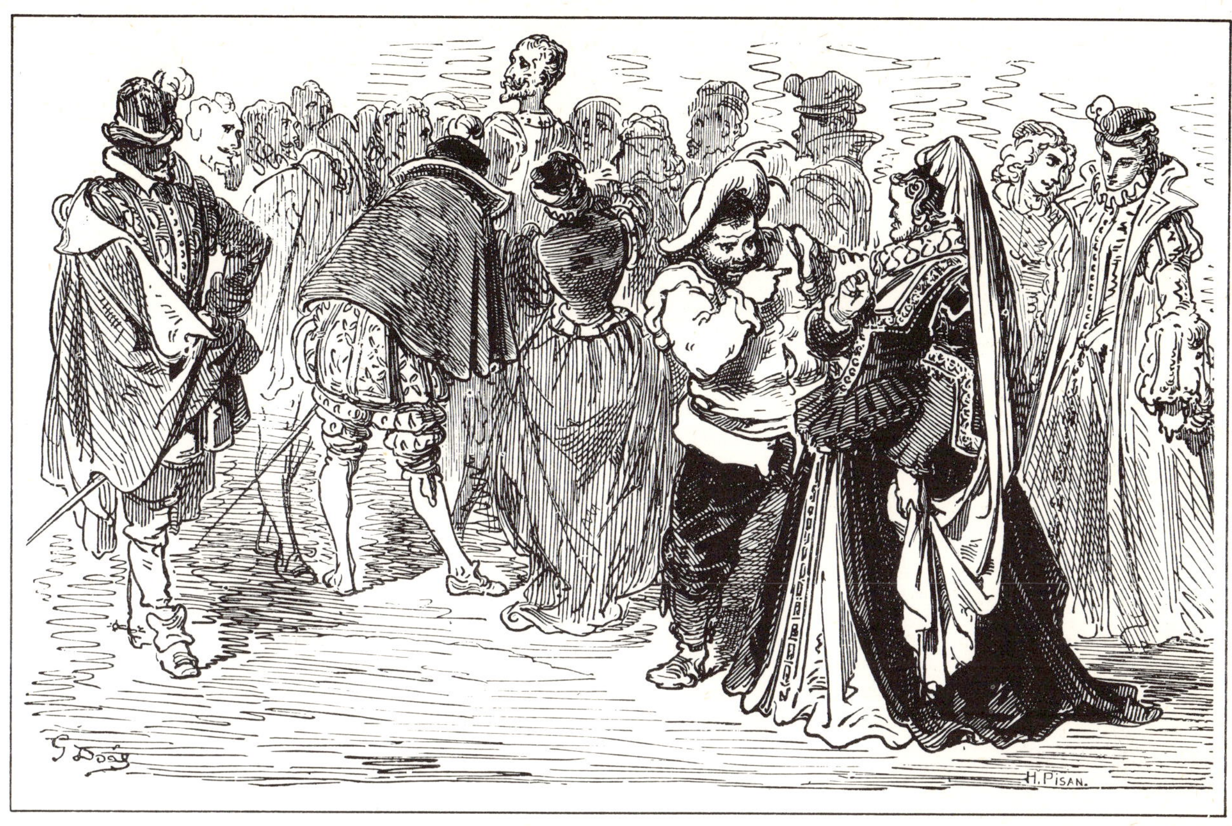

otherwise an unusually happy life. At his death in 1883, his commercial success seemed little compensation for the academic esteem which had eluded him.

Doré's great achievement clearly lay in linear rather than painterly form, and here he exerted a strong influence on the history of engraving and illustration. His rigorous demands on craftsmen and later his experiments with large scale engravings generated a greater elaboration of detail and gave to wood engraving some of the effects of painting. This technical achievement is clearly evident in the illustrations to *Don Quixote,* where, to ensure uniformity, Doré commissioned all 231 illustrations of the original edition from a single engraver, Héliodore Joseph Pisan.

These illustrations for Cervante's masterpiece mark a special achievement in Doré's career. *Don Quixote* seemed to draw upon aspects of Doré's imagination which no other piece of literature managed to tap. His response to the gentle knight, who, fired by medieval romances, undertook a series of exploits totally at variance with the standards of late Renaissance society, brought forth a visual image of Quixote and Sancho Panza which was devoid of the mannerisms and the stock apparatus apparent in his earlier work. Drawing upon memories of his travels through Spain, Doré produced designs which, with their realism and authenticity married to a sympathetic portrait of the Don, have become the most popular and widely accepted graphic image of Quixote. The source for this current collection of Doré illustrations is the English version of *Don Quixote*, edited by J. W. Clark and published in London in 1880 by Cassell, Petter and Galpin.

Gustave Doré's reputation has been one of the chief beneficiaries of the revival of interest in the art of Victorian England and Second Empire France. The bitter disappointment which marked his last years has been redressed by the reappraisal of a different epoch, and many of the paintings which Doré thought most worthy of his vision have come to receive the acclaim and appreciation he always felt they deserved. Yet among Doré's oeuvre, the designs for *Don Quixote* will always rank as one of his most striking masterpieces, remarkable for the totality, complexity, authenticity and human compassion of the vision of one of the most outstanding illustrators of the mid-nineteenth century.

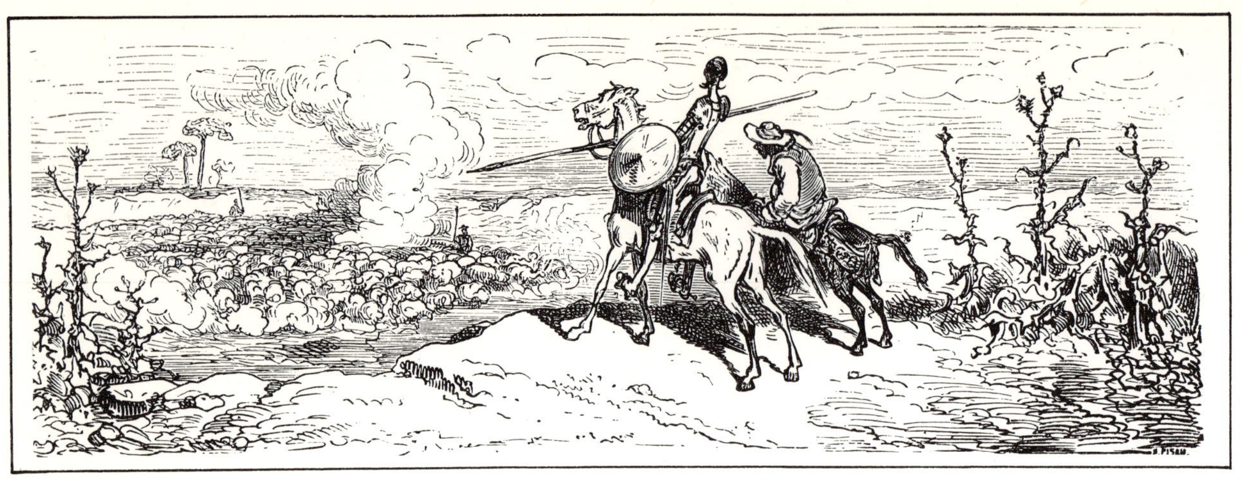

Brief Bibliography

Jacques Bainville, 'Gustave Doré et l'Alsace', *l'Alsace française,* 17 October 1925

Jacques Bainville, 'Gustave Doré', *Revue Alsacienne Illustrée,* vol. X, 1908

Henri Beraldi, *Gustave Doré,* Paris 1888

F. Courboin, *Histoire illustrée de la graveur en France,* vol. III, Paris 1926

Lucien de Dardel, 'Gustave Doré: Caricatures from his School Days', *Internationale Zweimonatscrift für freie Graphik und Gebauchsgraphik,* vol. VIII, no. 43, 1952

Alexandre Dumas *fils* (ed.), *Catalogue des Tableaux, Etudes et Esquisses, Aquarelles, Dessins et Sculptures, laissés dans son atelier par le feu Gustave Doré,* Paris 1885

G. Duplessis (ed.), *Catalogue des Dessins, aquarelles et estampes de Gustave Doré esposés dans les Salons du Cercle de la Librairie,* Paris 1885

Exposition rétrospective Gustave Doré, Palais des Beaux-Arts catalogue, Paris 1932

Konrad Farner, *Gustave Doré, der industrialisierte Romantiker,* Dresden 1963

Nigel Gosling, *Gustave Doré,* London 1973

P. Gusman, *La Graveur sur bois en France au XIXe siècle,* Paris 1925

G. F. Hartlaub, *Gustave Doré,* Leipzig 1924

Marina Henderson, *Gustave Doré,* London 1971

Blanchard Jerrold *Life of Gustave Doré,* London 1891

H. Leblanc, *Catalogue de l'oeuvre complet de Gustave Doré,* Paris 1931

H. Lehmann-Haupt, *The Terrible Gustave Doré,* New York 1943

Pierre Mornand, *Gustave Doré,* Paris 1946

Michel Ragan, 'Gustave Doré, un dessinateur frénétique', *L'Œuil,* no. 3, 1955

Blanche Roosevelt, *Life and Reminiscences of Gustave Doré*, London 1885

Milicent Rose, *Gustave Doré,* London 1946

A. Rümann, *Das illustrierte Buch des 19. Jahrhunderts in England, Frankreich und der Schweiz,* Leipzig 1930

A. Rümann, *Gustave Doré: Bibliographie der Erstausgaben,* Munich 1921

Max Sander, *Les Livres illustrés français du dix-neuvième siècle,* Stuttgart n.d. (1923)

J. Valmy-Baysse and Louis Dézé, *Gustave Doré,* Paris n.d. (1930)

PLATES

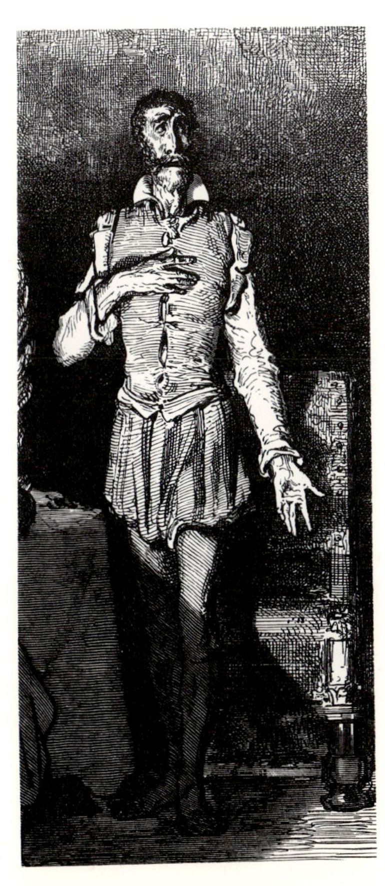

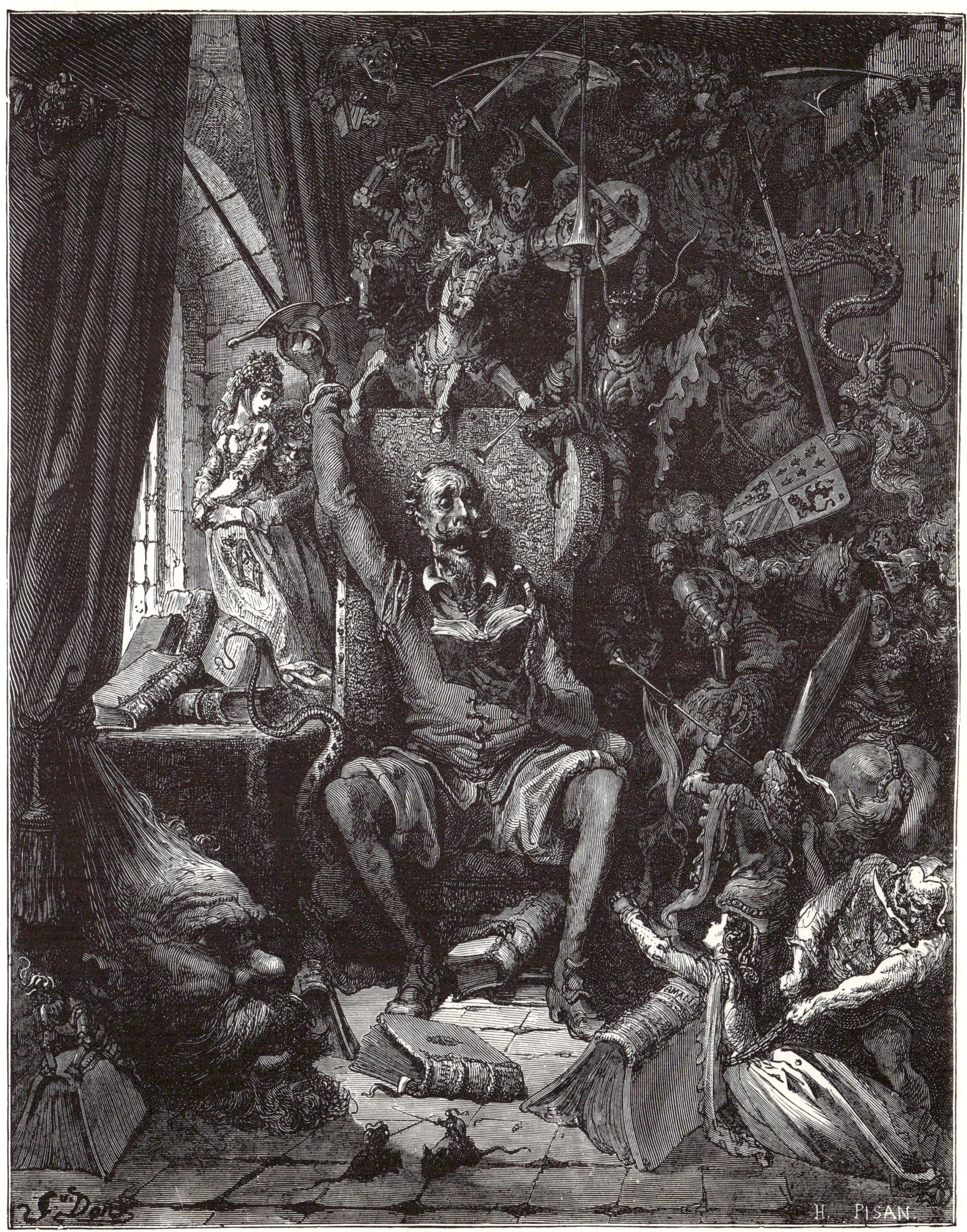

'A world of disorderly notions, picked out of his books, crowded into his imagination.'

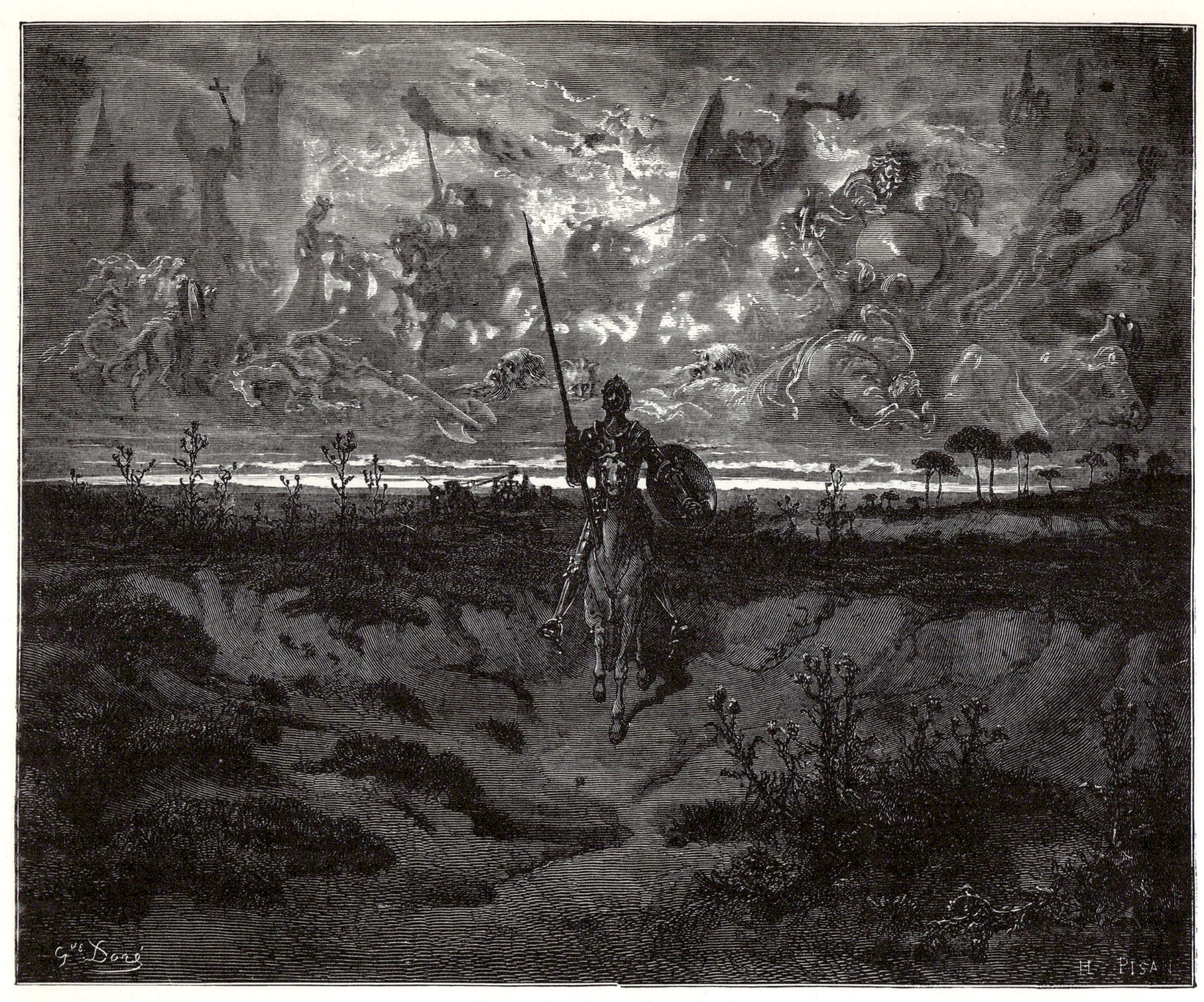

‘He travelled almost all that day.’

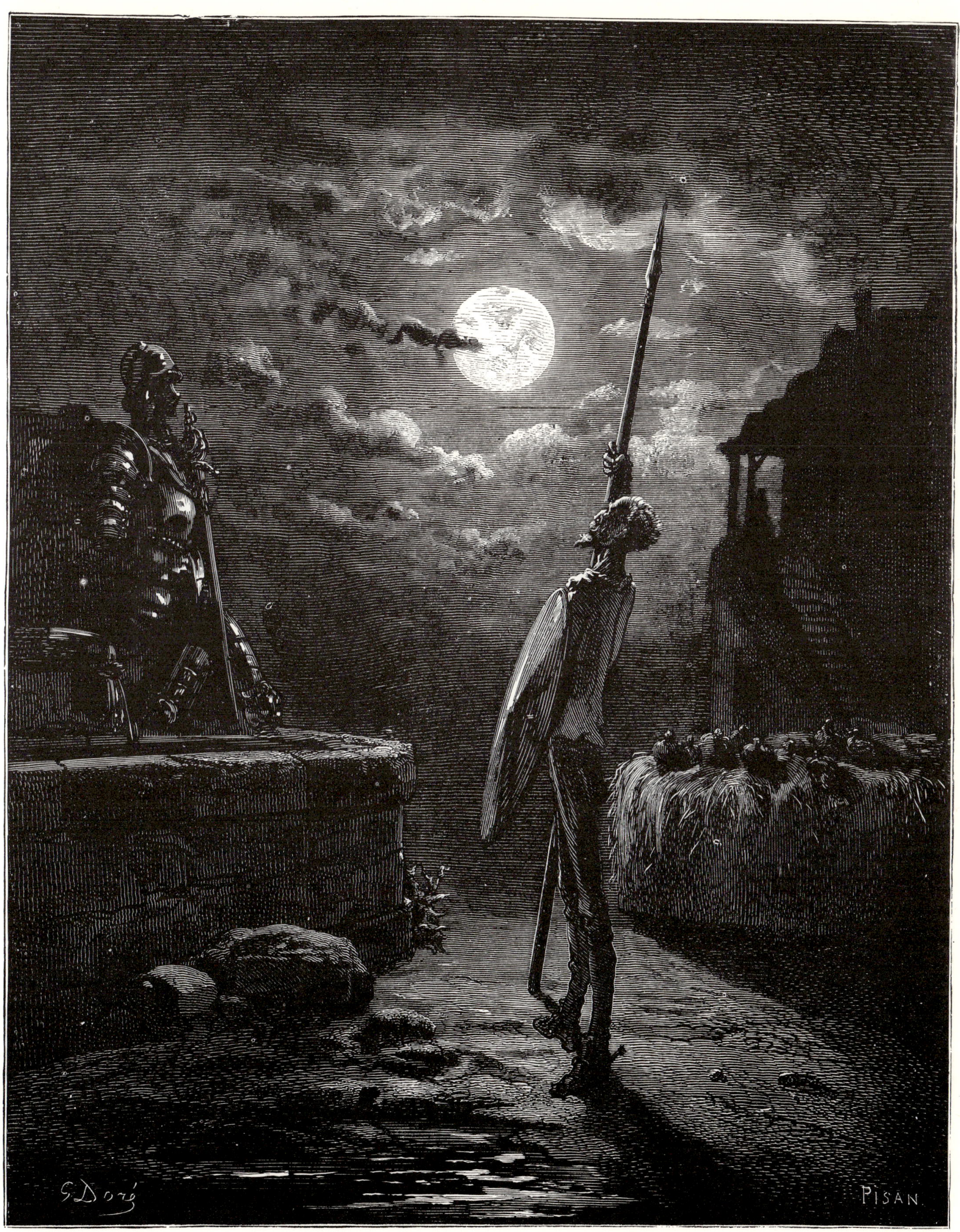

'He began to walk about by the horse-trough with a graceful deportment.'

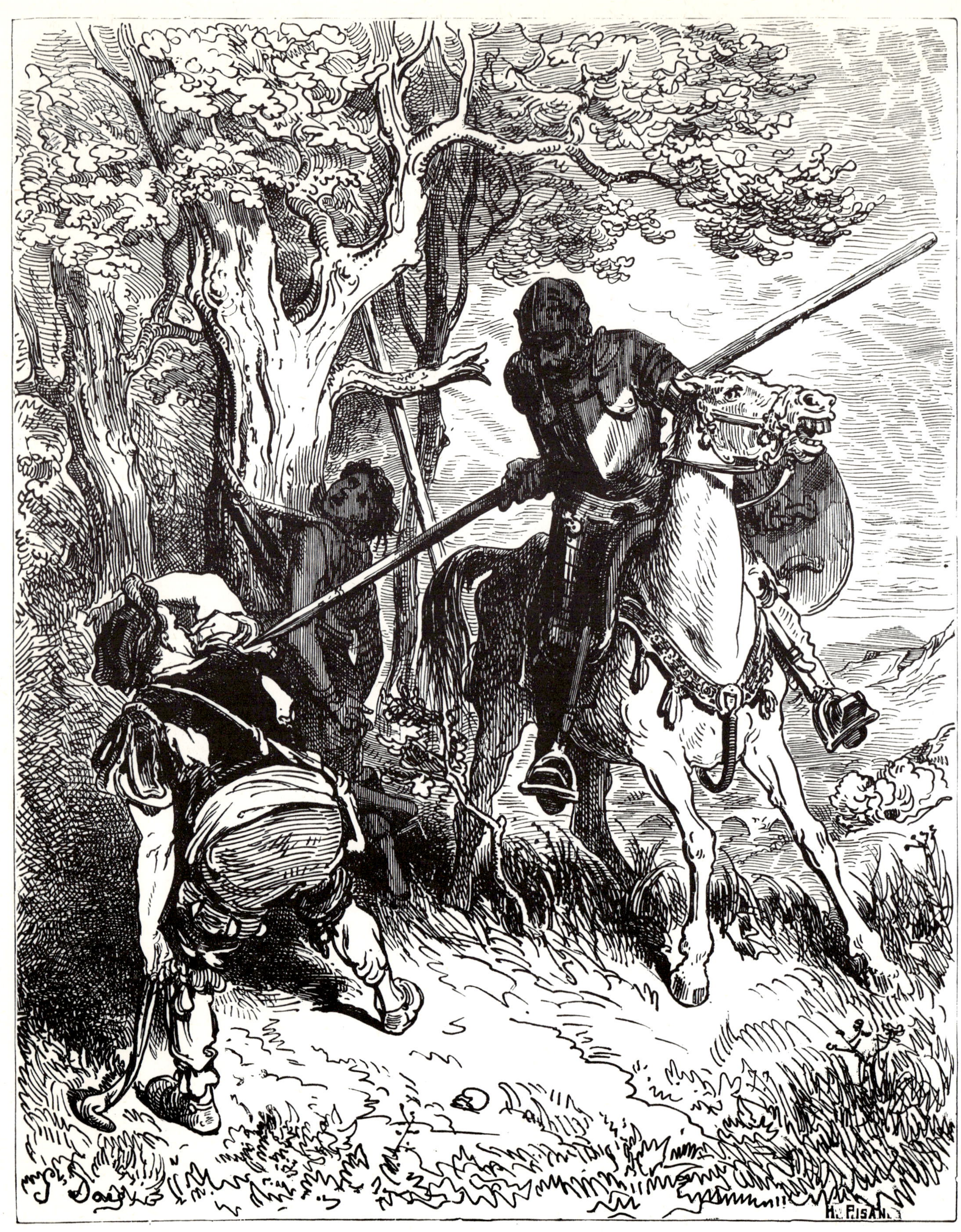

'By the sun that shines, I have a good mind to run thee through the body with my lance.'

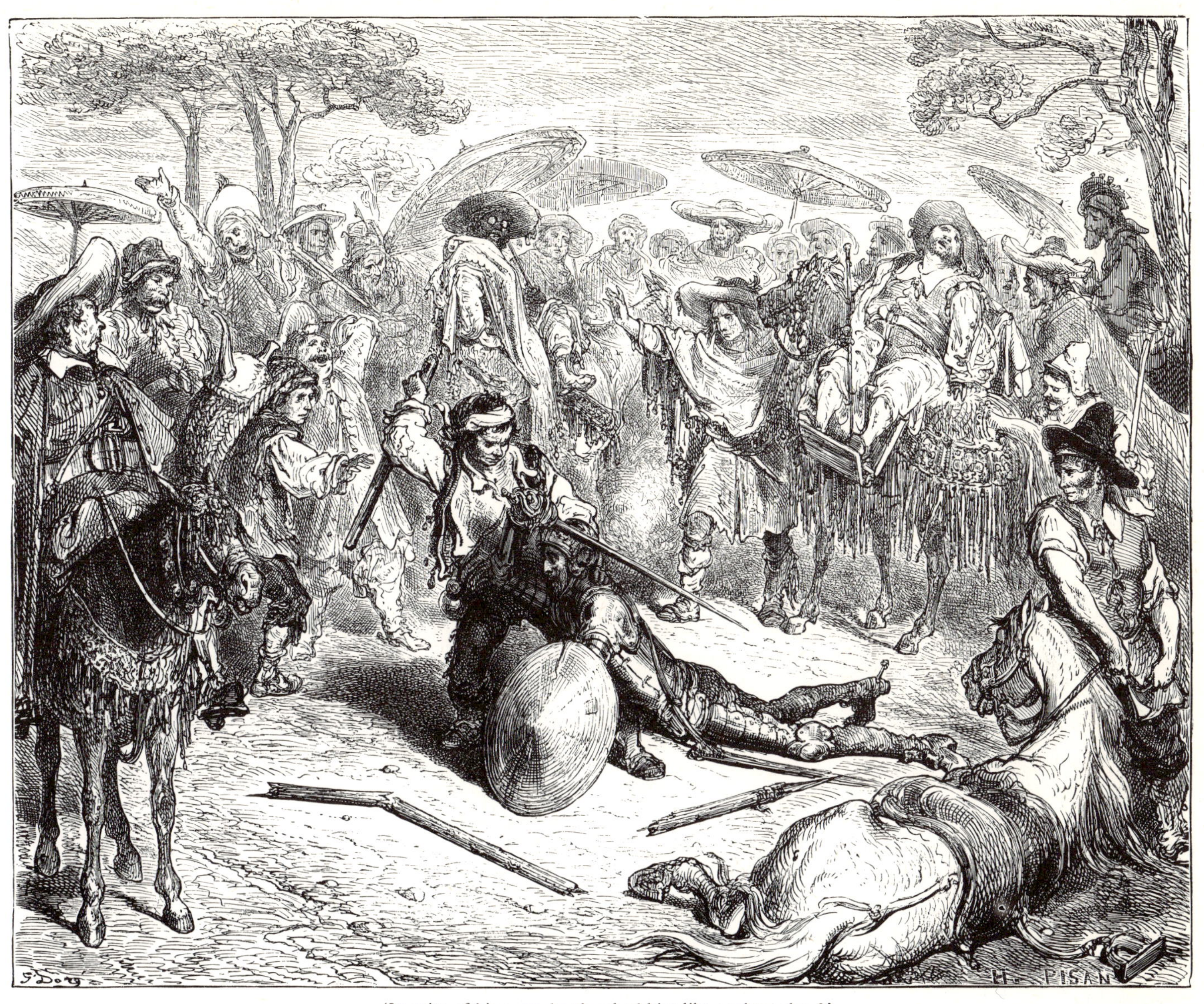

'In spite of his arms, he thrashed him like a wheat-sheaf.'

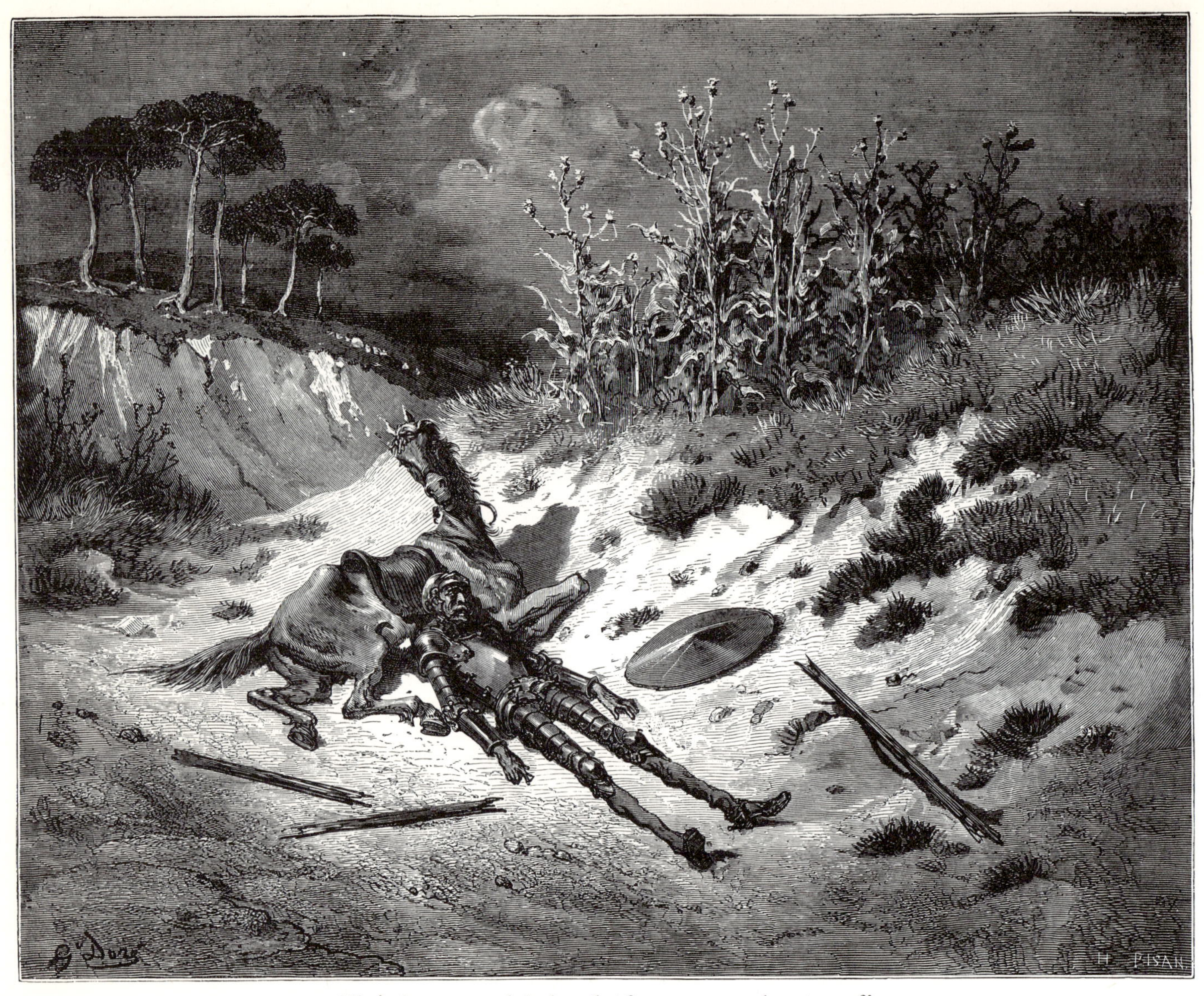

‘Alas! where are you, lady dear, that for my woe you do not moan?’

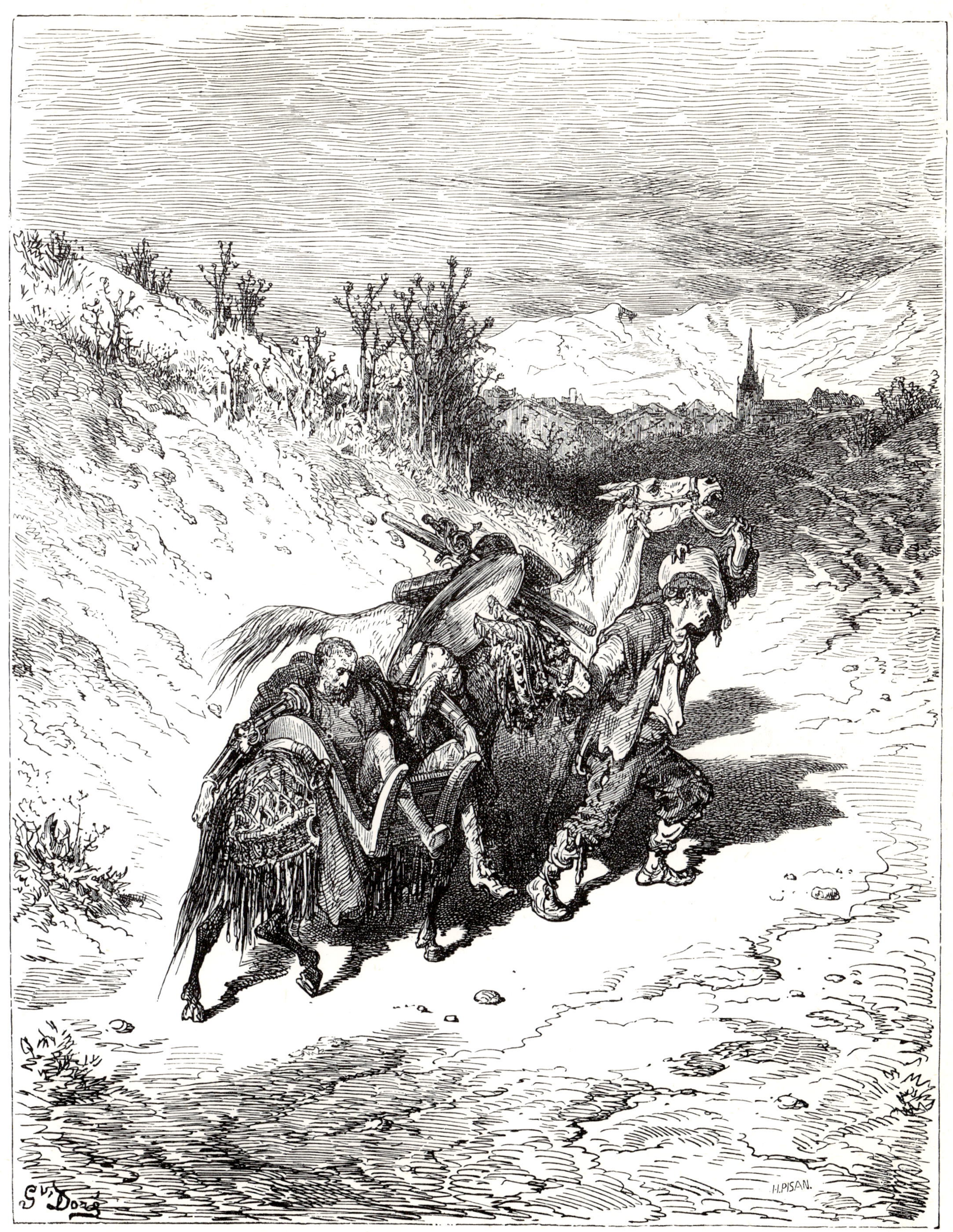

'He led them all towards the village, and trudged a-foot himself, very pensive.'

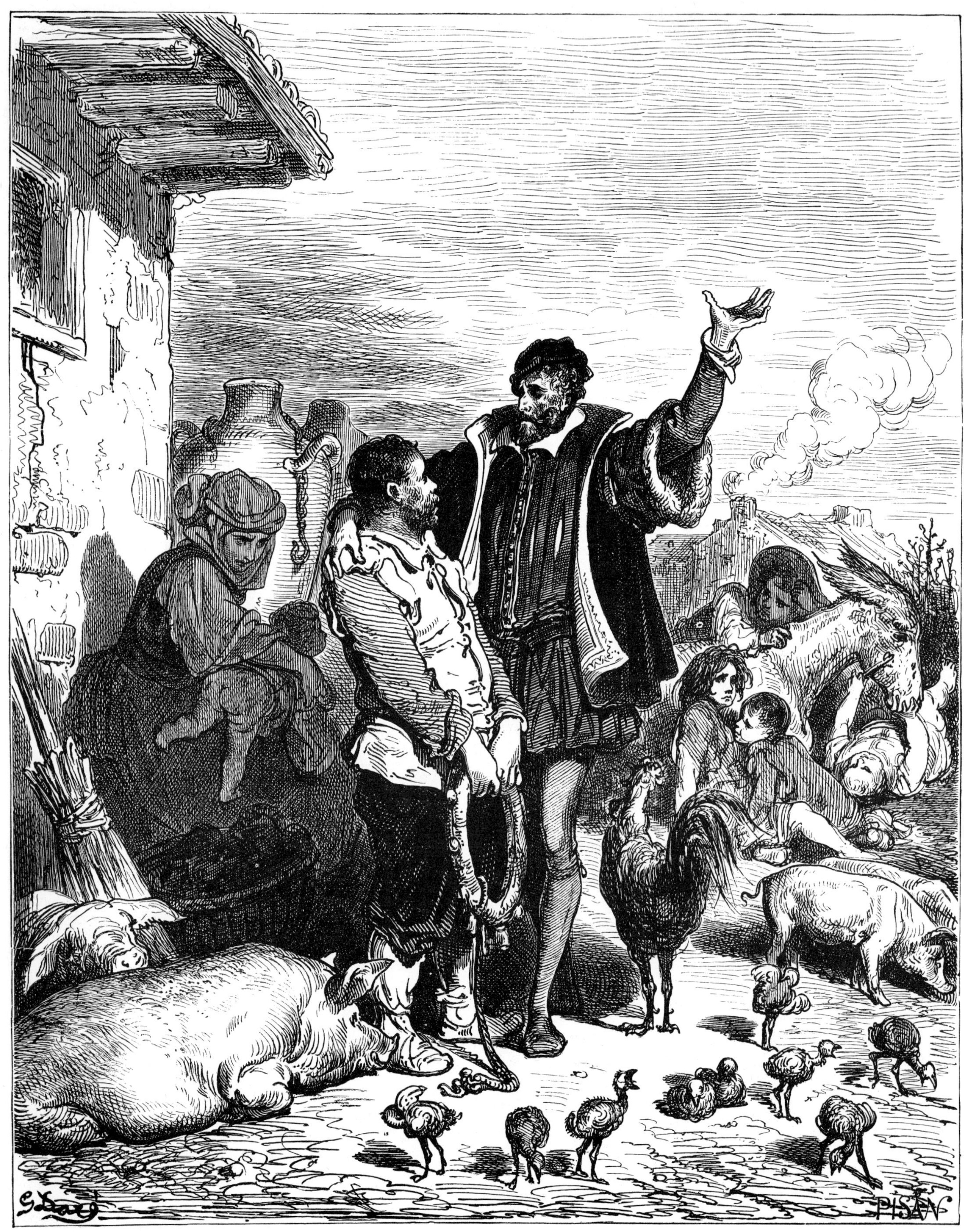

'The knight made him so many fair promises, that at last the poor silly clown consented to go along with him, and become his squire.'

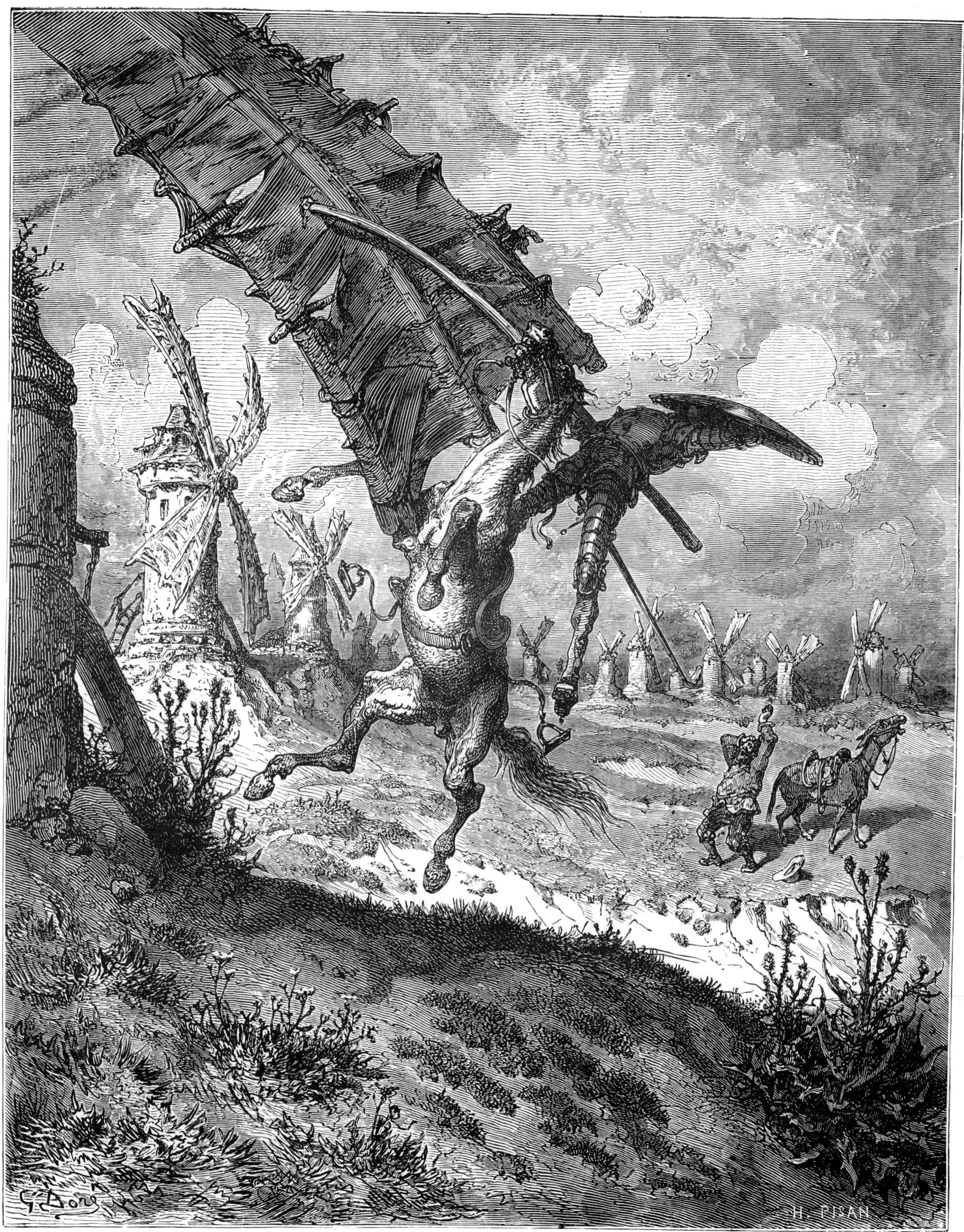

'The sail hurled away both knight and horse along with it.'

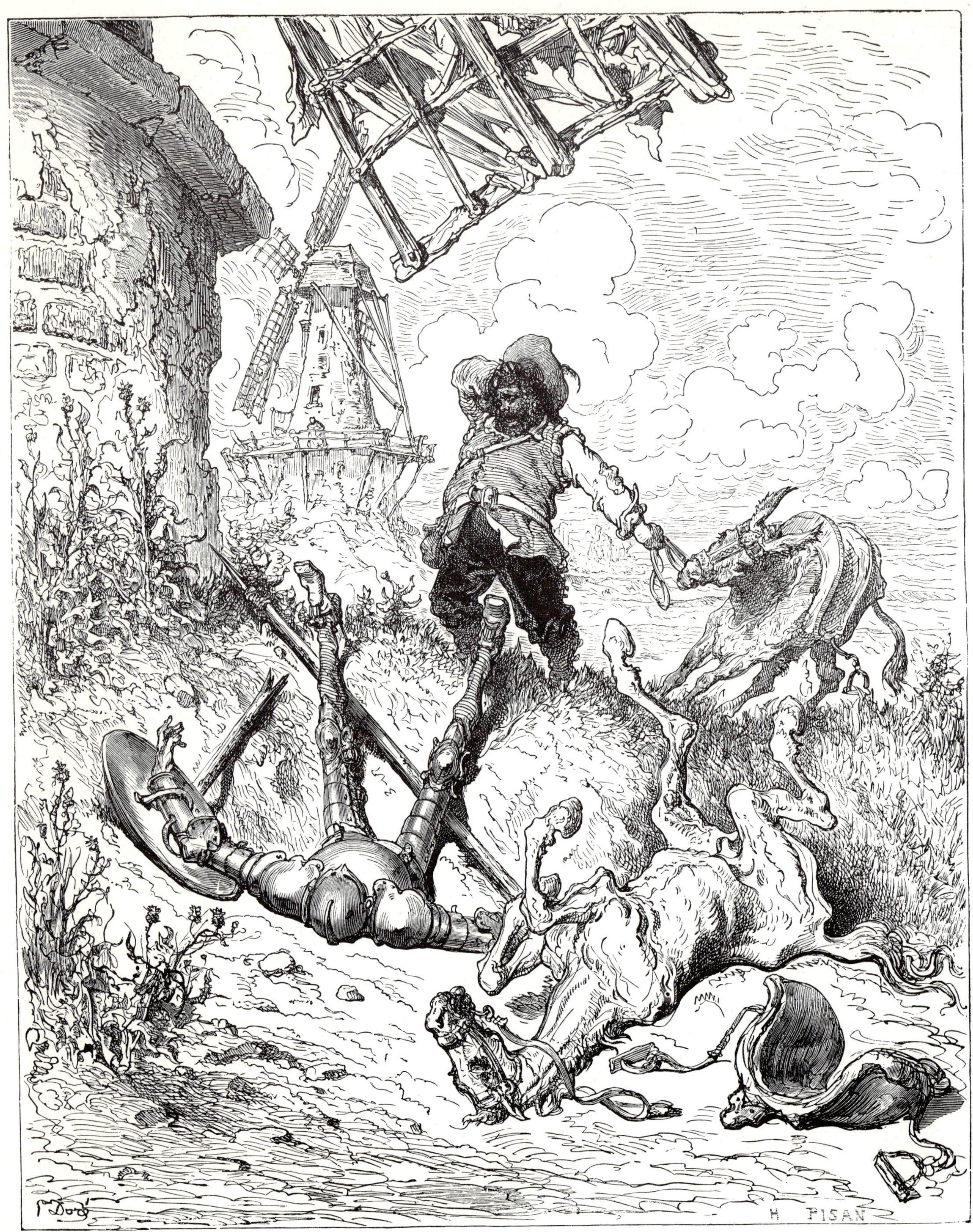

'Sancho ran as fast as his ass could drive, to help his master.'

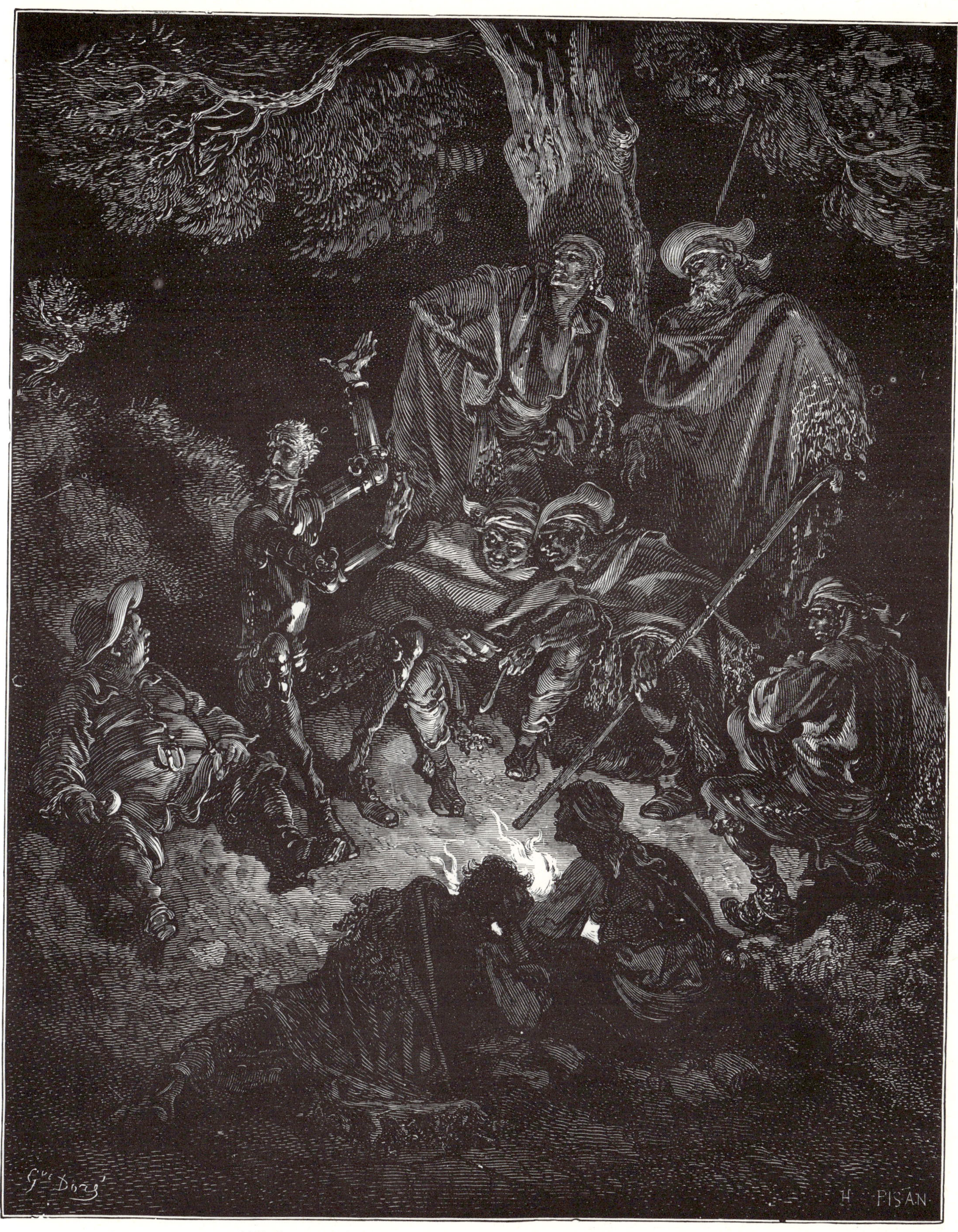

''Oh, happy age,' cried he, 'which our first parents called the age of gold!''

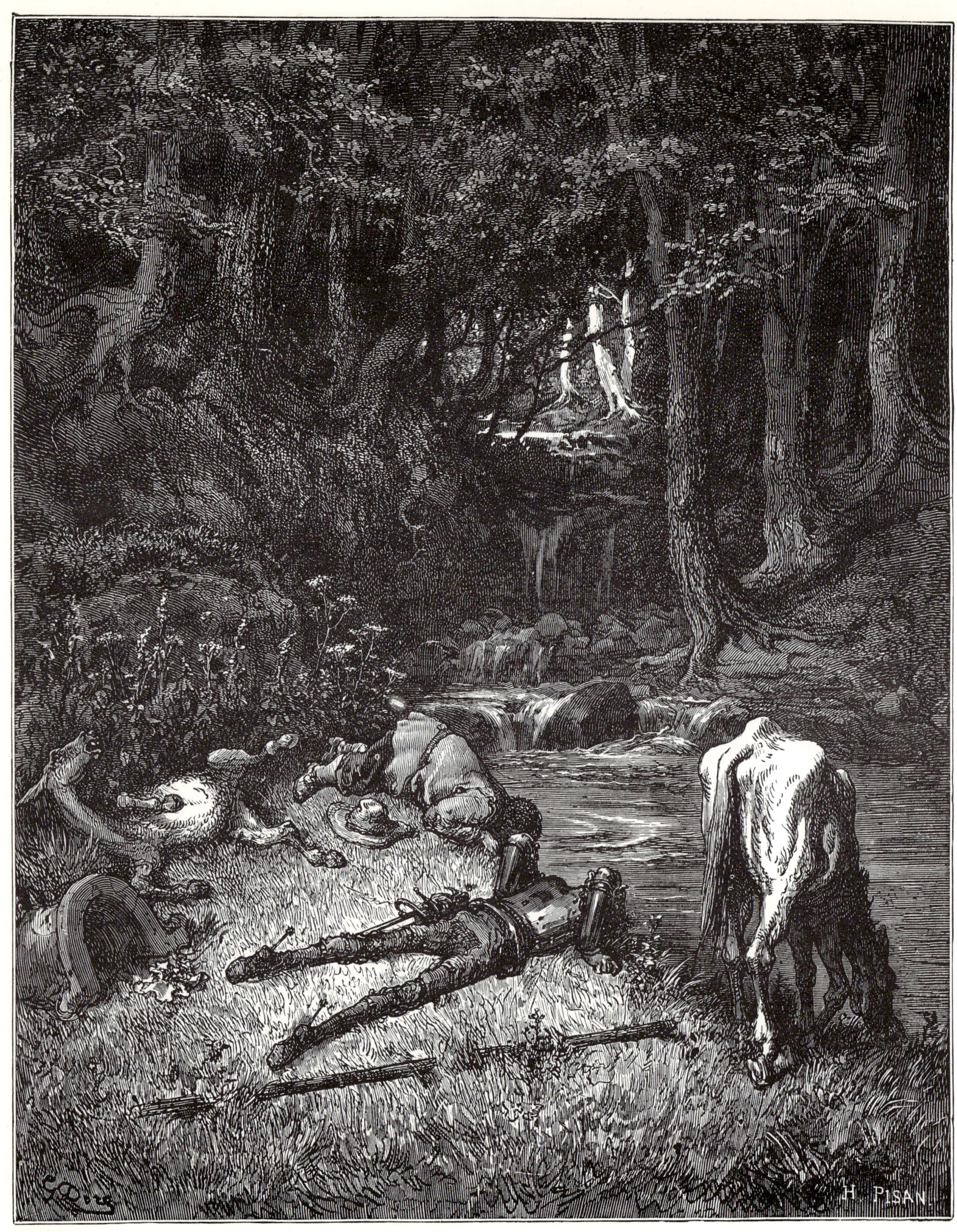

'A meadow watered with a rivulet, invited them to alight.'

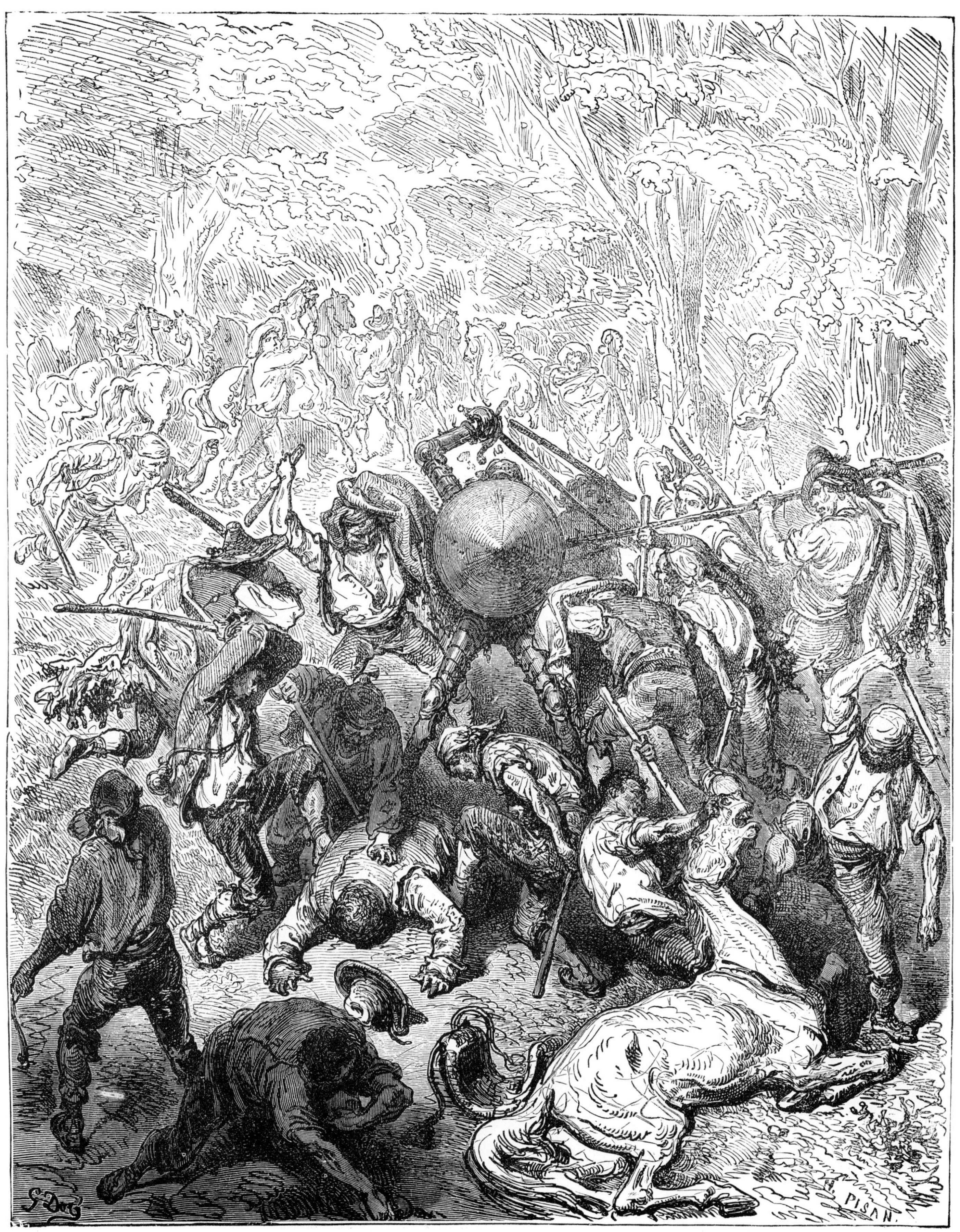

'The Yanguesians betook themselves to their levers and pack-staves.'

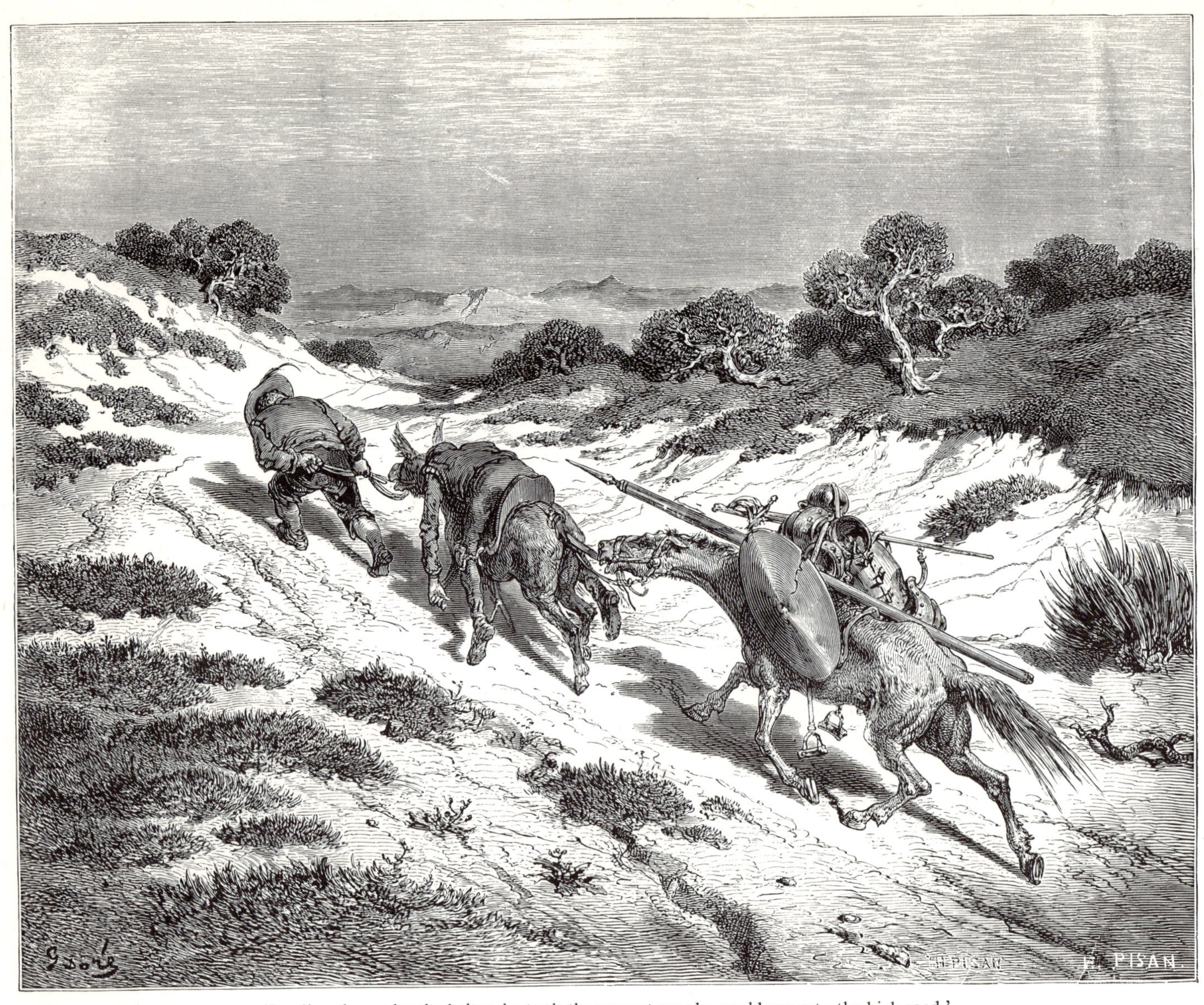

'Leading the ass by the halter, he took the nearest way he could guess to the high road.'

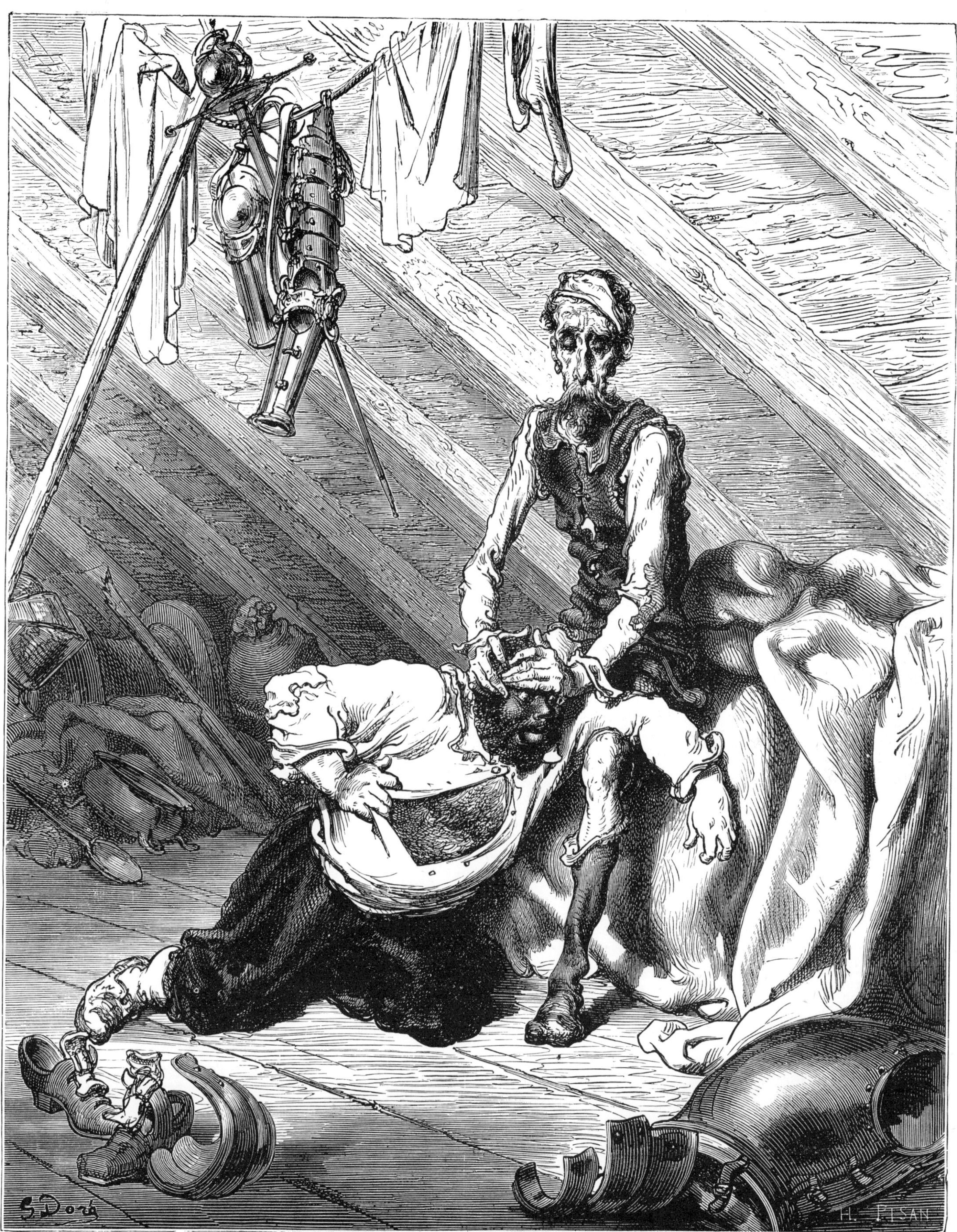

'He verily believed his last hour was come.'

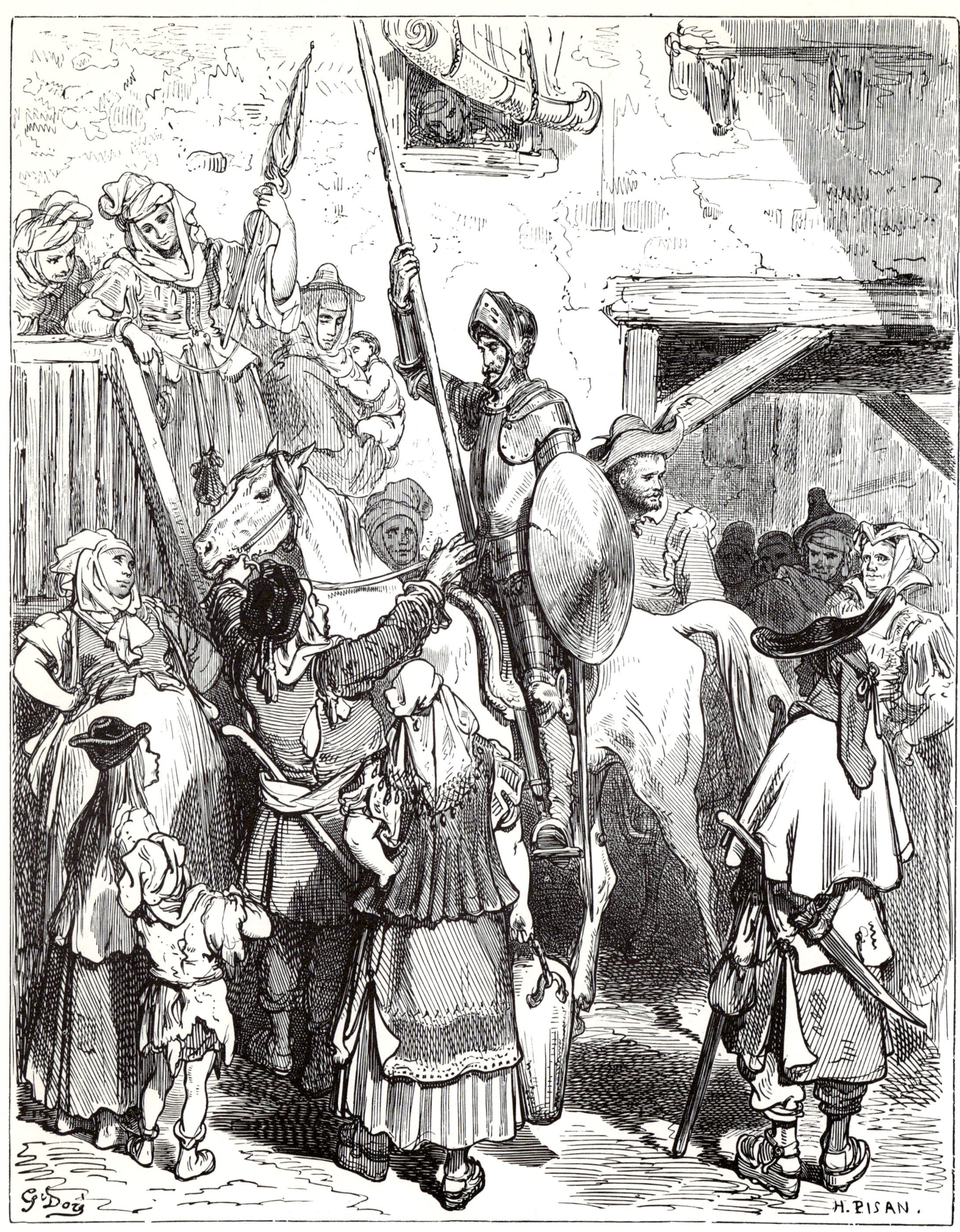

' 'I have nothing to do with all this,' cried the innkeeper: 'pay your reckoning.' '

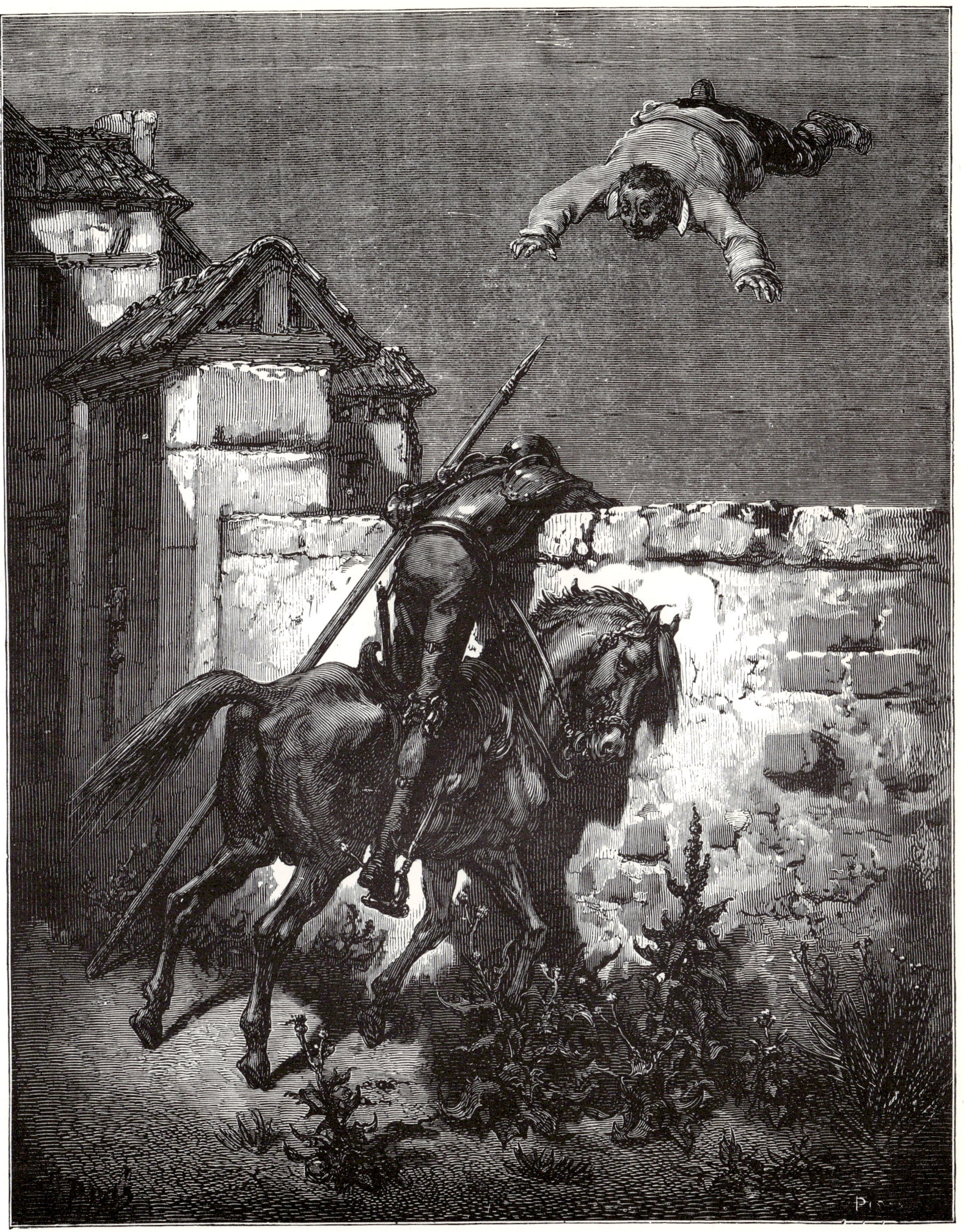

'The more he stormed, the more they tossed and laughed.'

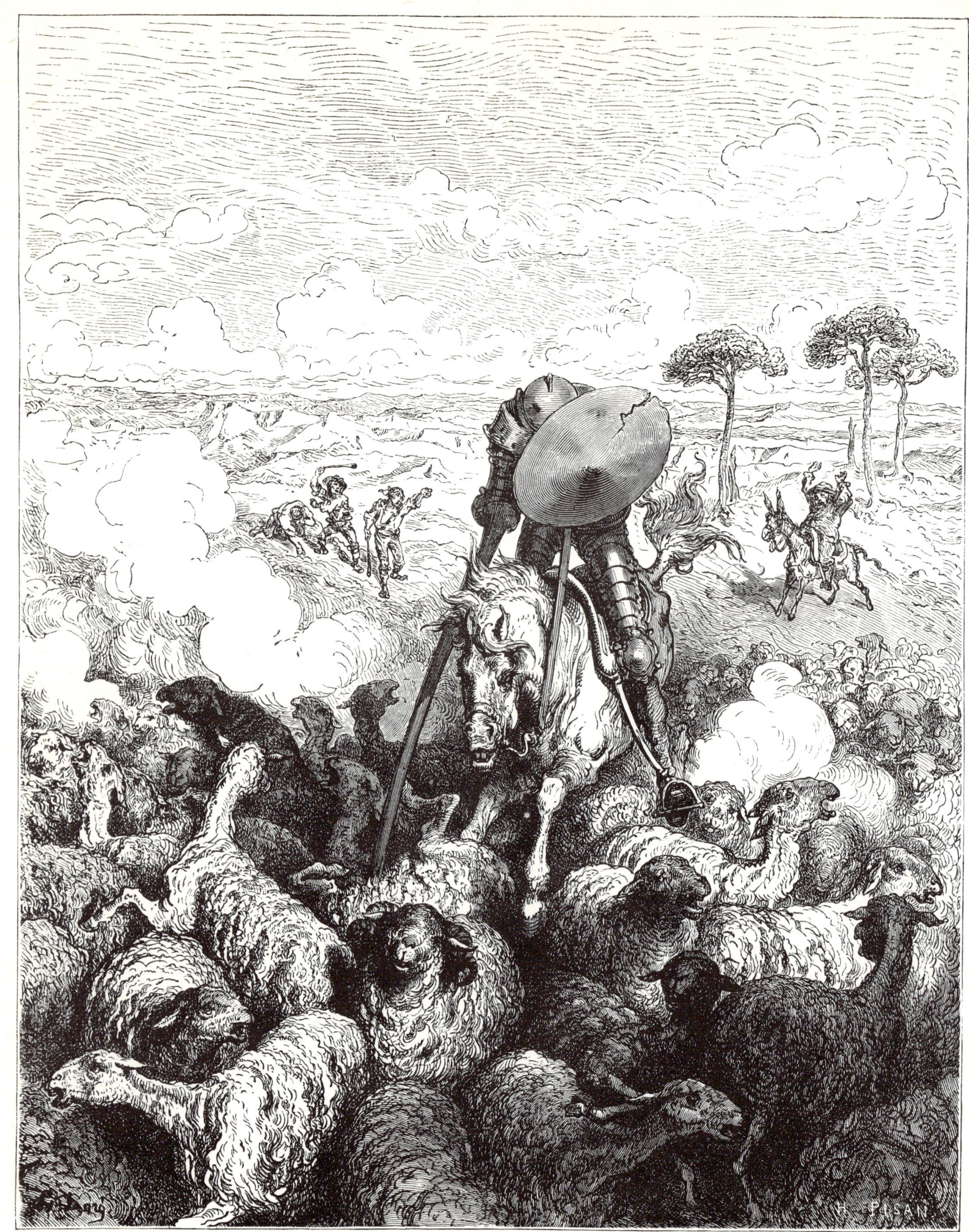

'He charged the squadron of sheep.'

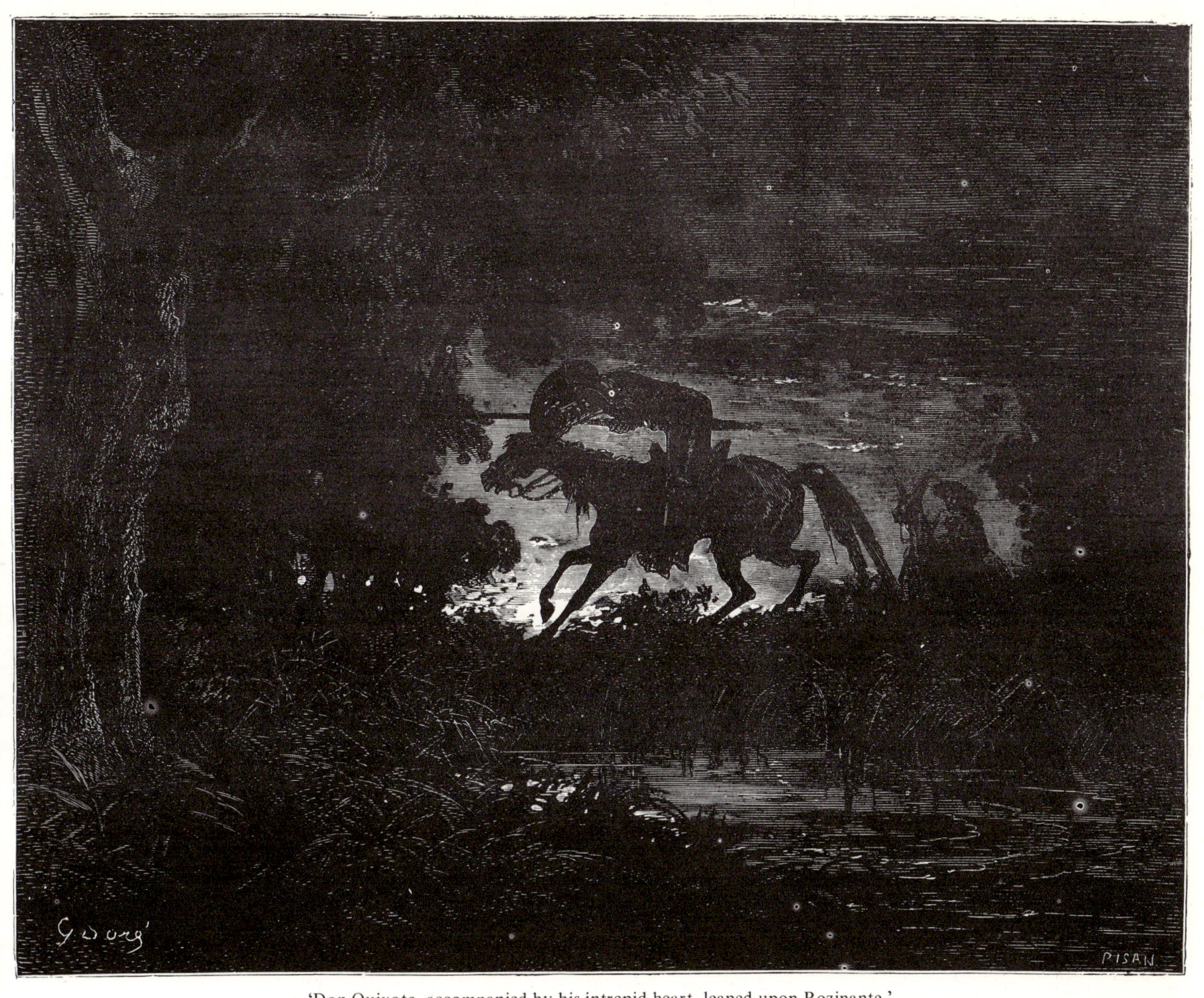

'Don Quixote, accompanied by his intrepid heart, leaped upon Rozinante.'

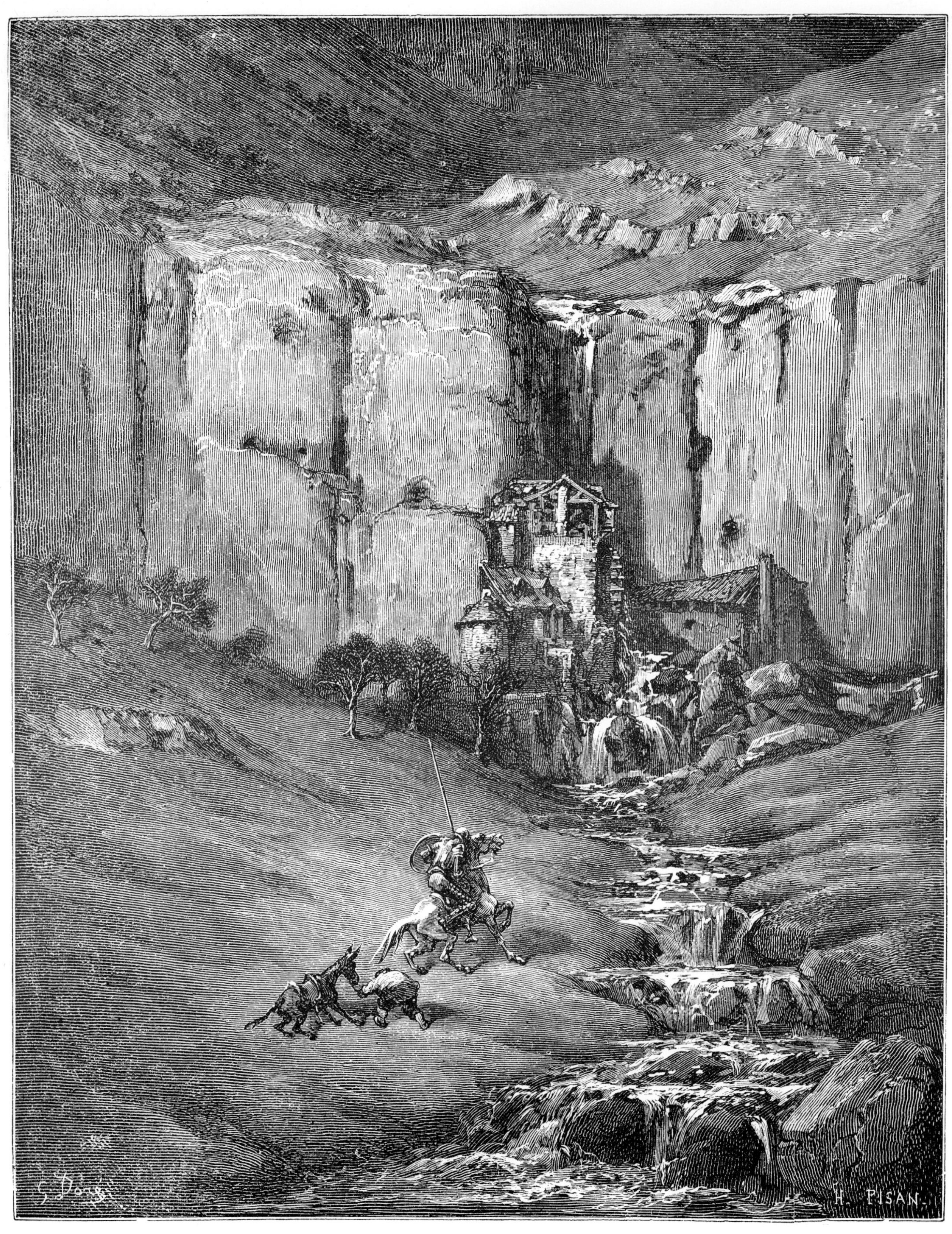

'When they came nearer, even patient Rozinante himself started at the dreadful sound.'

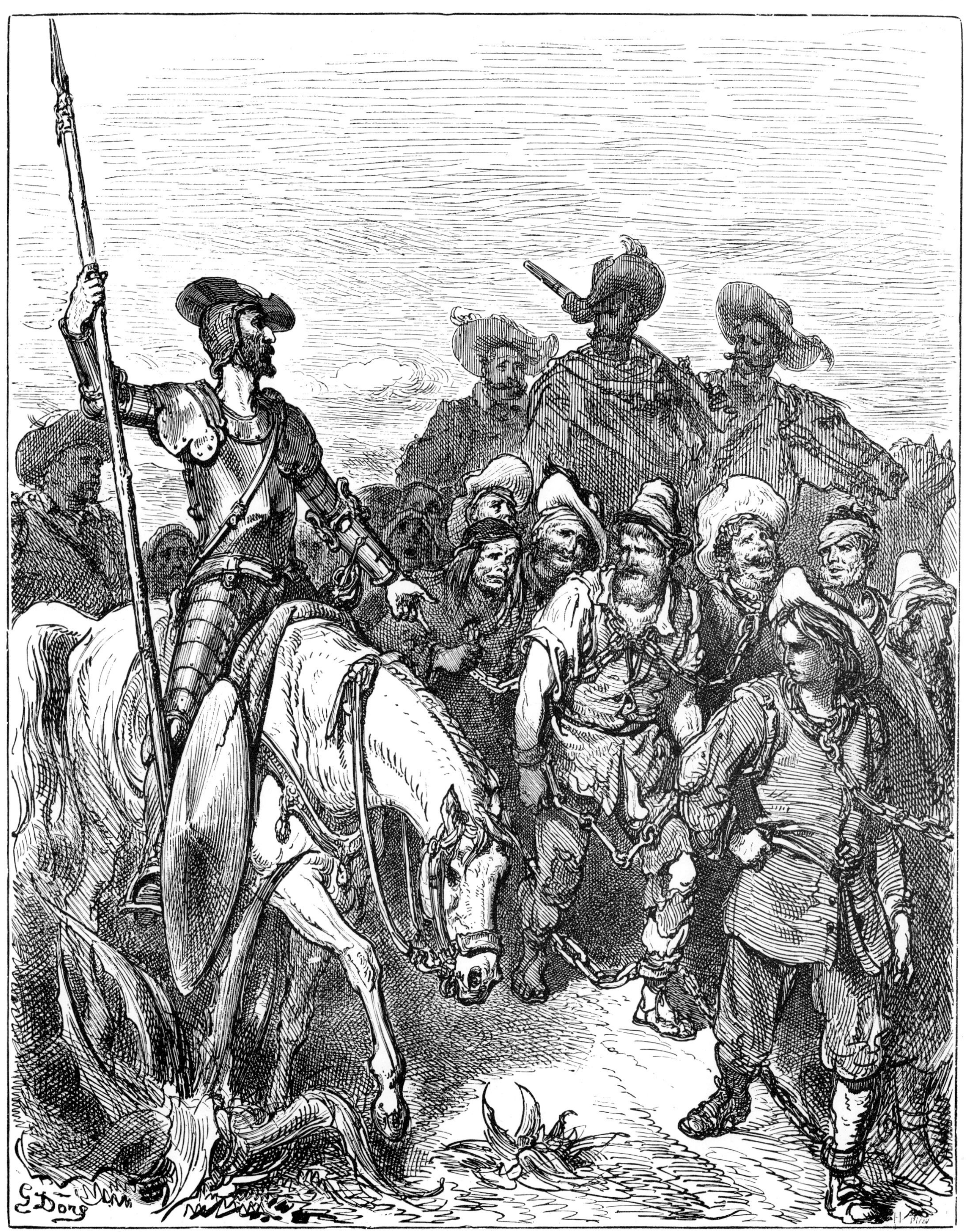

'Don Quixote asked the first for what crimes he was in these miserable circumstances.'

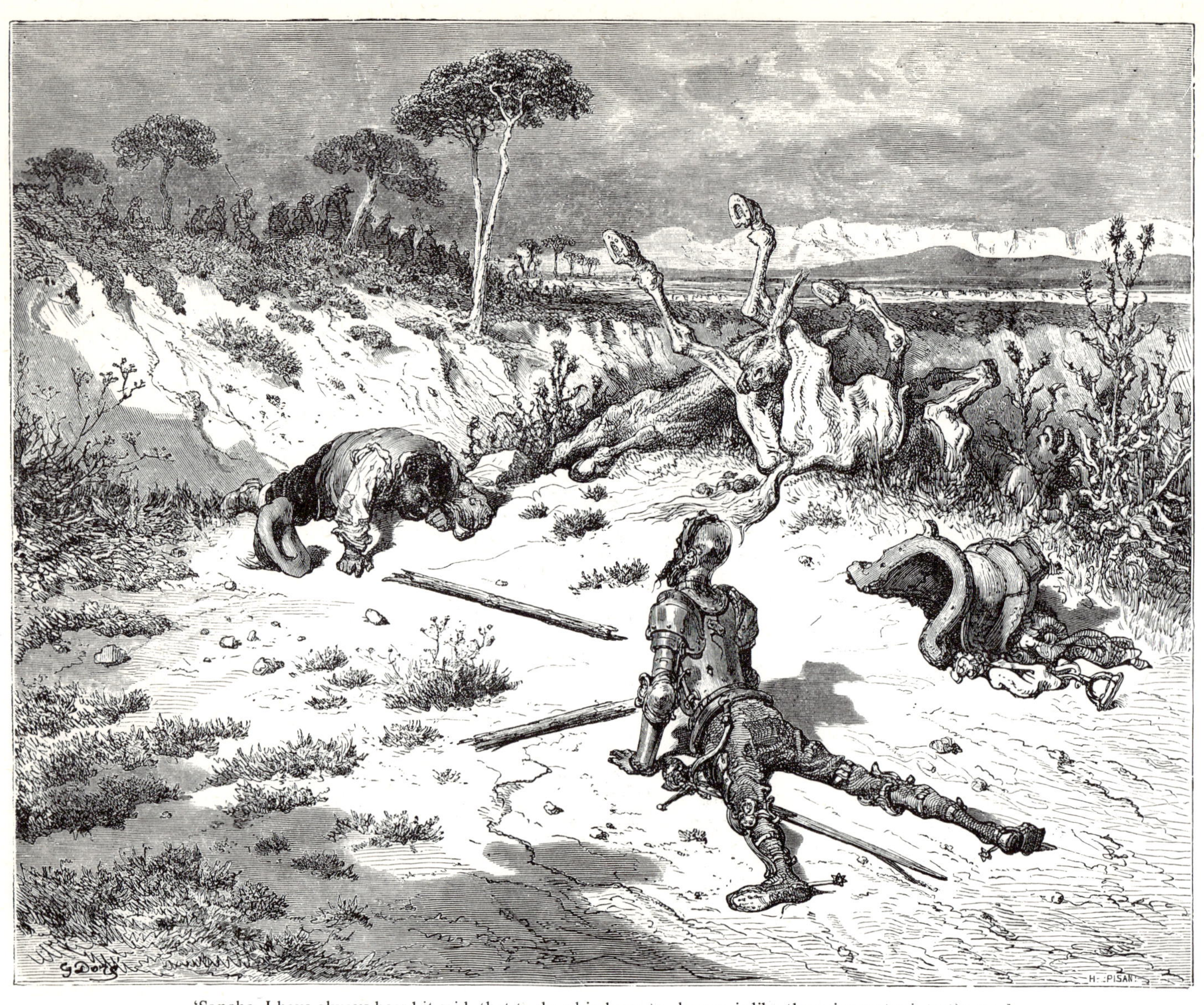

'Sancho, I have always heard it said, that to do a kindness to clowns, is like throwing water into the sea.'

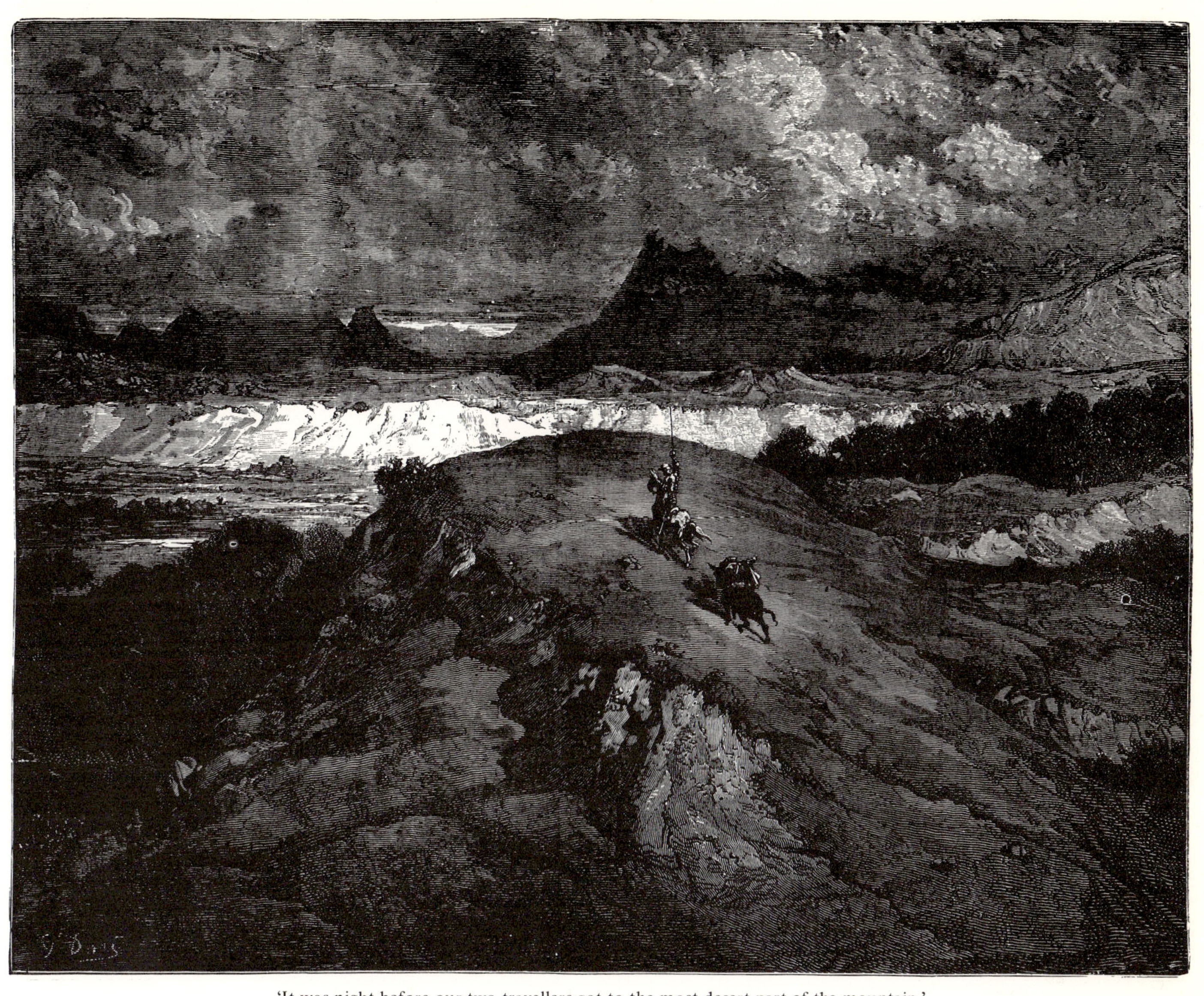

'It was night before our two travellers got to the most desert part of the mountain.'

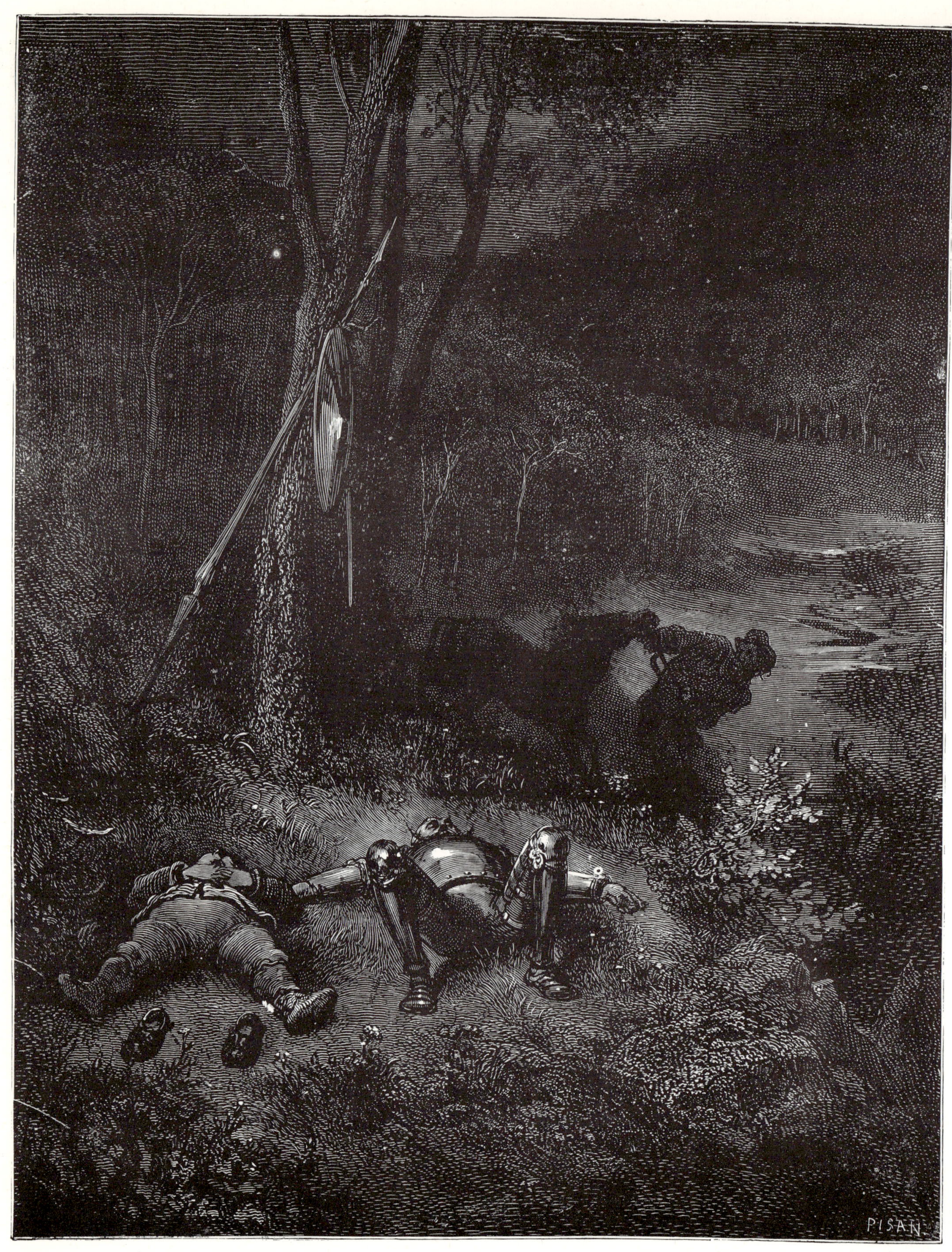

'Gines, who was a stranger both to gratitude and humanity, resolved to ride away with Sancho's ass.'

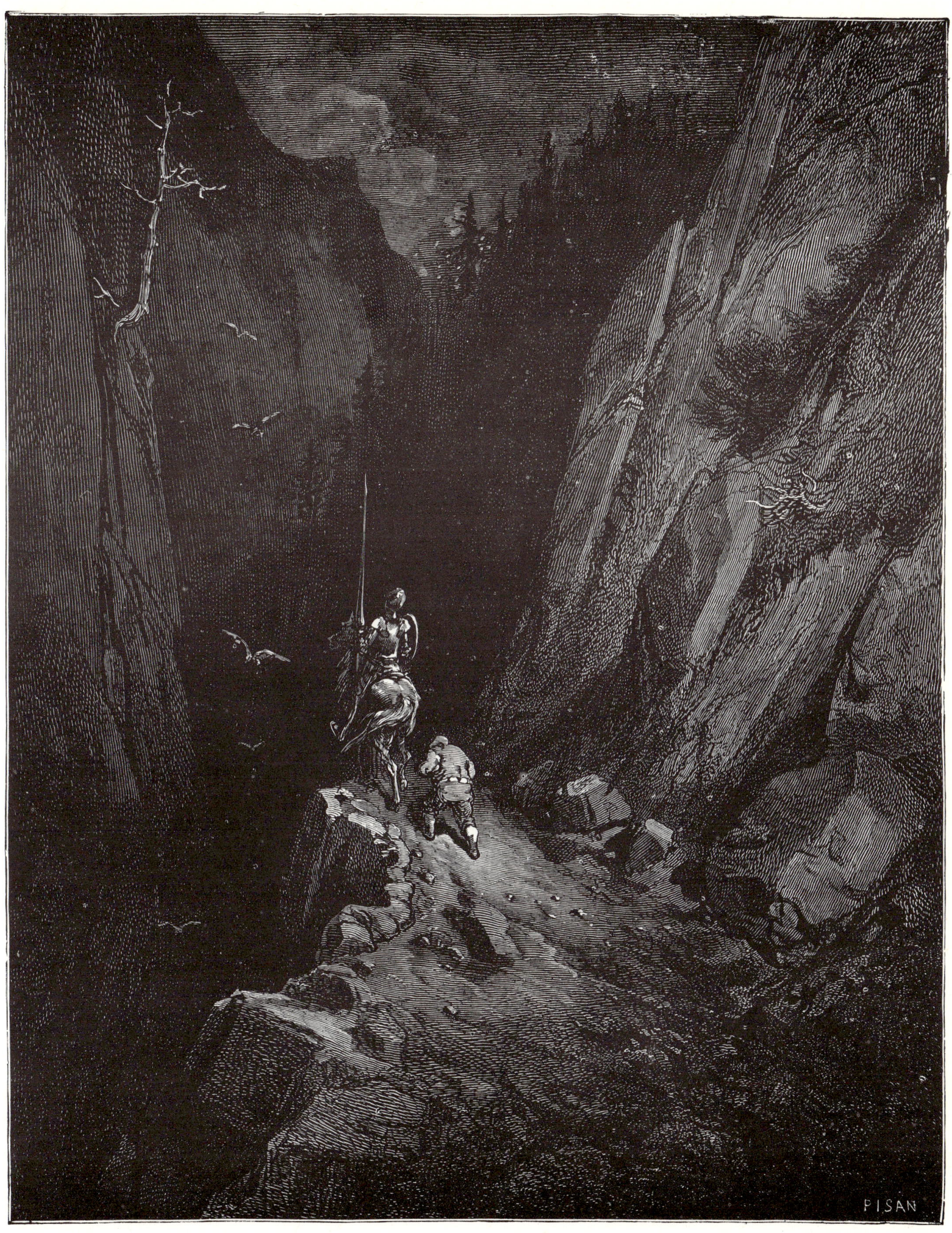

'Don Quixote was transported with joy to find himself where he might flatter his ambition with the hopes of fresh adventures.'

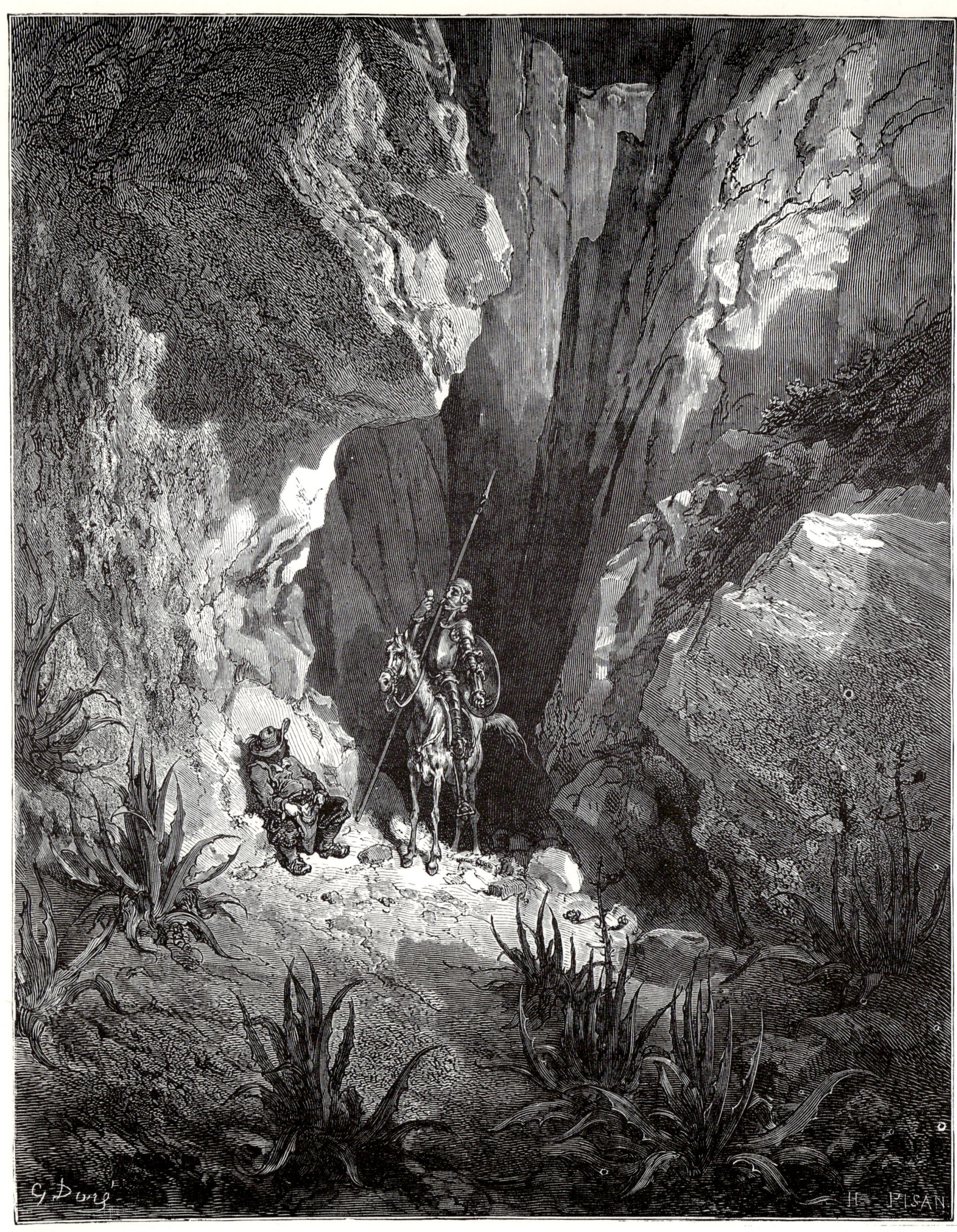

'The first thing he found was the rough draught of a sonnet; so he read it aloud.'

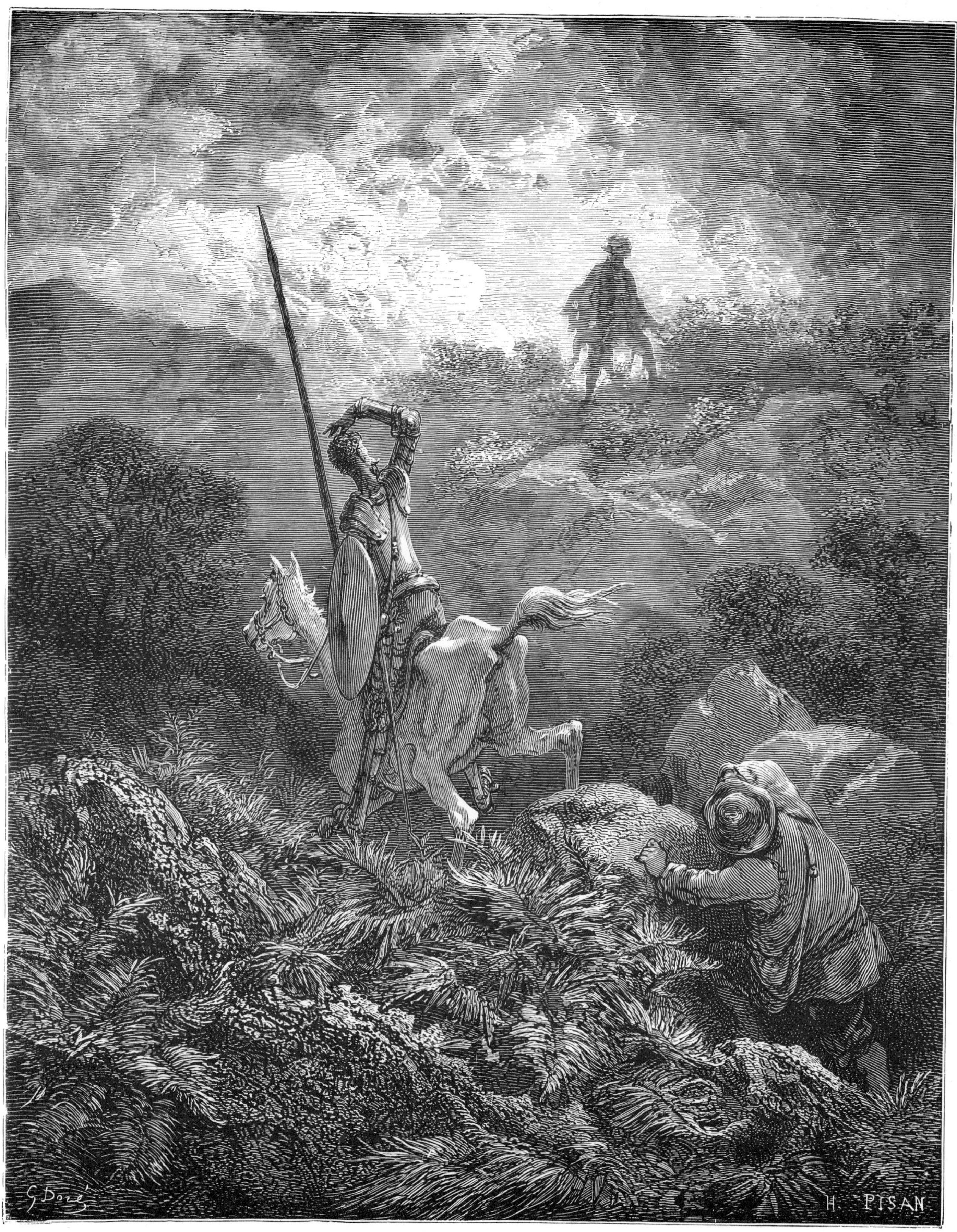

‘He spied upon the top of a stony crag just before him a man that skipped from rock to rock with wonderful agility.’

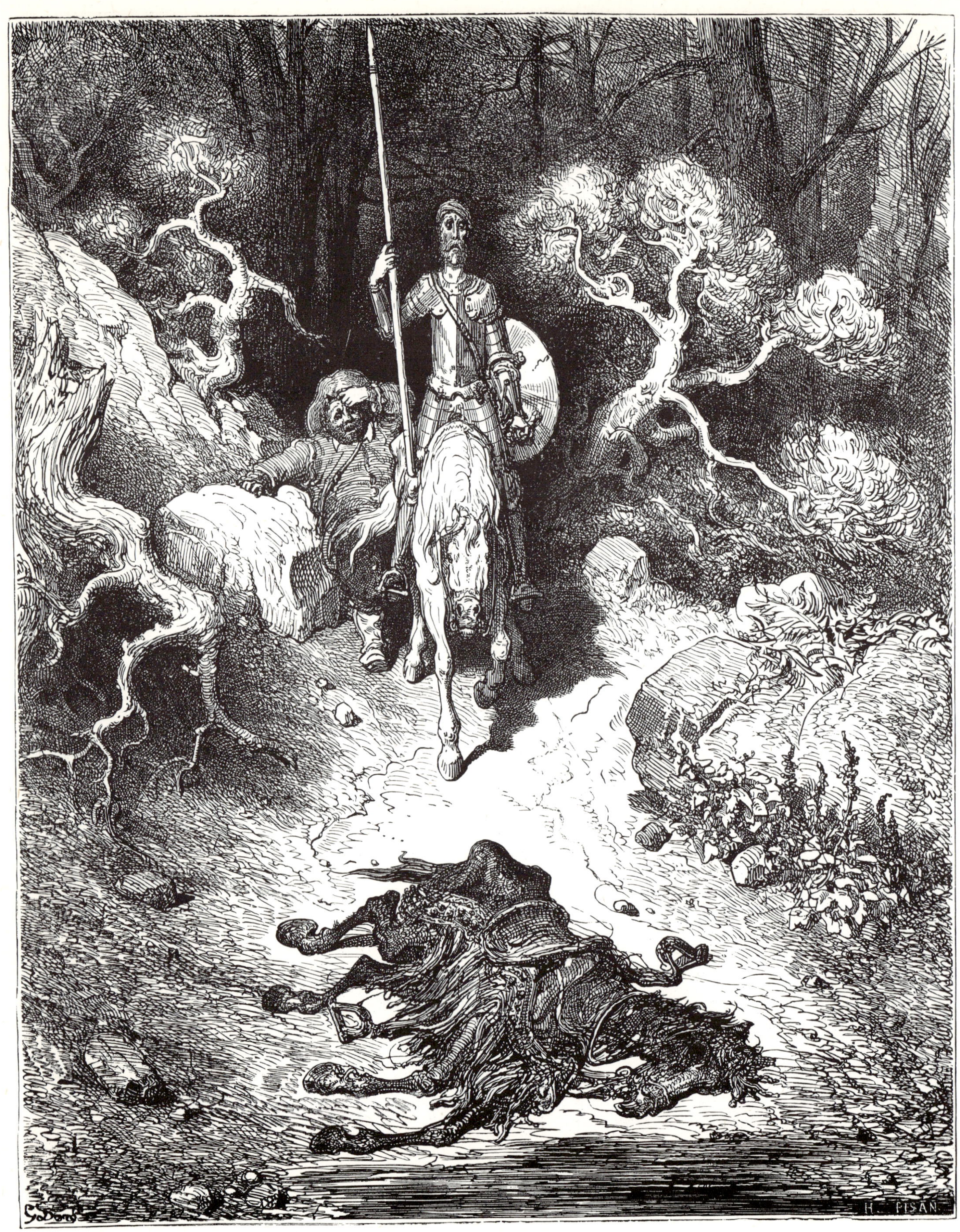

'They came to a park, where they found a mule lying dead.'

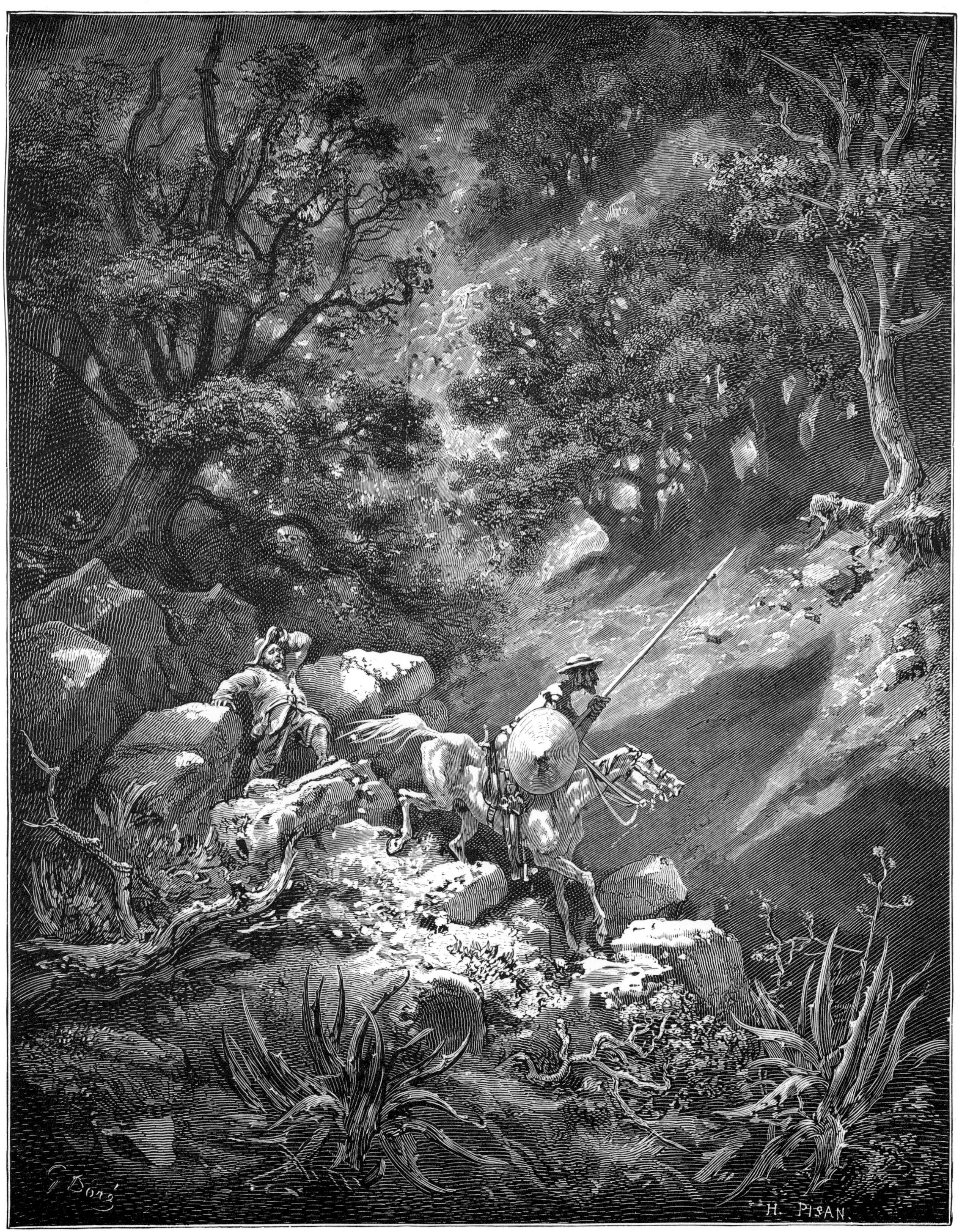

''But pray, sir,' quoth Sancho, 'is it a good law of chivalry that says we shall wander up and down, over bushes and briars, in this rocky wilderness?''

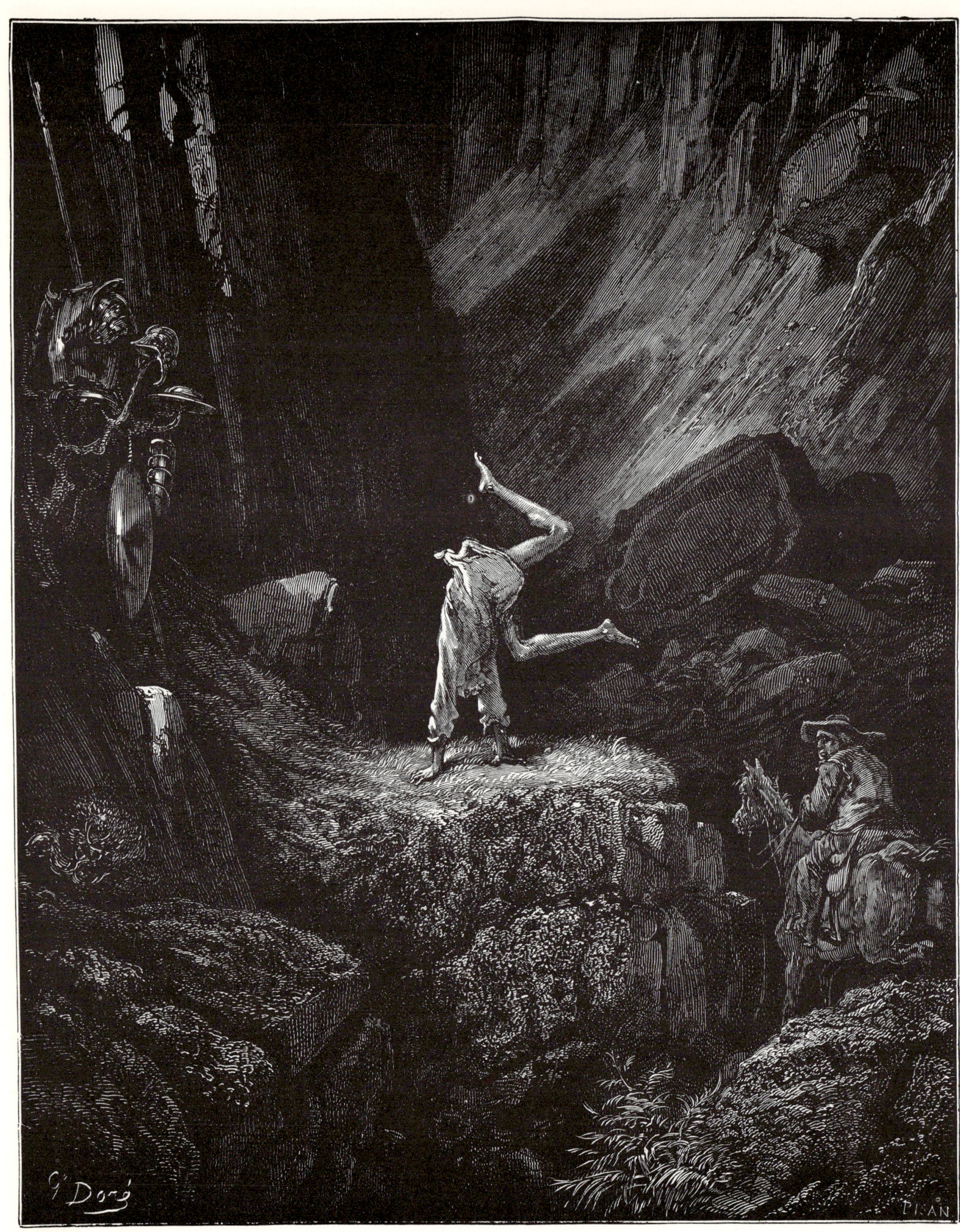

'He gave two or three frisks in the air, and then pitching on his hands, he fetched his heels over his head twice together.'

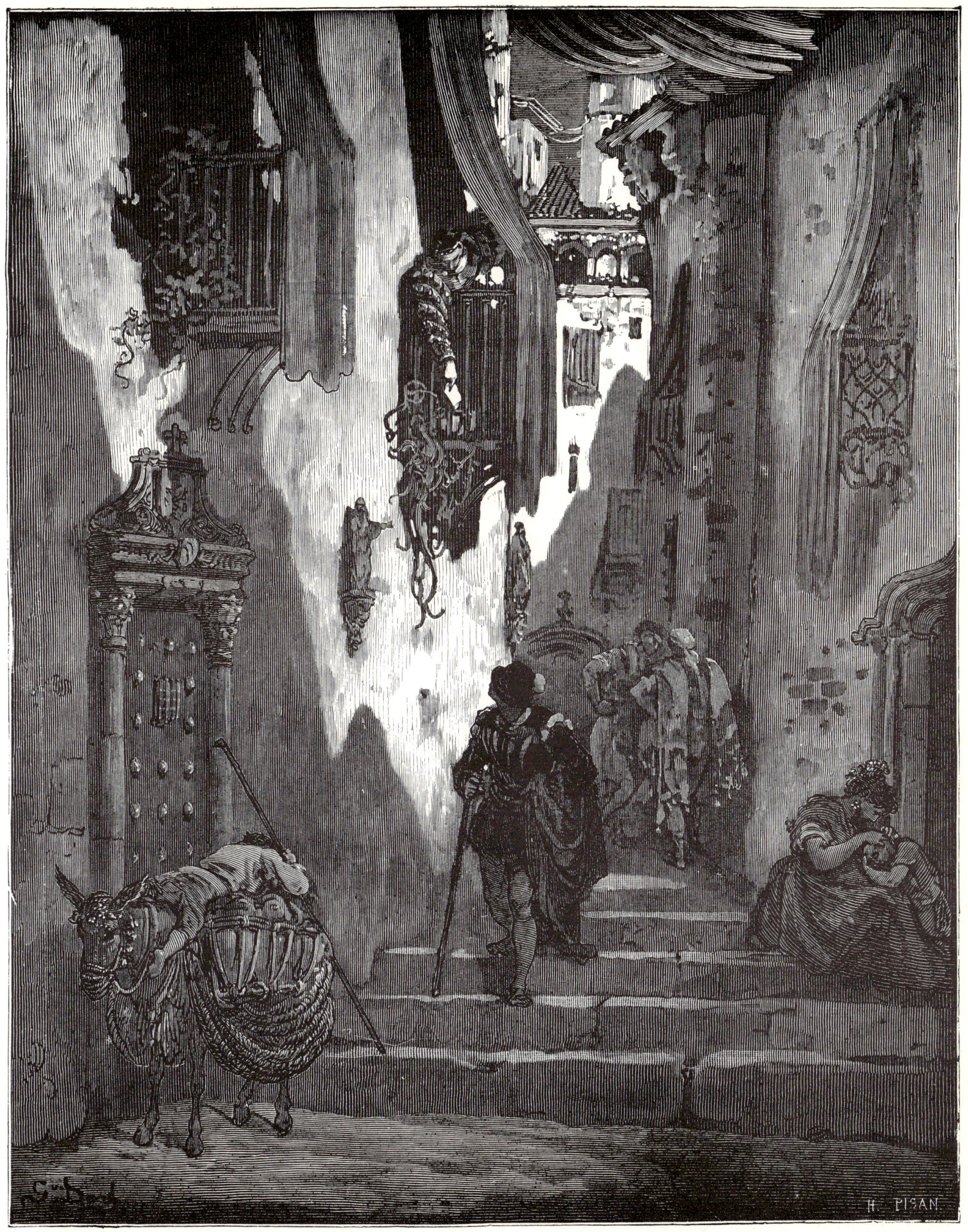

'He got a number of love-letters transmitted to me, every one full of the tenderest expressions.'

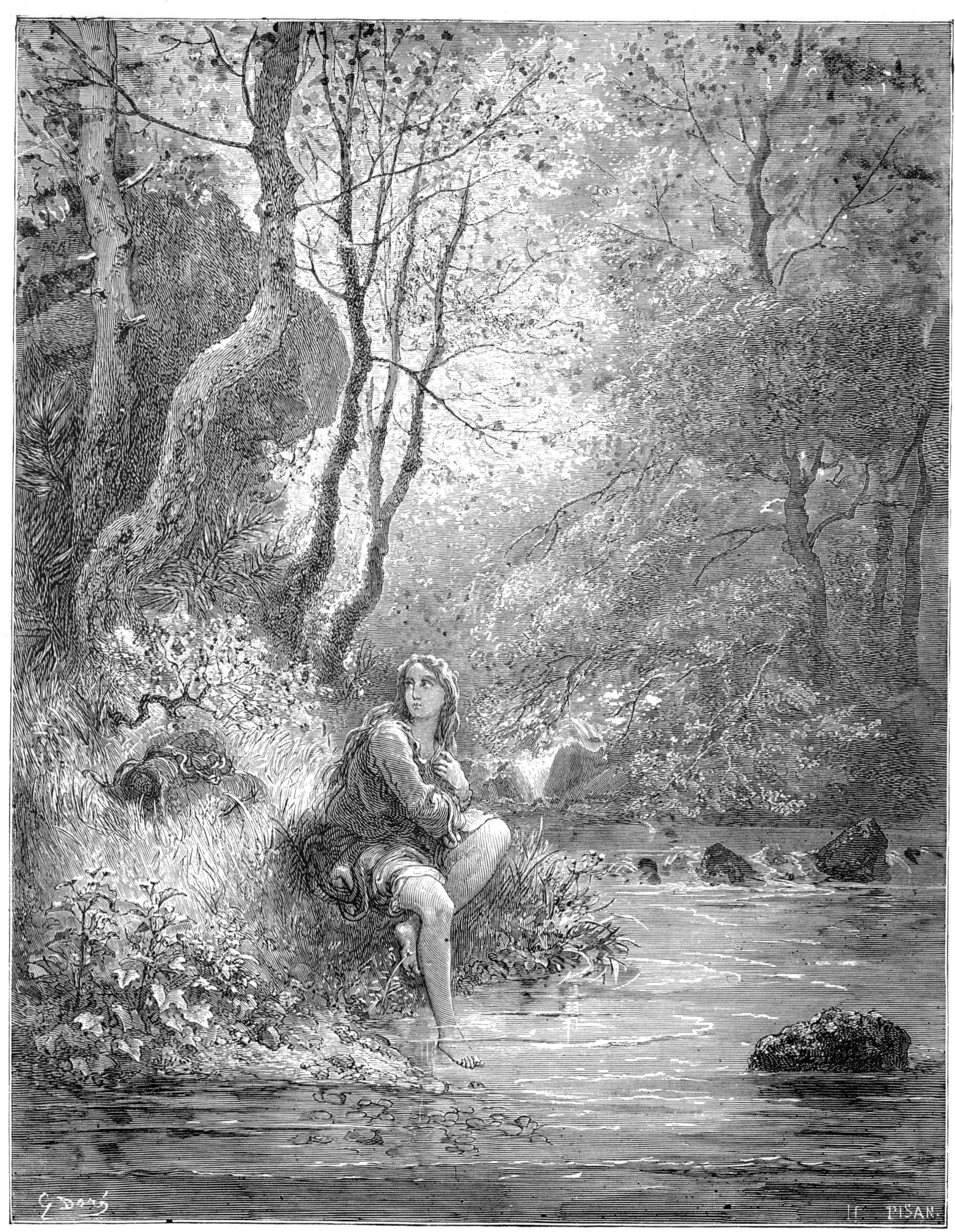

'They spied a youth in a country habit, sitting at the foot of a rock behind an ash-tree.'

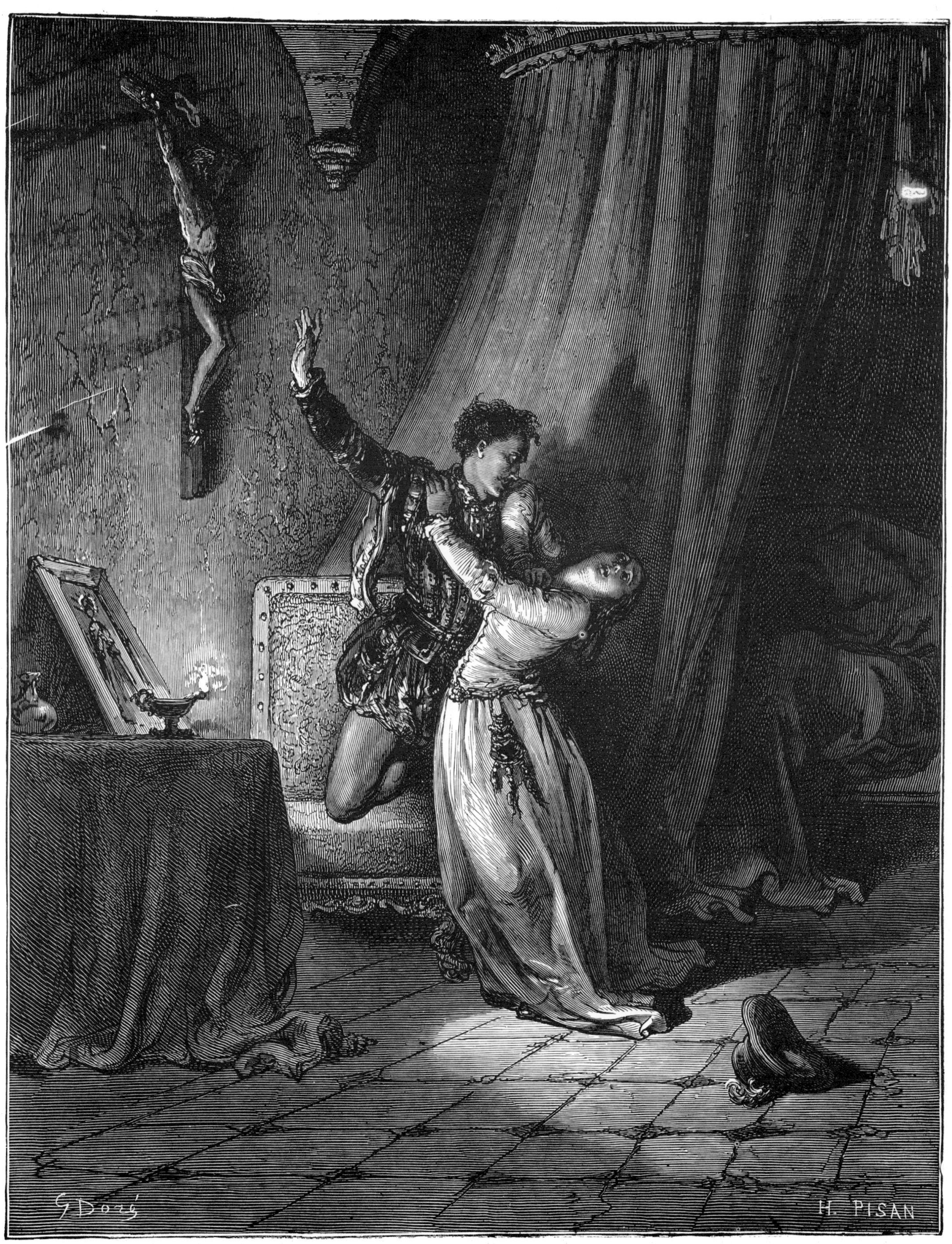

'I am yours this moment, beautiful Dorothea: see, I give you here my hand to be yours.'

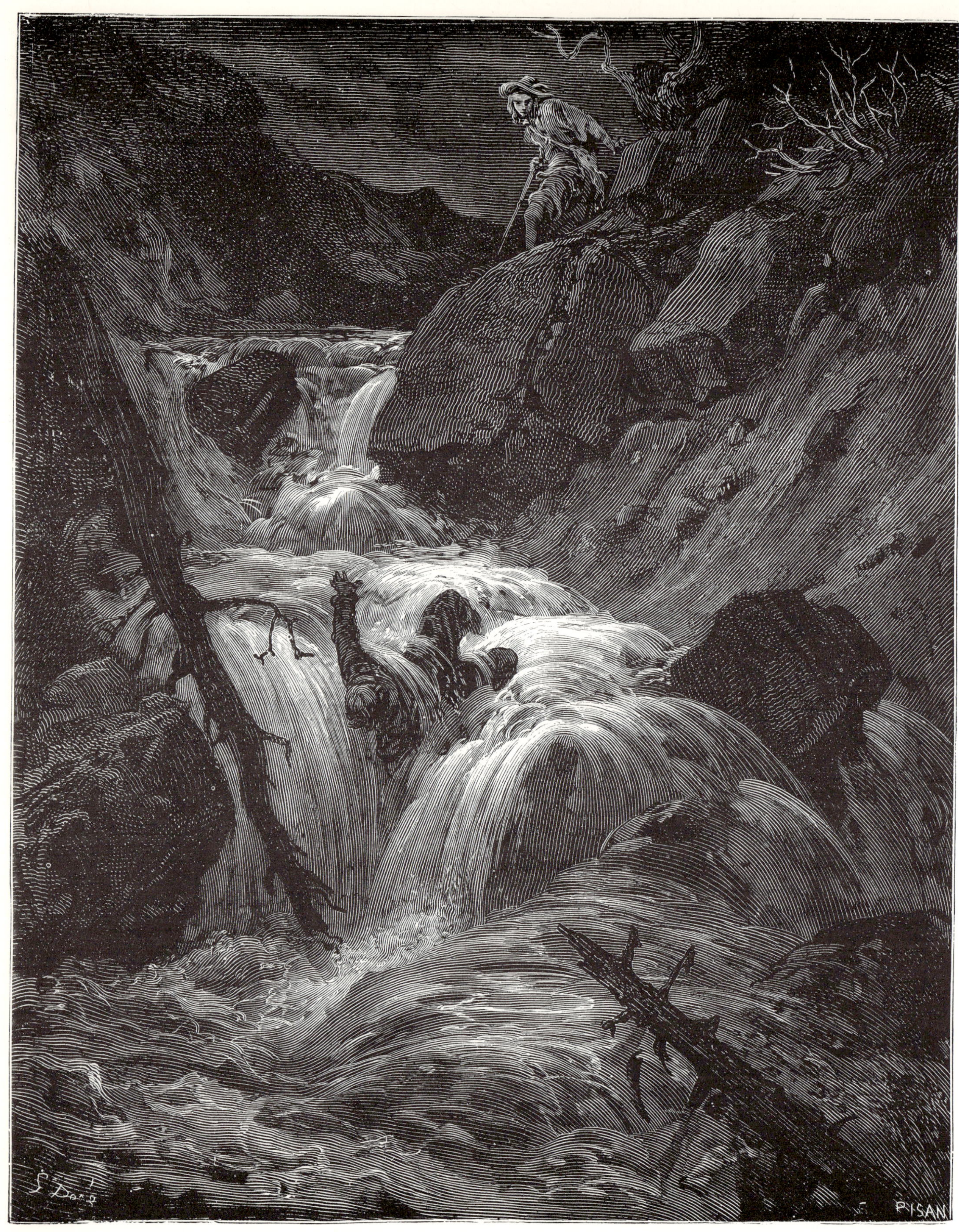

‘With the little strength I had I pushed him down a precipice, where I left him.’

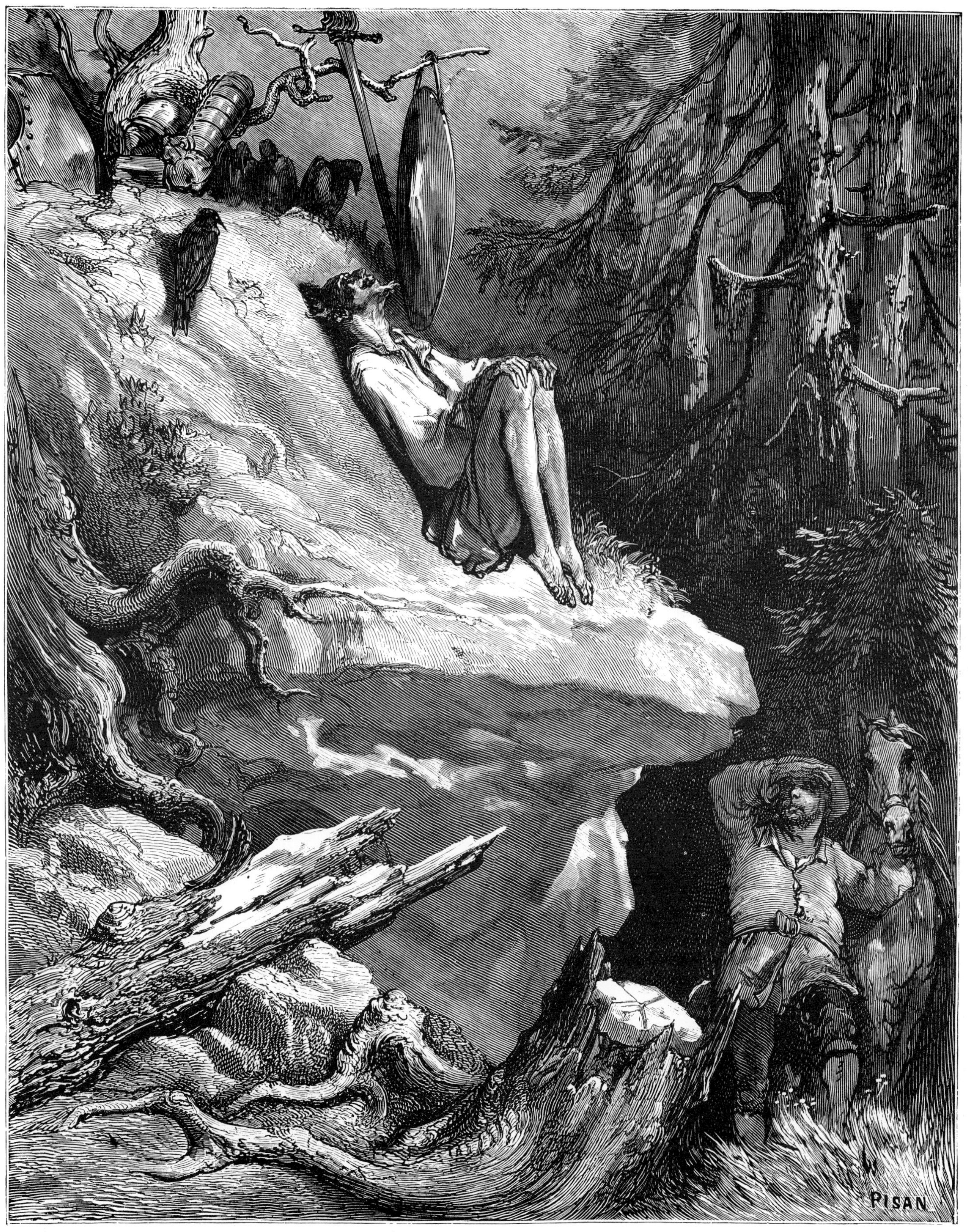

''Alas!' answered Sancho, 'I found him in his shirt, lean, pale, and almost starved, sighing for his Lady Dulcinea.''

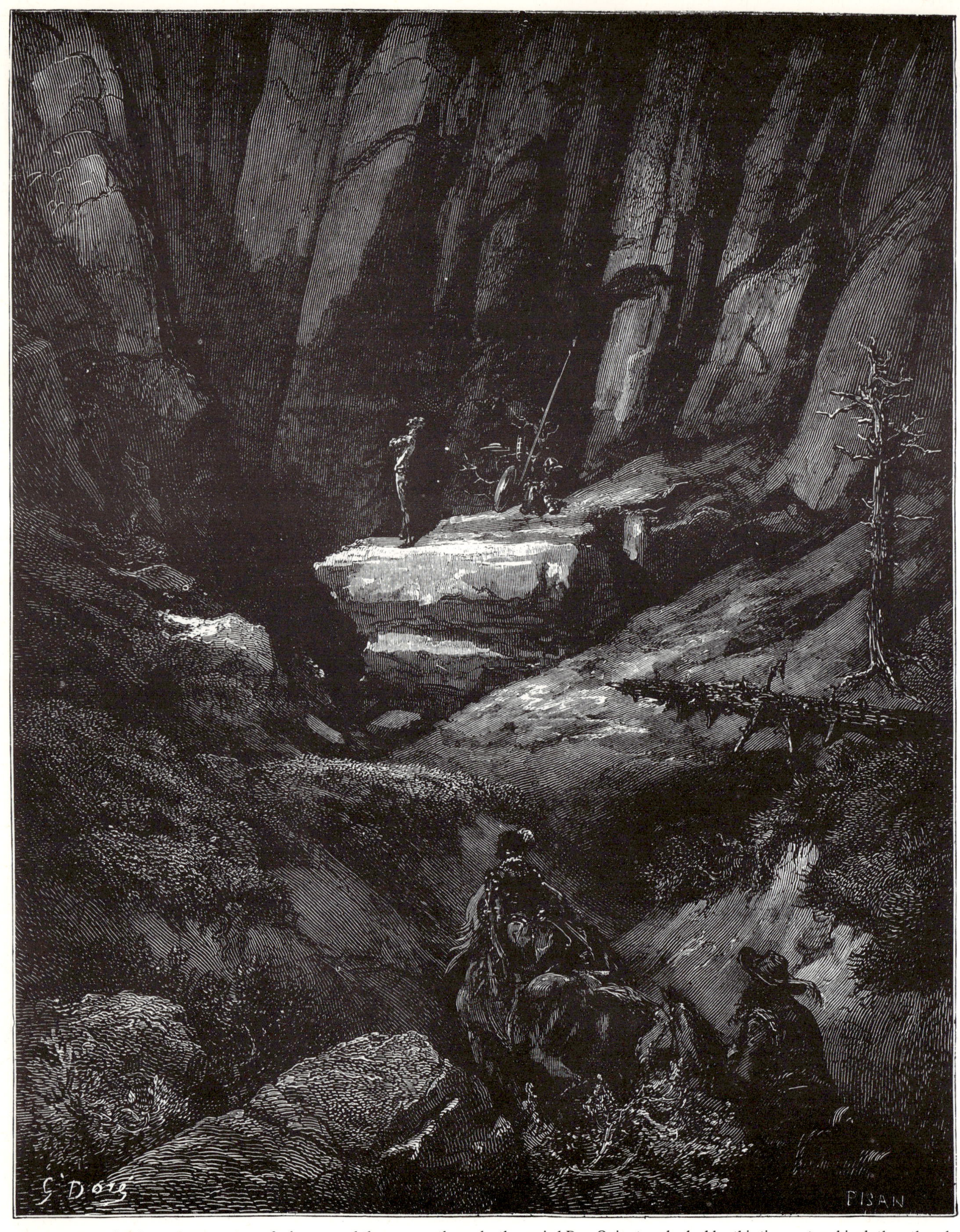

'They went on for about three quarters of a league, and then among the rocks they spied Don Quixote, who had by this time put on his clothes, though not his armour.'

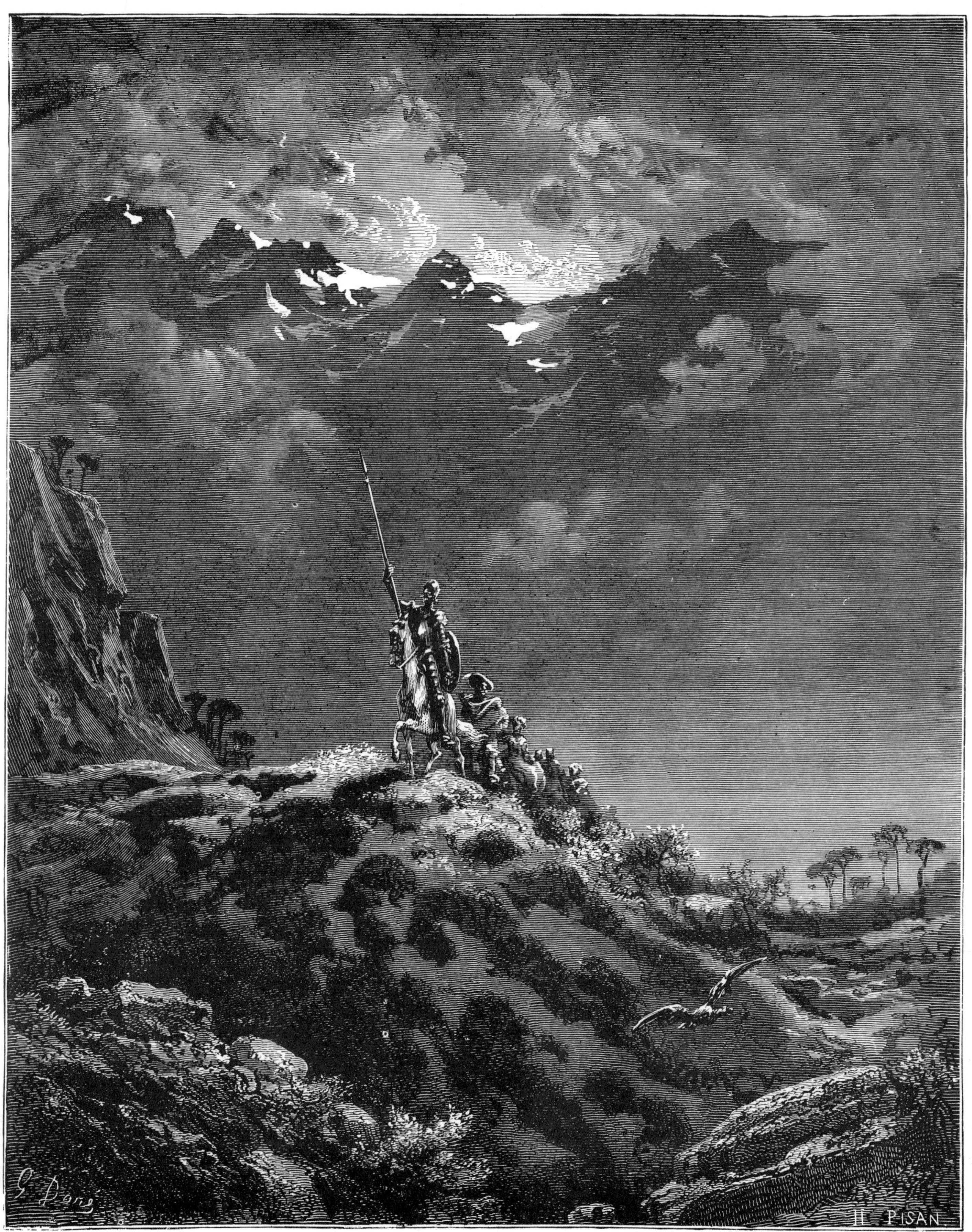

'Towards the kingdom of Micomicon.'

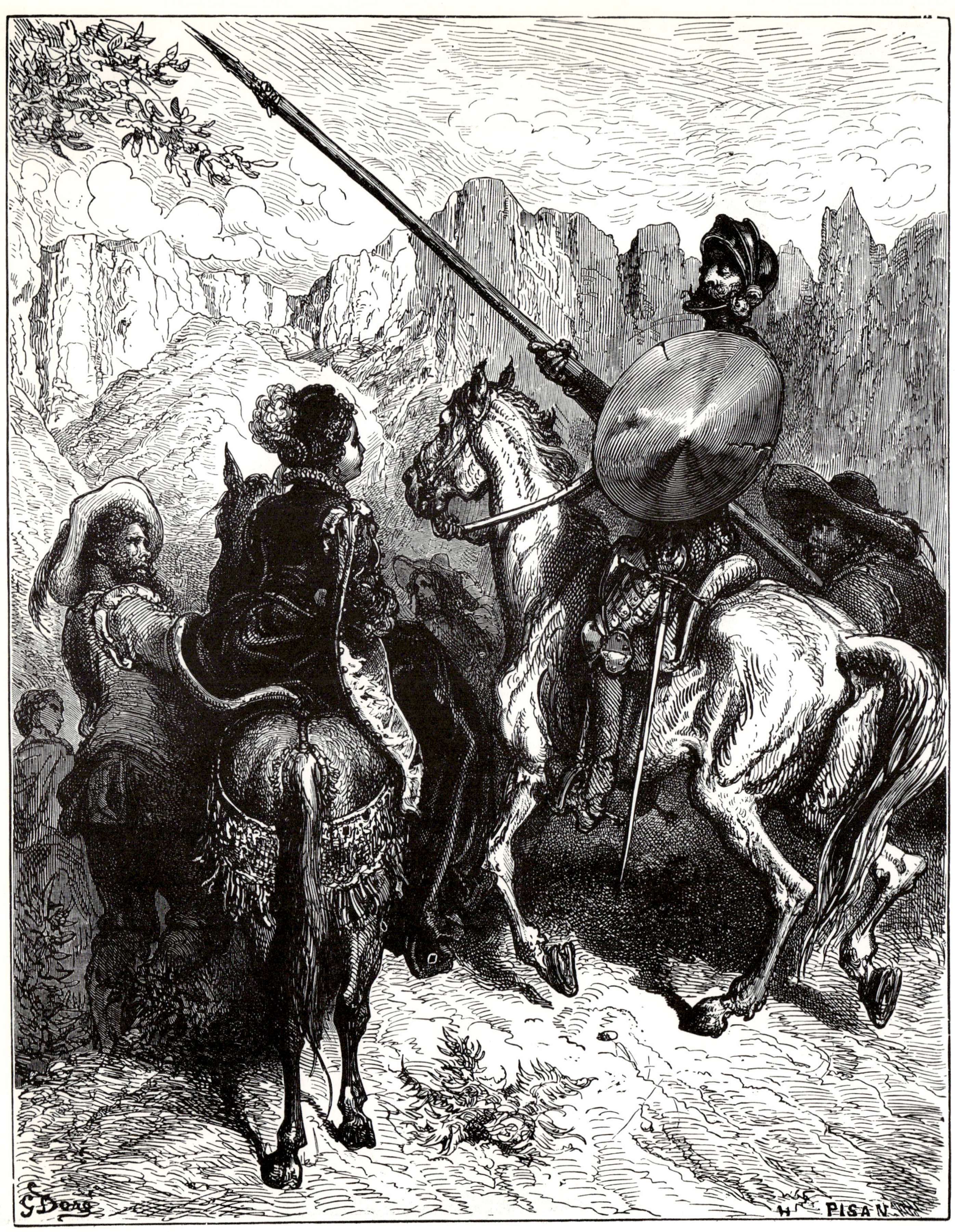

' 'Now lady,' said Don Quixote, 'let me entreat your greatness to tell me which way we must go, to do you service.' '

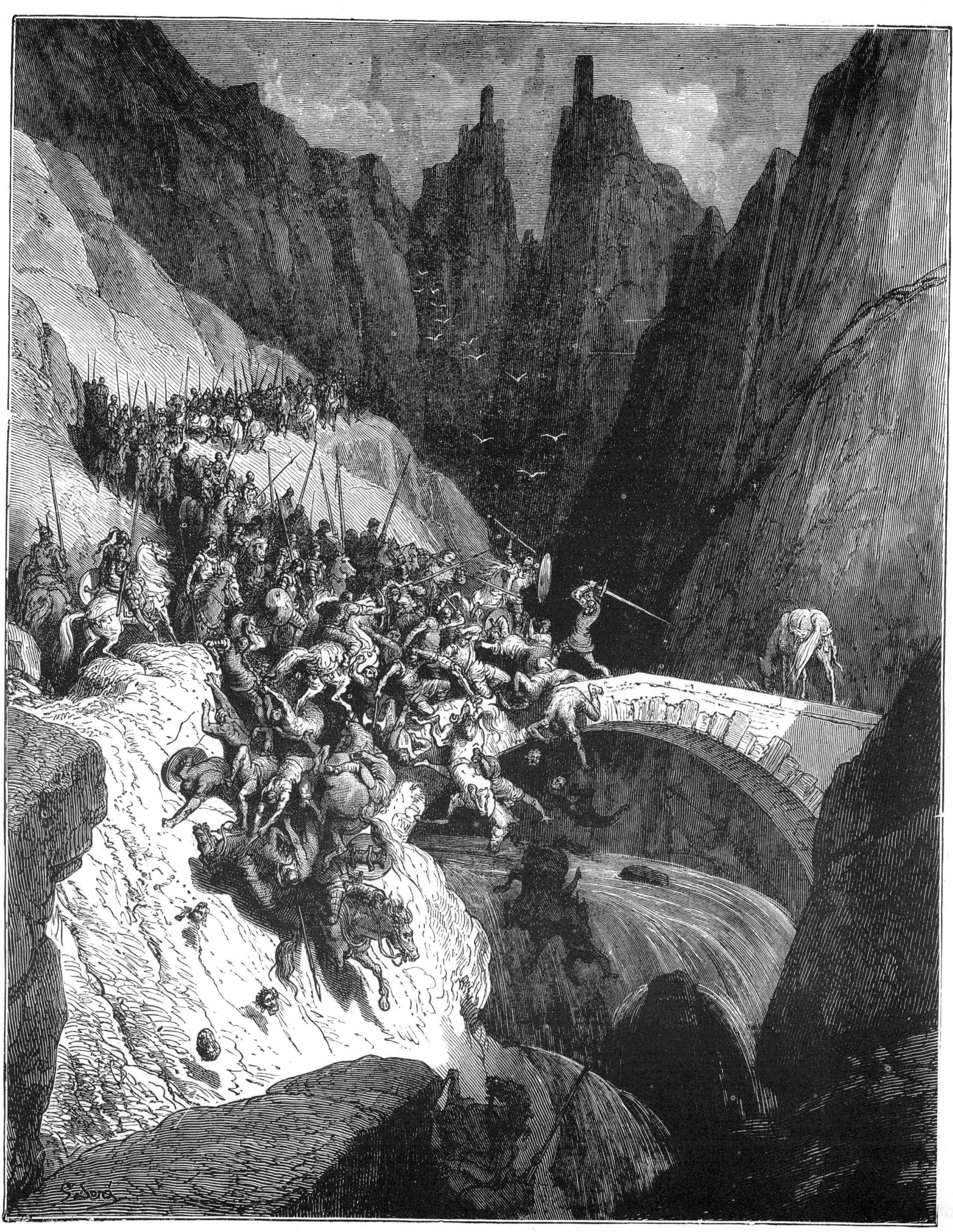

'How Don Diego Garcia with his single force defended the passage of a bridge against a great army.'

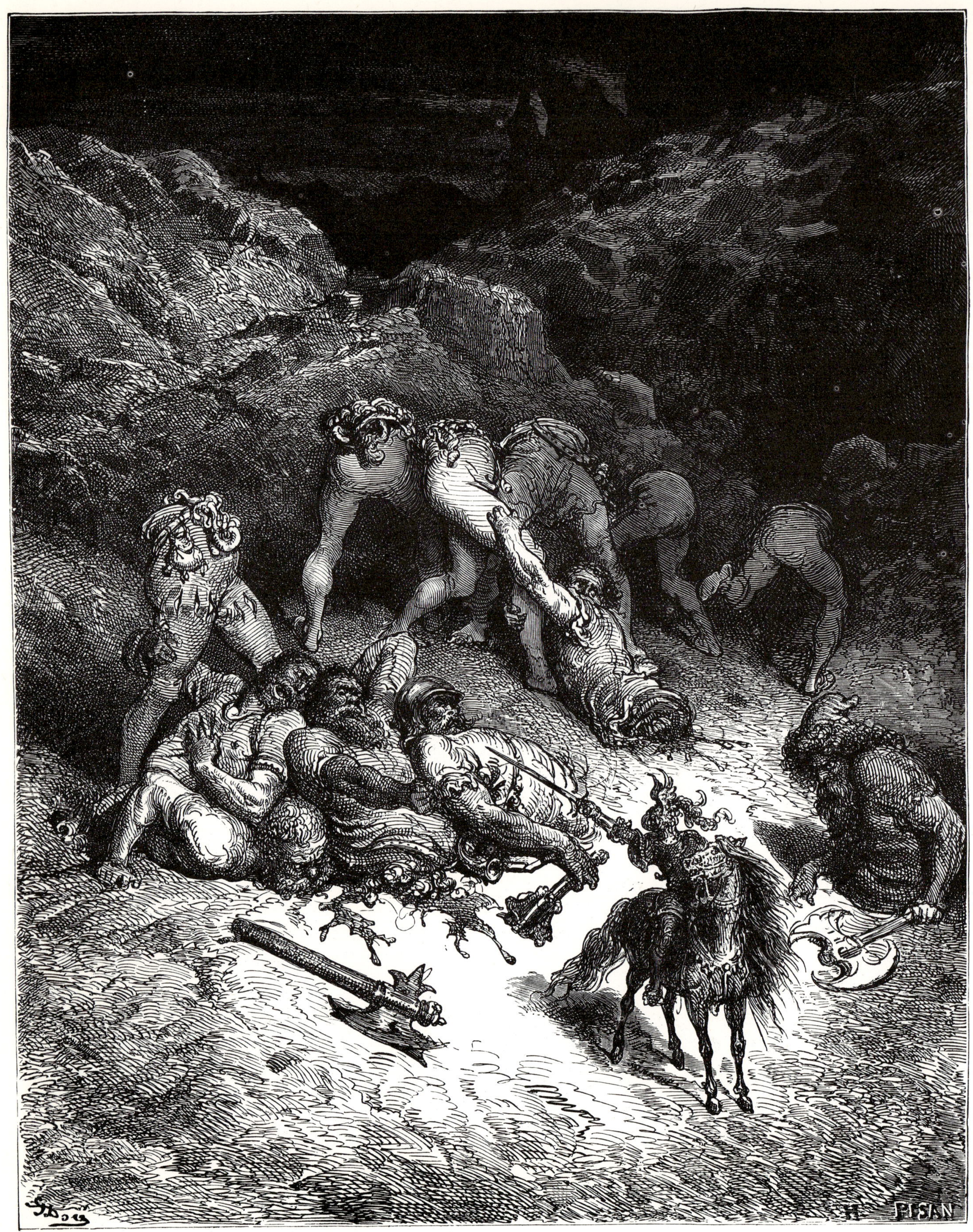

'How Felixmarte cut off five giants by the middle.'

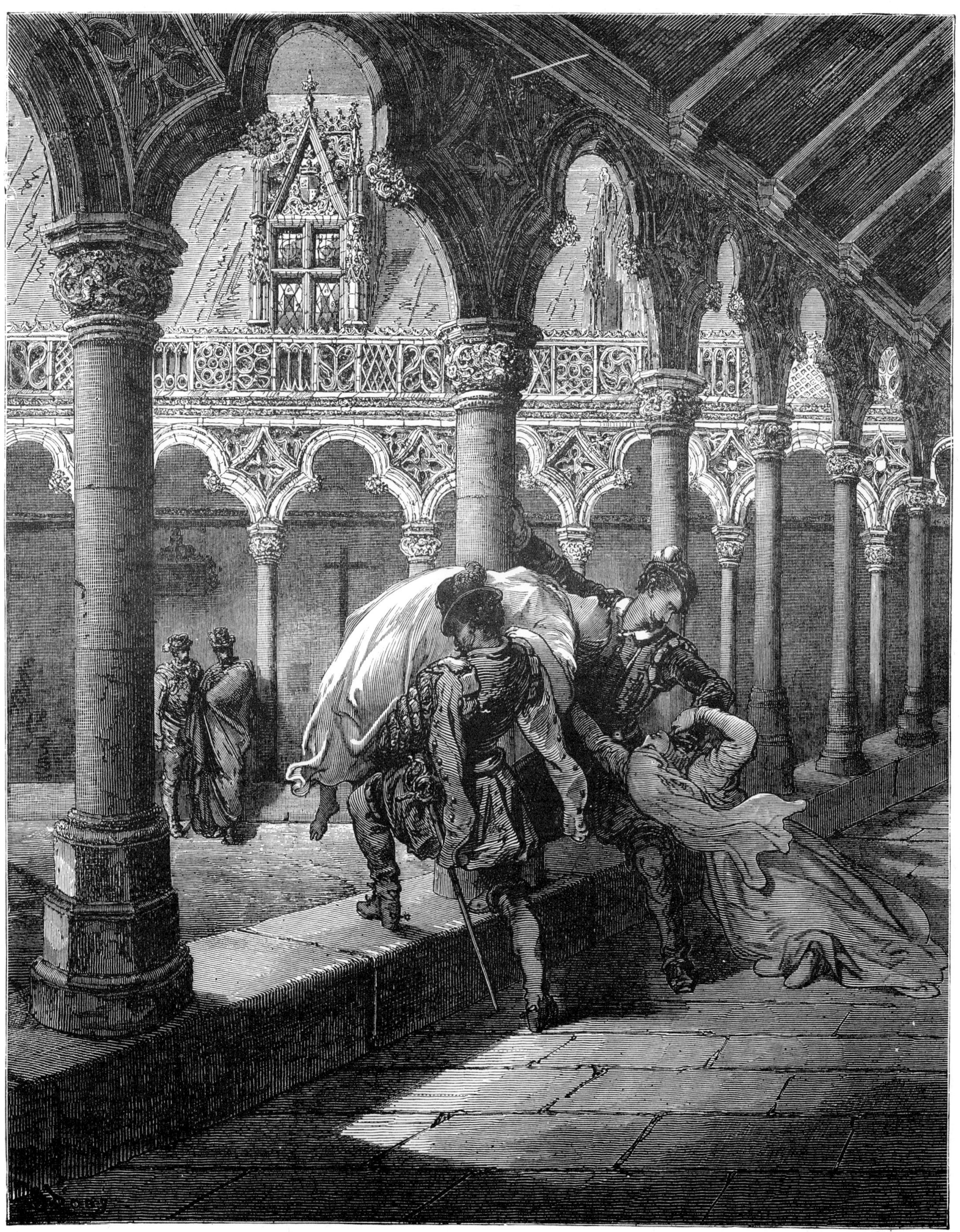

'Lucinda, finding herself in his power, fell into a swoon.'

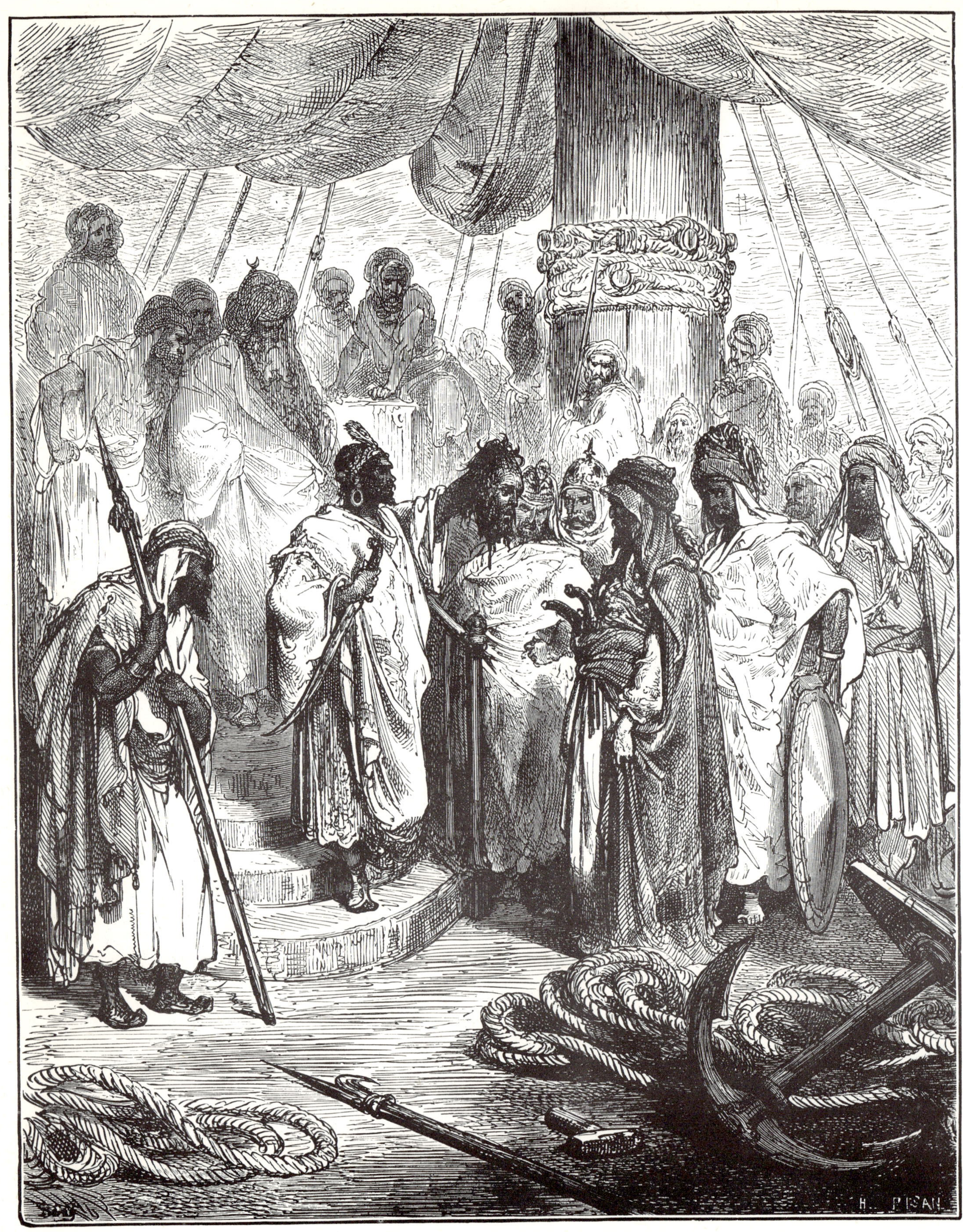

'They cut off his head, and brought it to the Turkish general.'

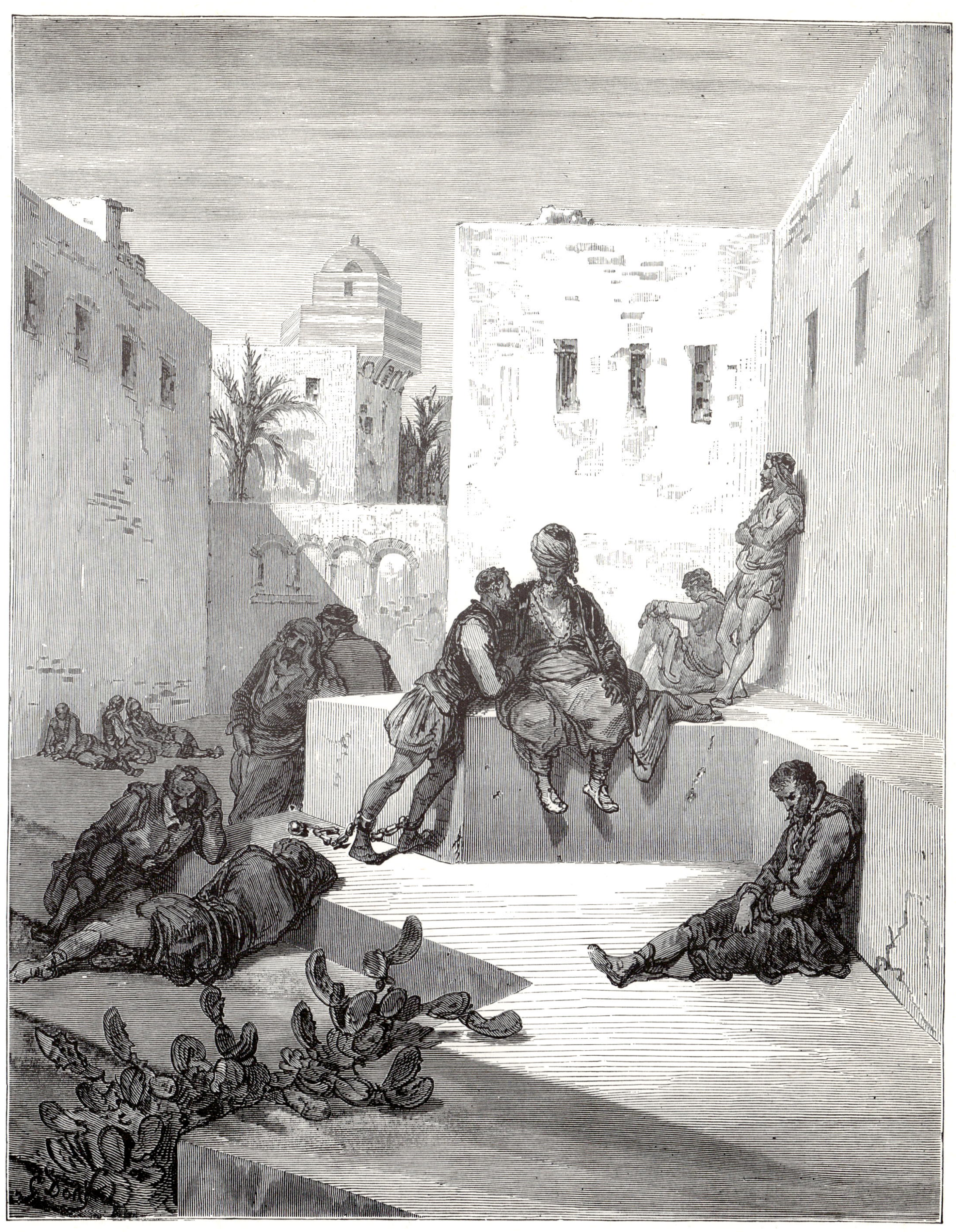

'At last I resolved to trust a renegade of Murcia, who had shown me great proofs of his kindness.'

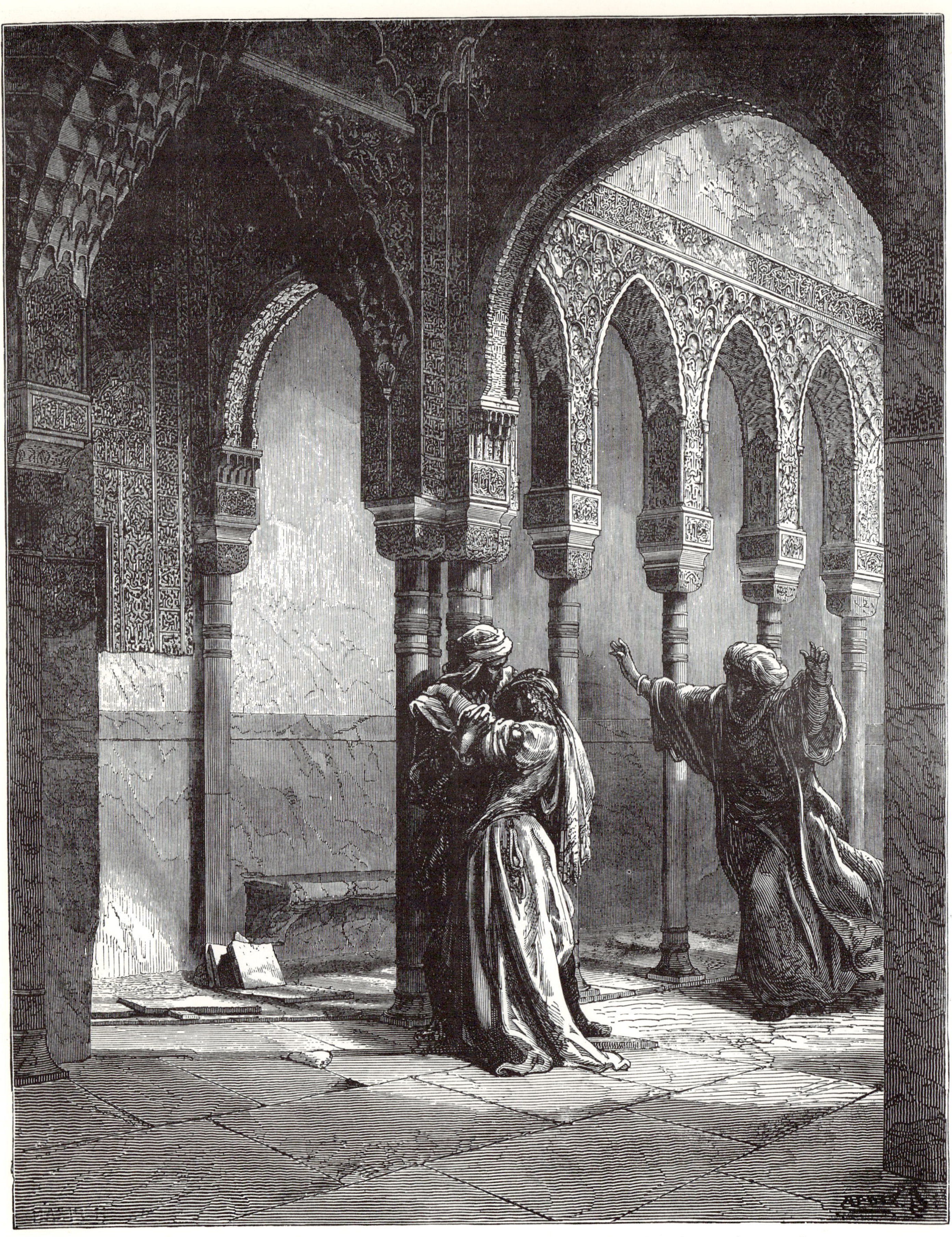

'Her father came hastily to us, and, seeing his daughter in this condition, asked her what was the matter.'

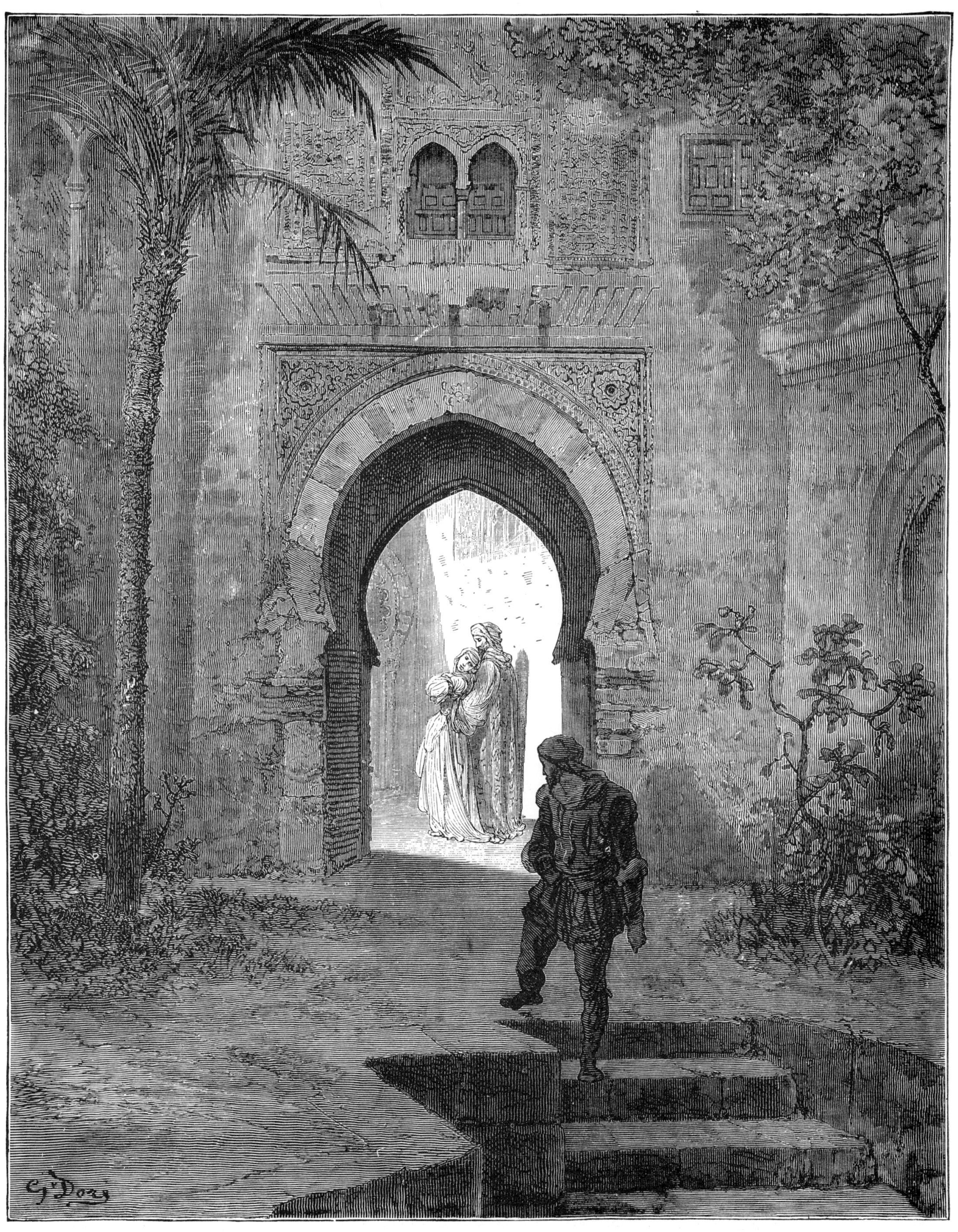

'Zoraida, showing trouble in her looks, went away with her father.'

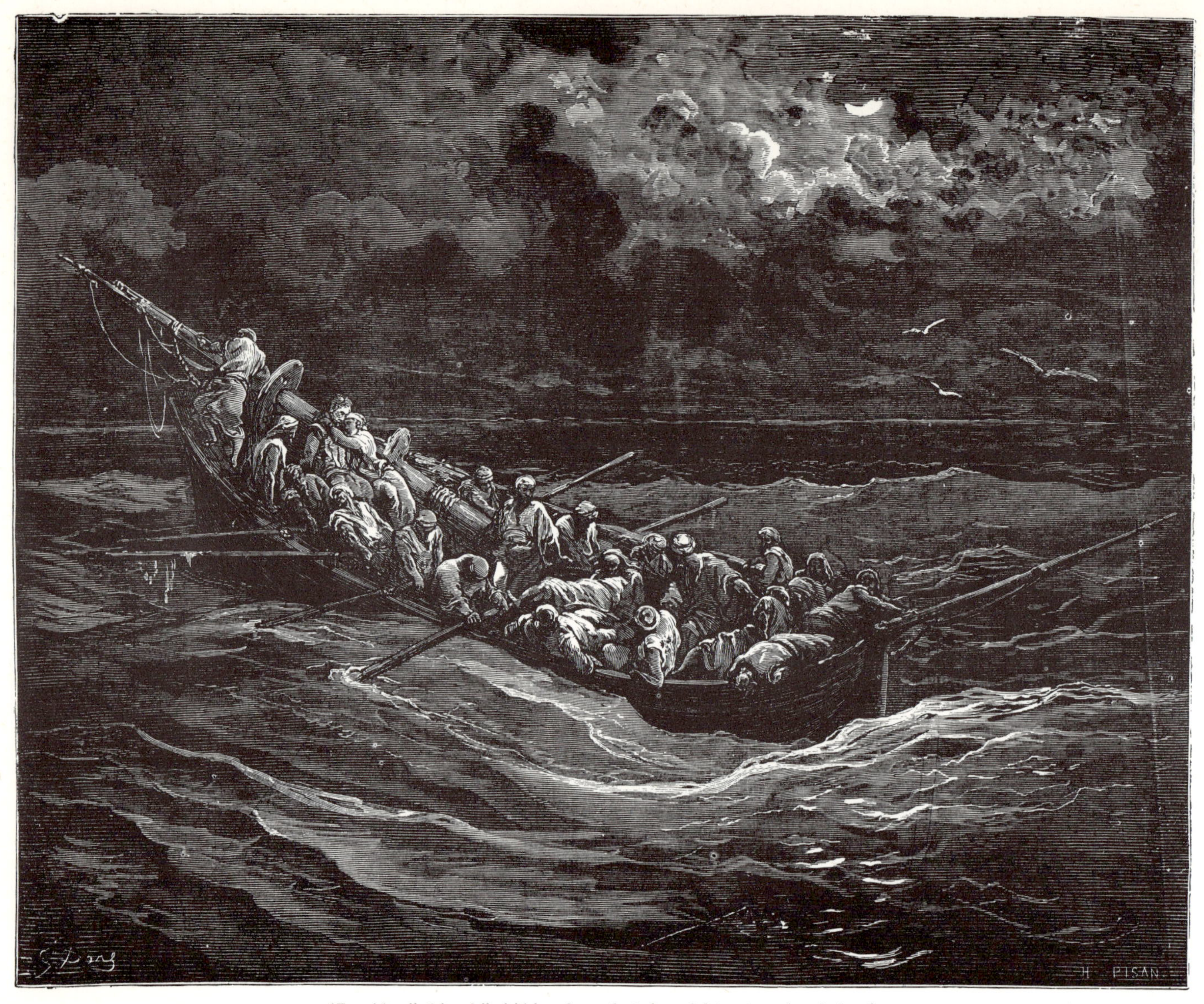

'Zoraida all this while hid her face, that she might not see her father.'

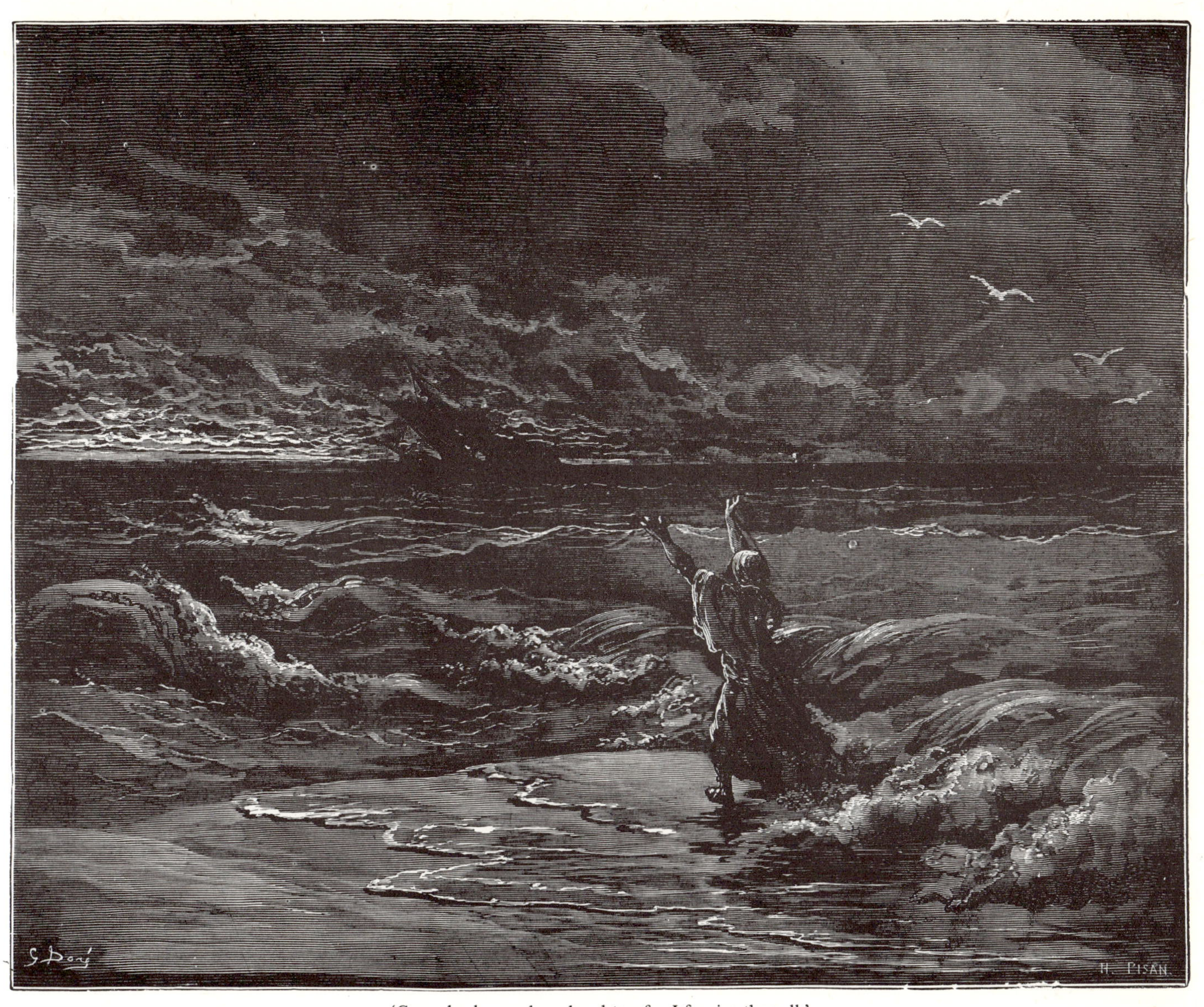

'Come back, my dear daughter, for I forgive thee all.'

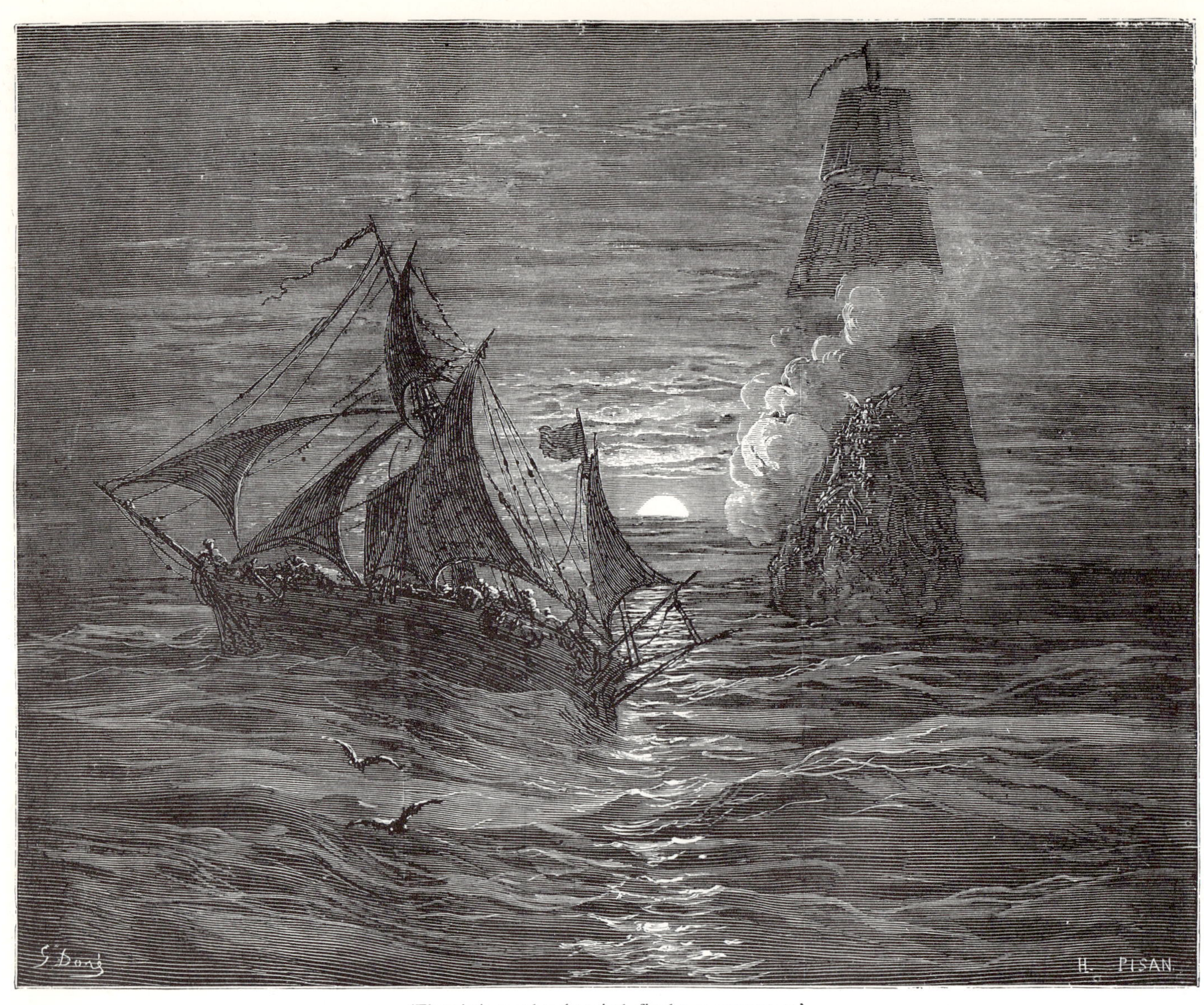

'They being under the wind, fired two guns at us.'

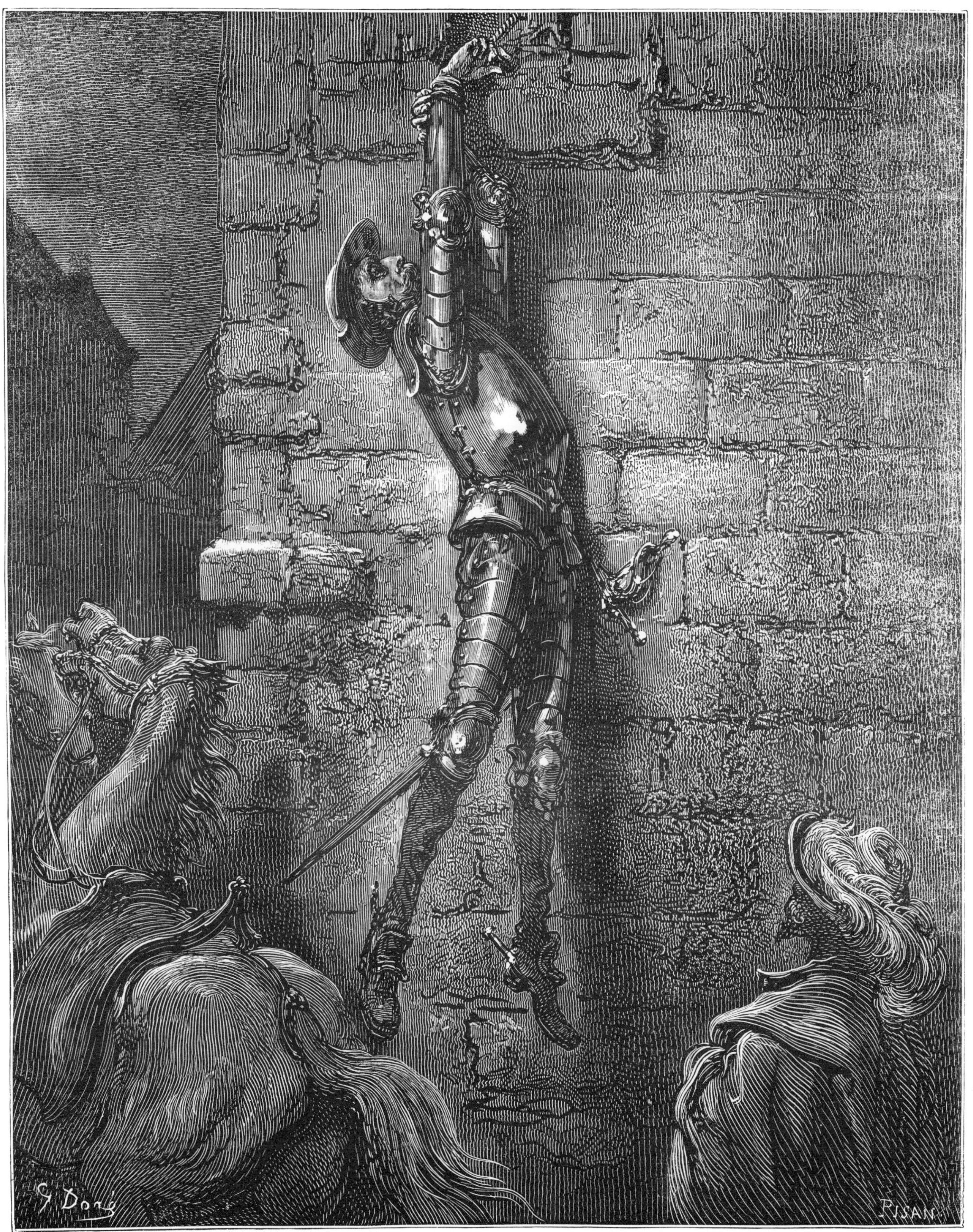

'He had inevitably fallen to the ground, had not his wrist been securely fastened to the rope.'

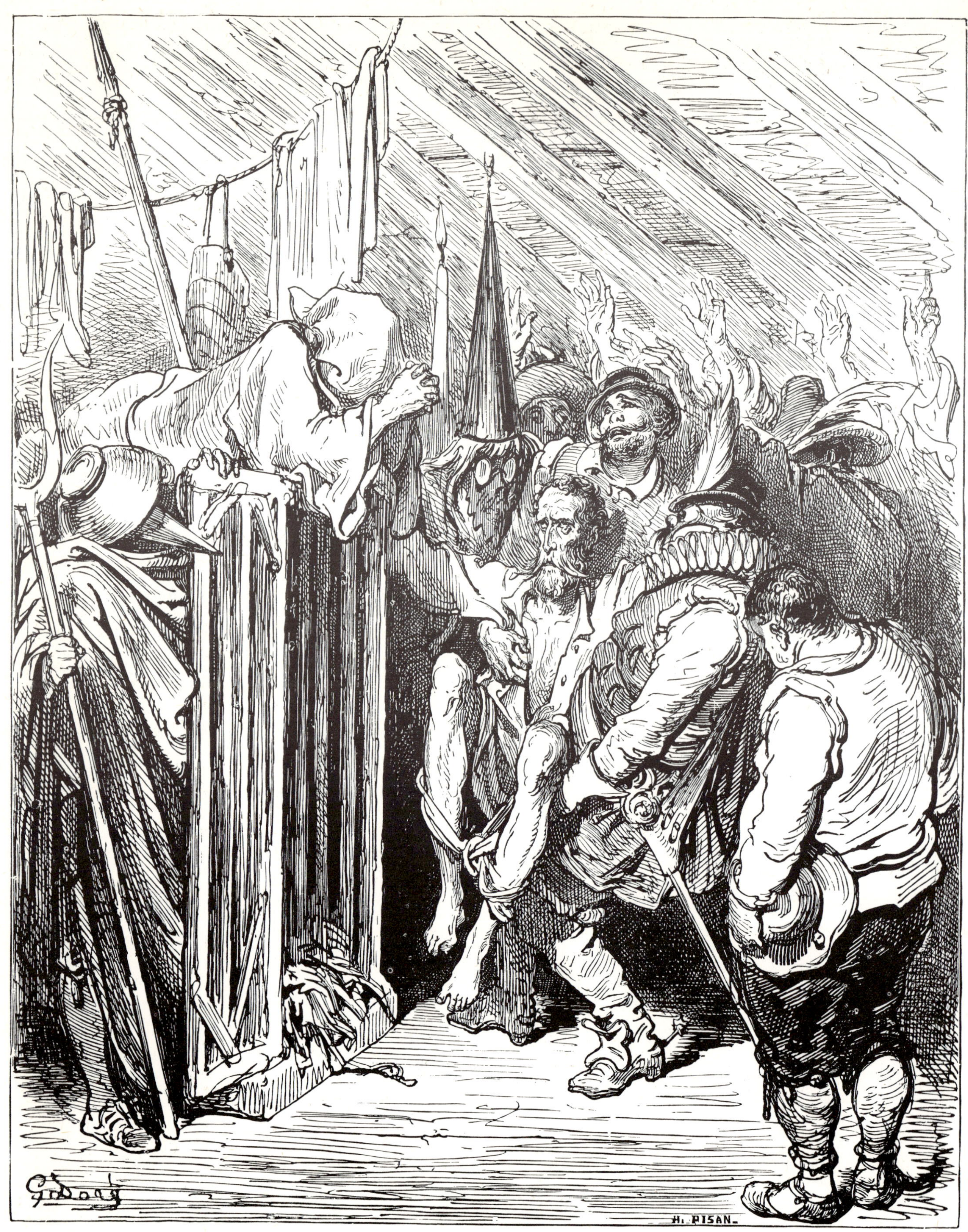

'Be not impatient, O Knight of the Woeful Figure, at your imprisonment.'

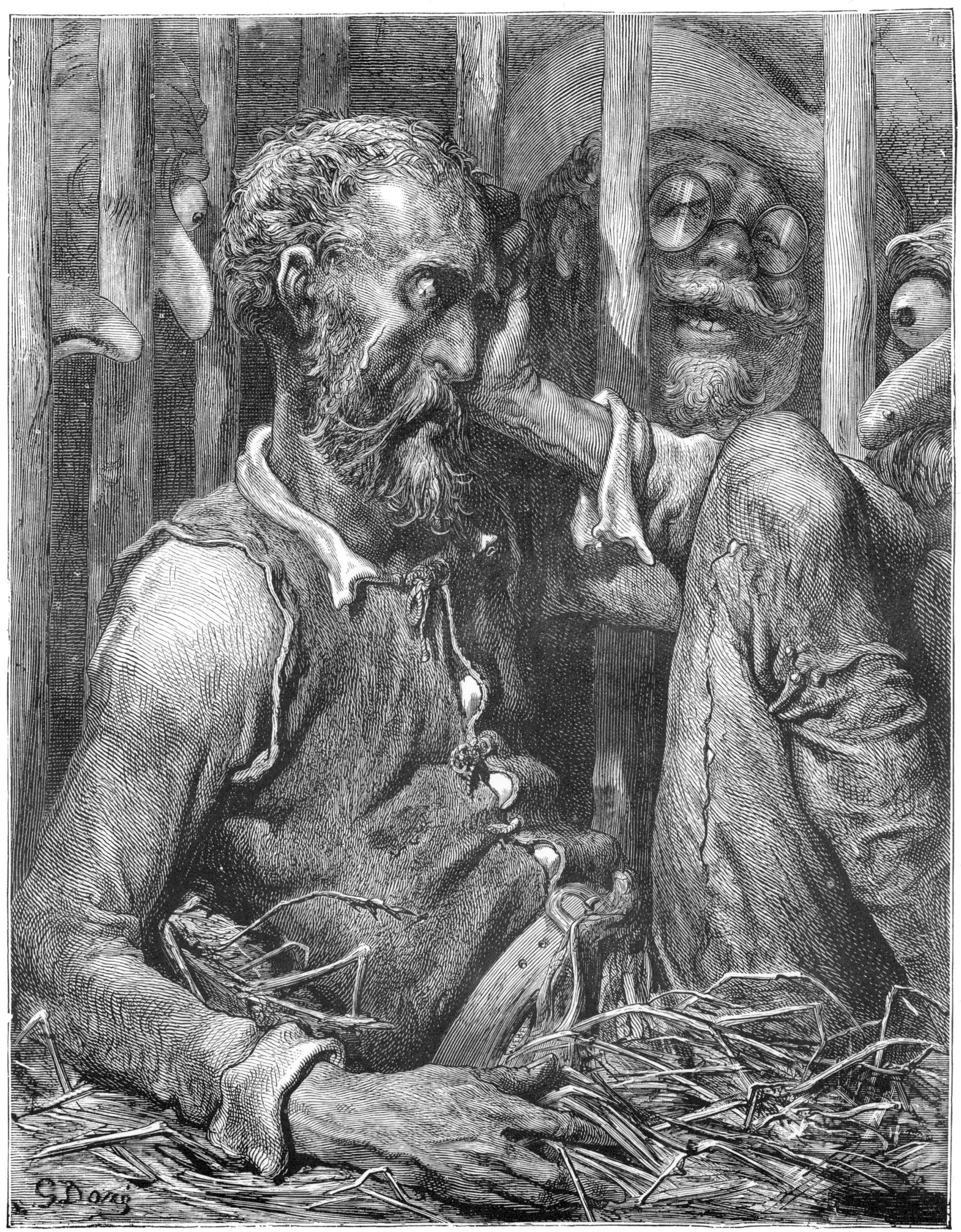

'Don Quixote was not so much amazed at his enchantment as at the manner of it.'

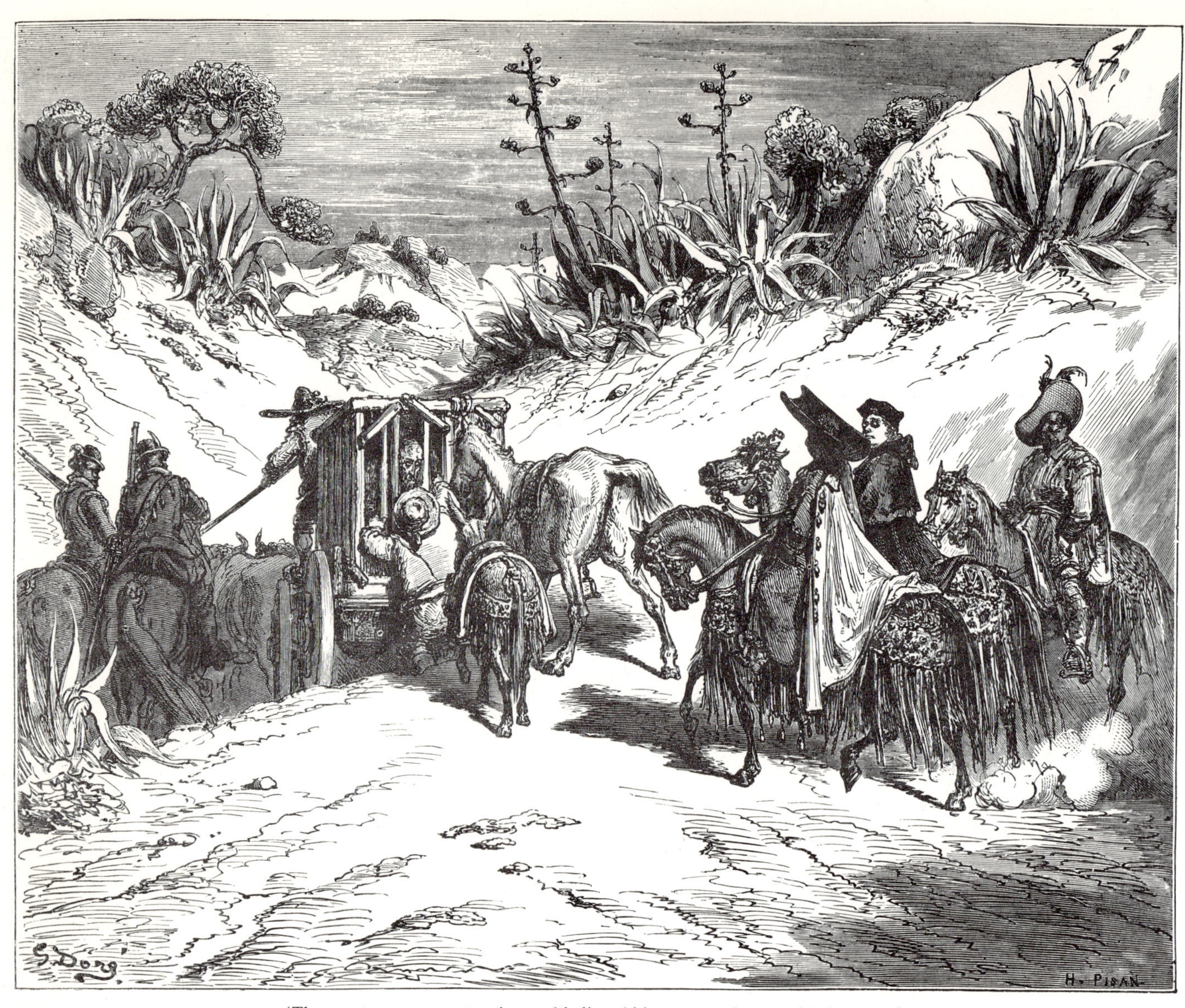

'The curate was very attentive, and believed him a man of a sound judgement.'

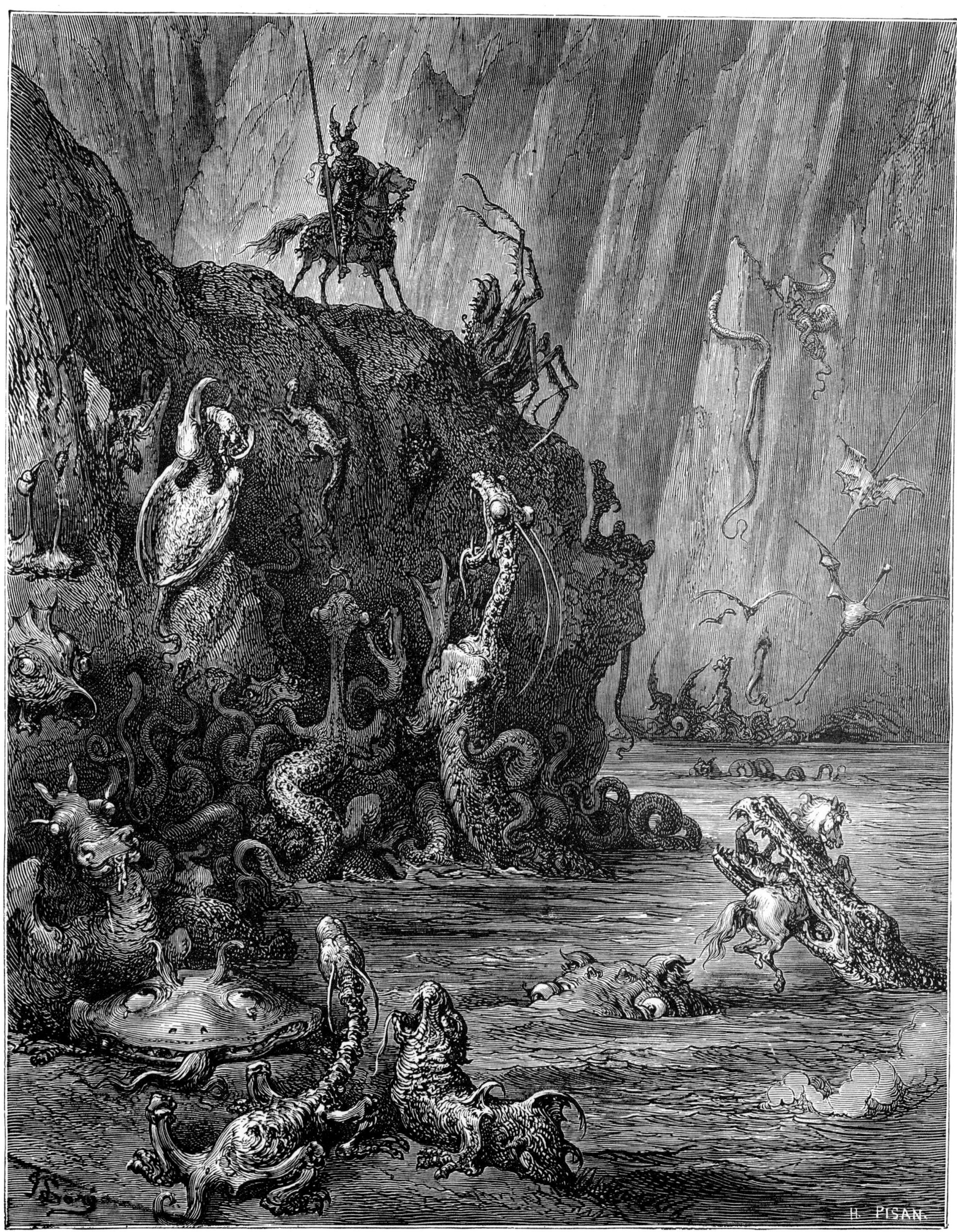

'A vast lake of boiling pitch, in which an infinite multitude of fierce and terrible creatures are traversing backwards and forwards.'

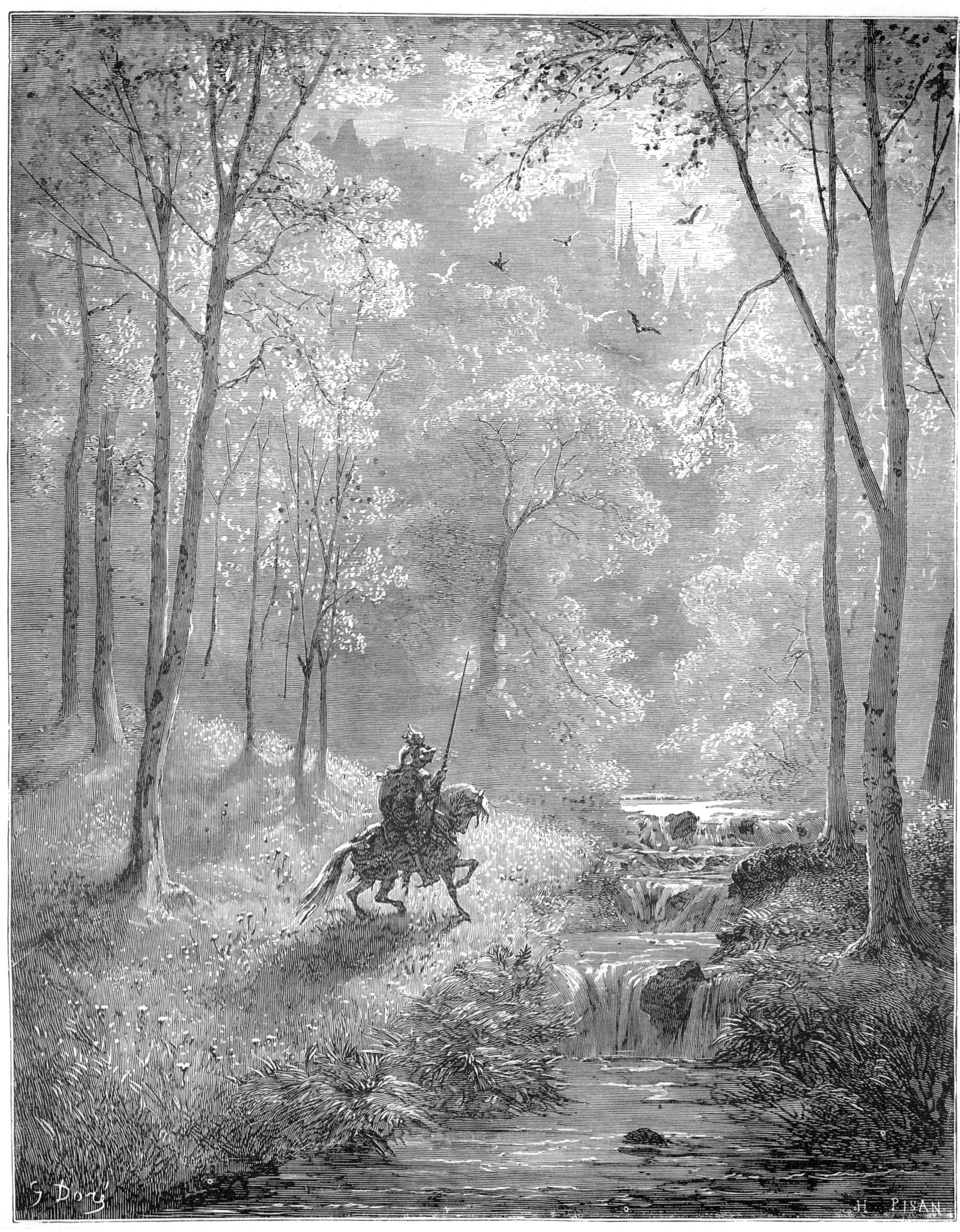

'The sky appears to him more transparent, and the sun seems to shine with a redoubled brightness.'

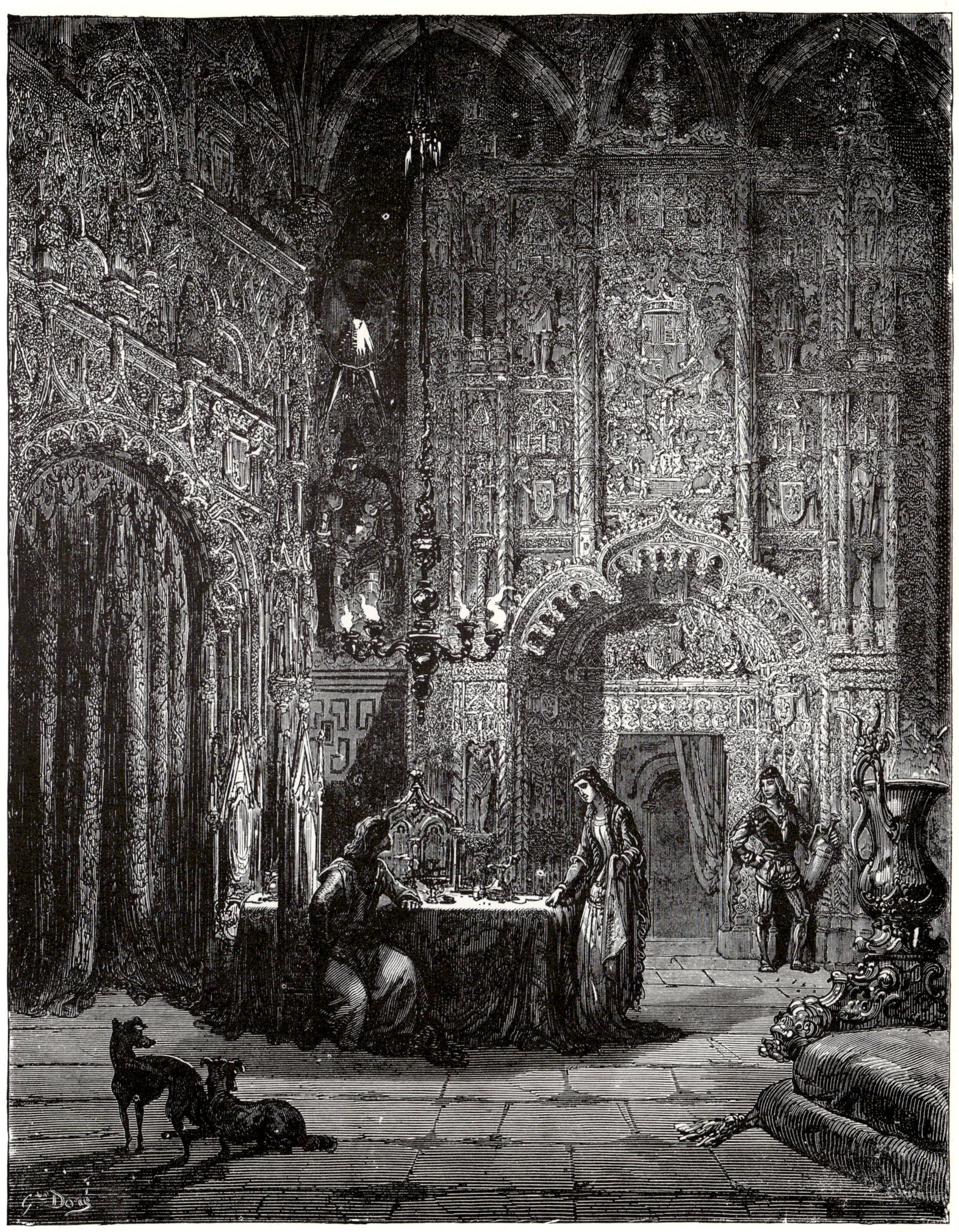

'Another damsel comes into the room, and begins to inform him what castle that is, and how she is enchanted in it.'

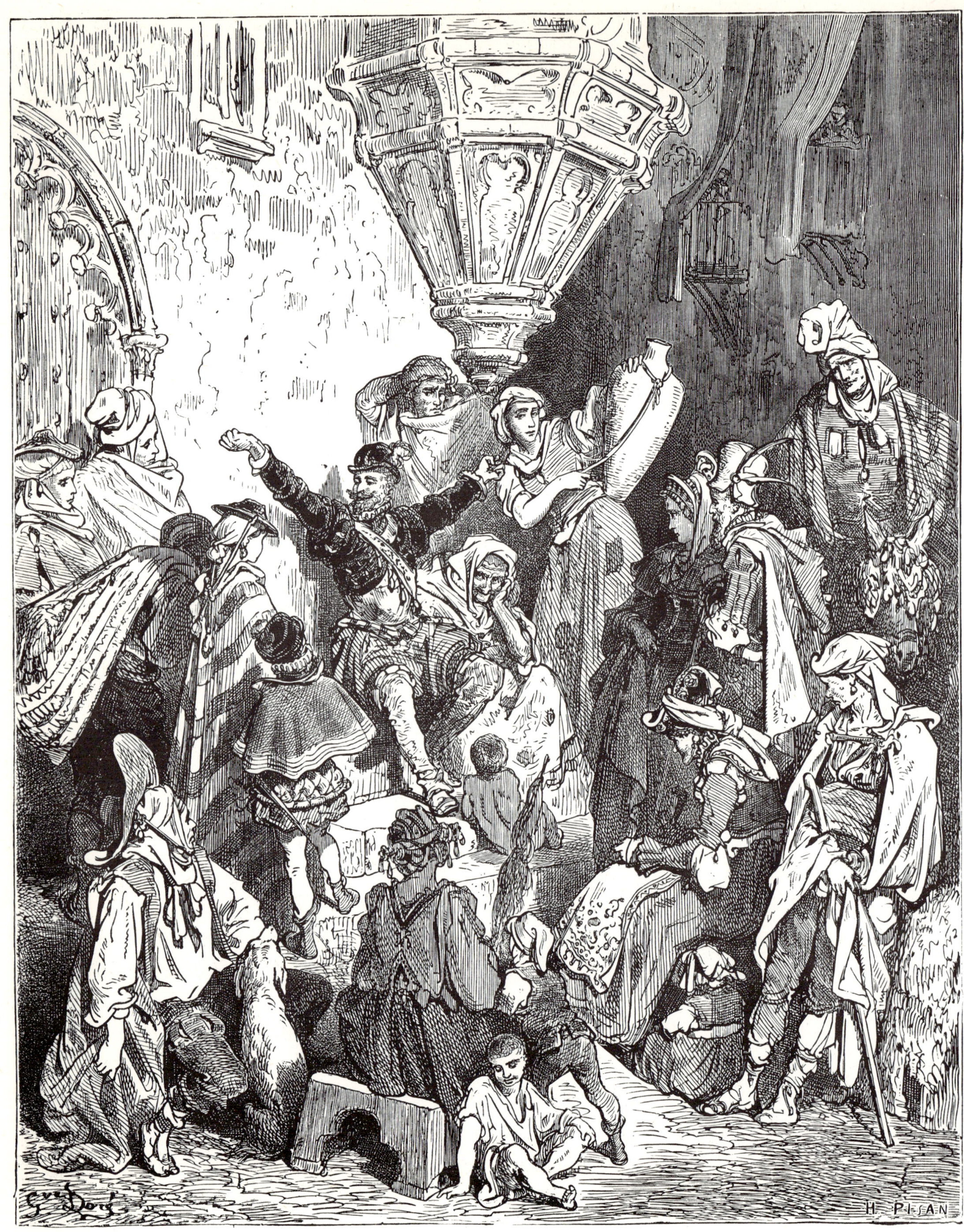

'There was not that country upon the face of the earth which he had not seen, nor battle which he had not been engaged in.'

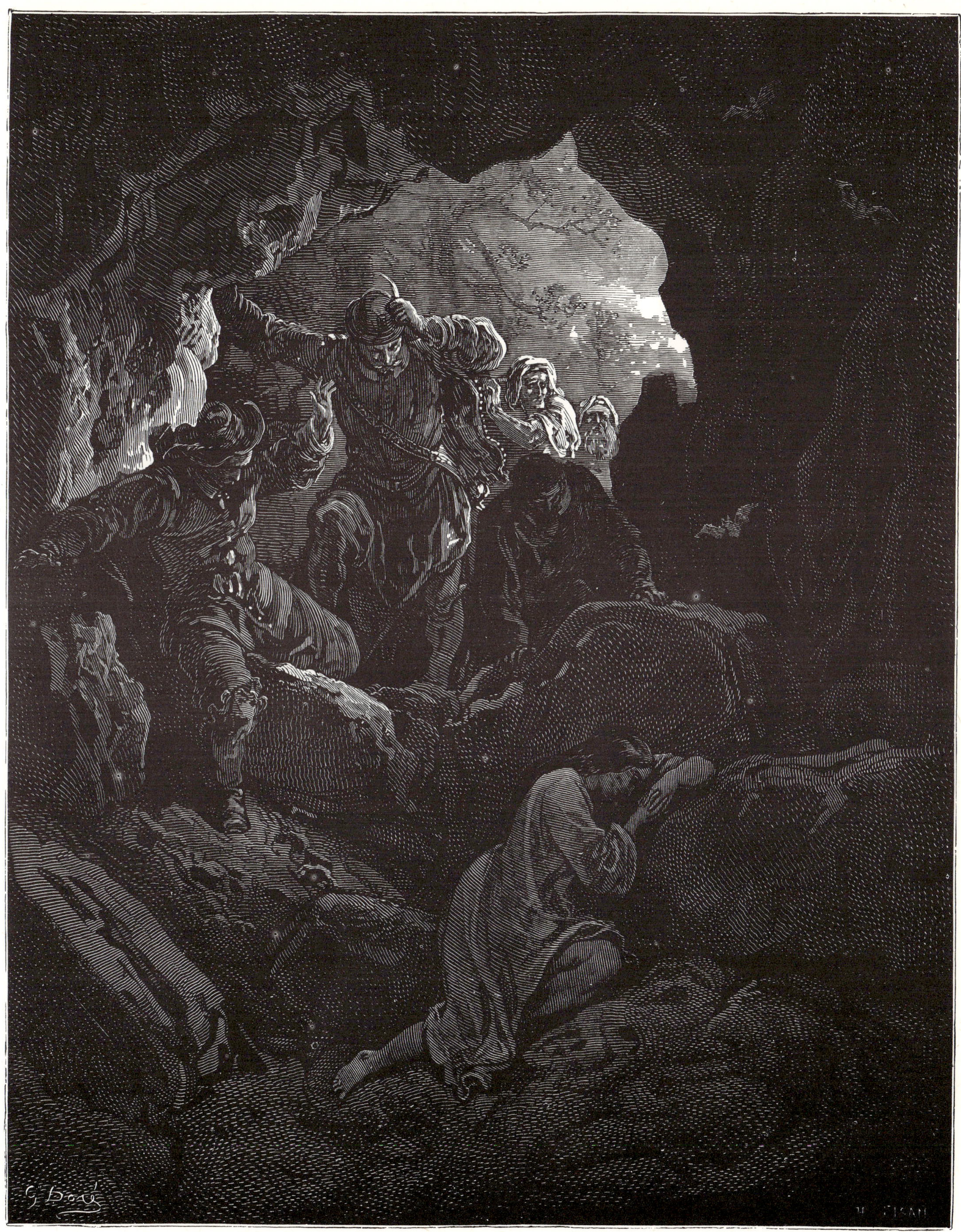

'A party with officers is sent out, who find the poor Leandra in a cave of one of the mountains.'

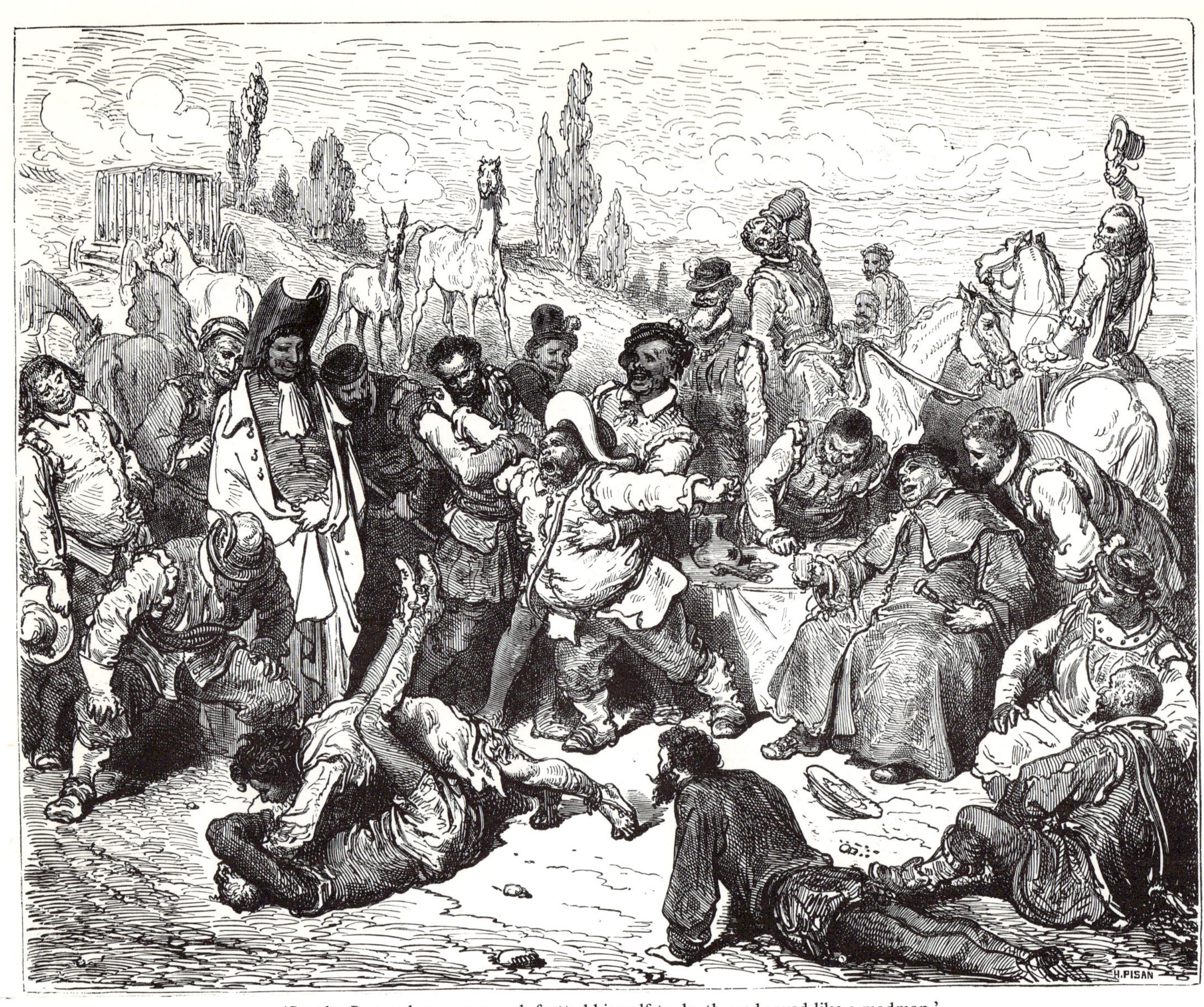

'Sancho Panza alone was vexed, fretted himself to death, and raved like a madman.'

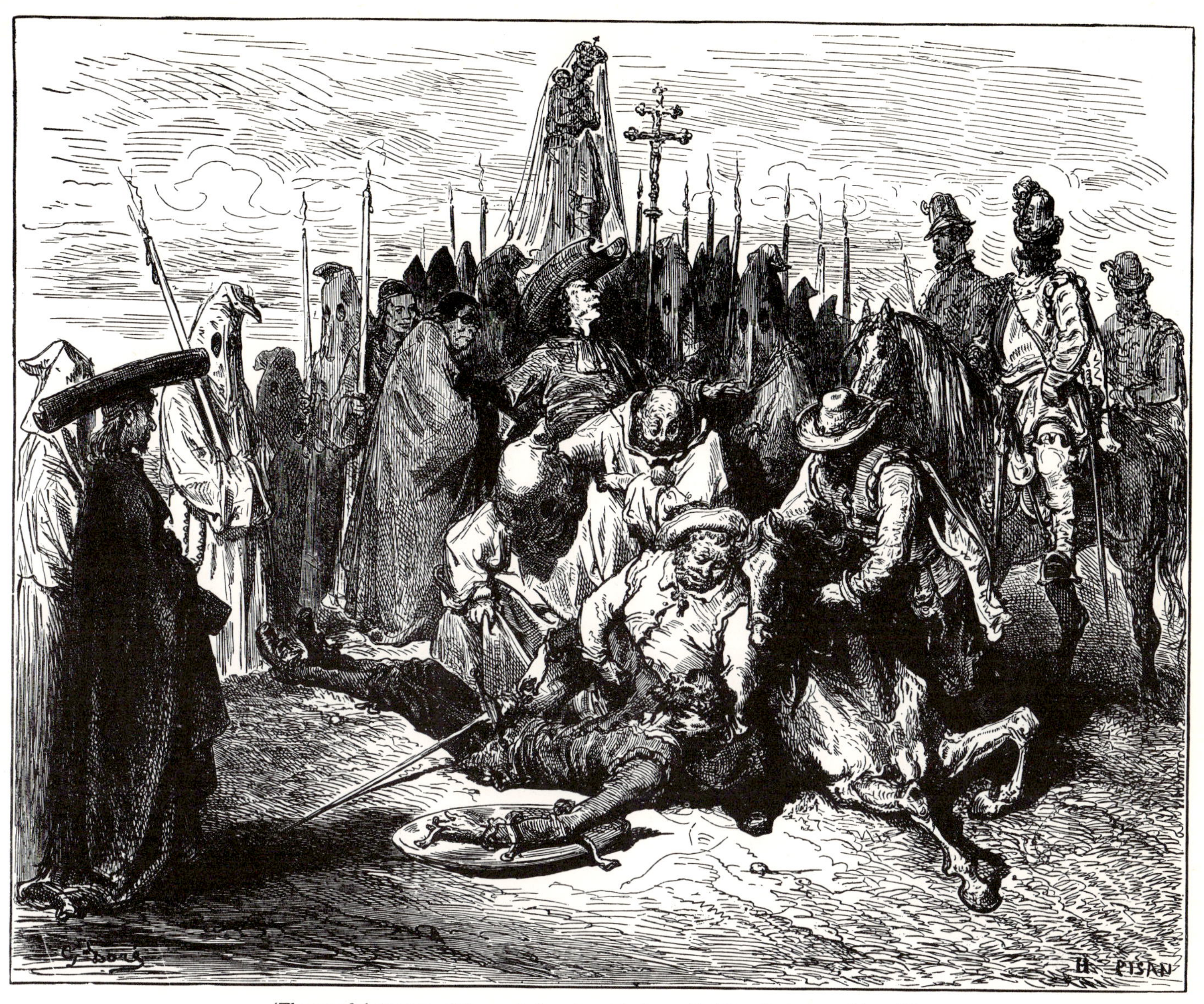

'The woeful accents of the squire's voice at last re-called Don Quixote to himself.'

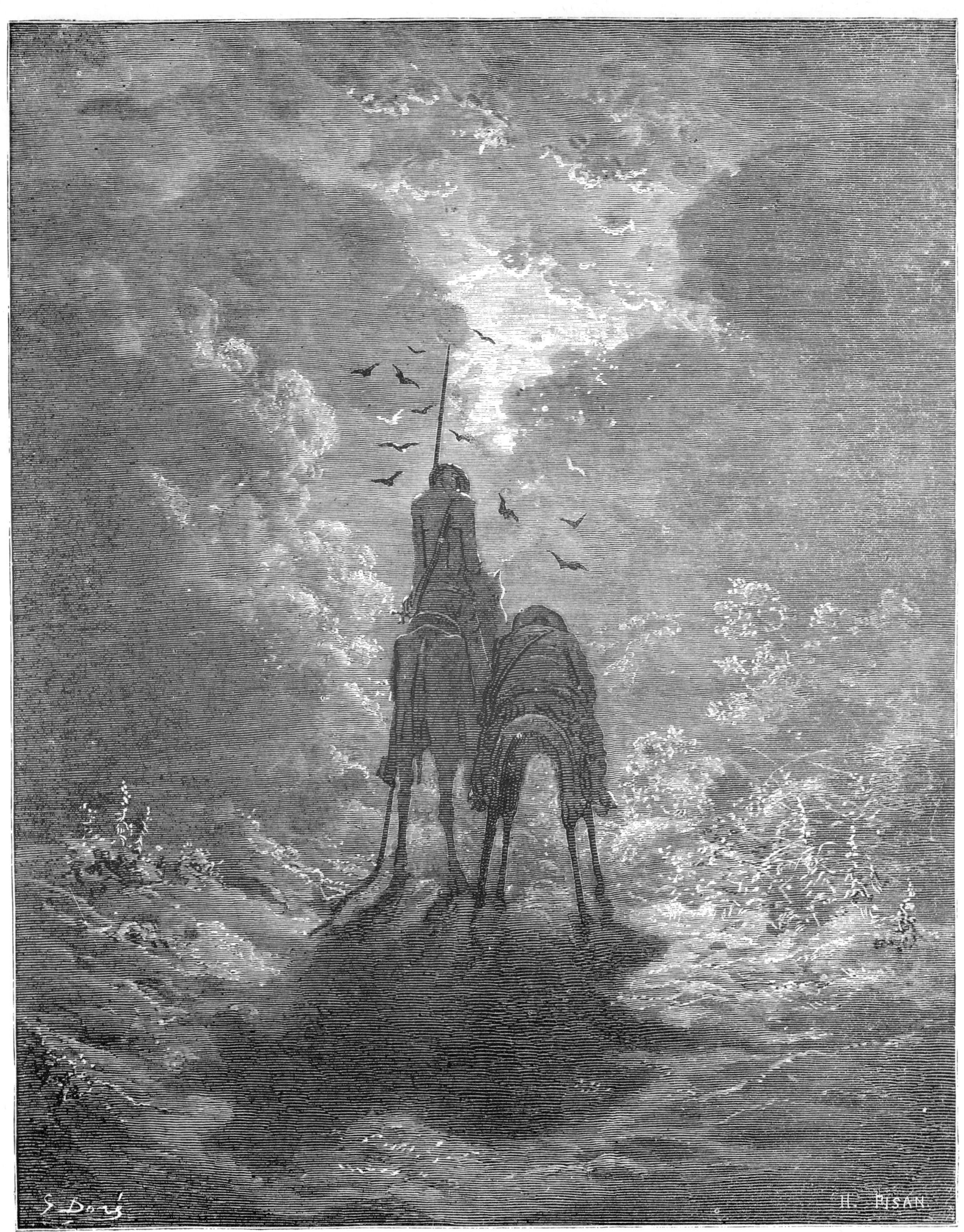

‘We slept as soundly as if we had four feather-beds under us.’

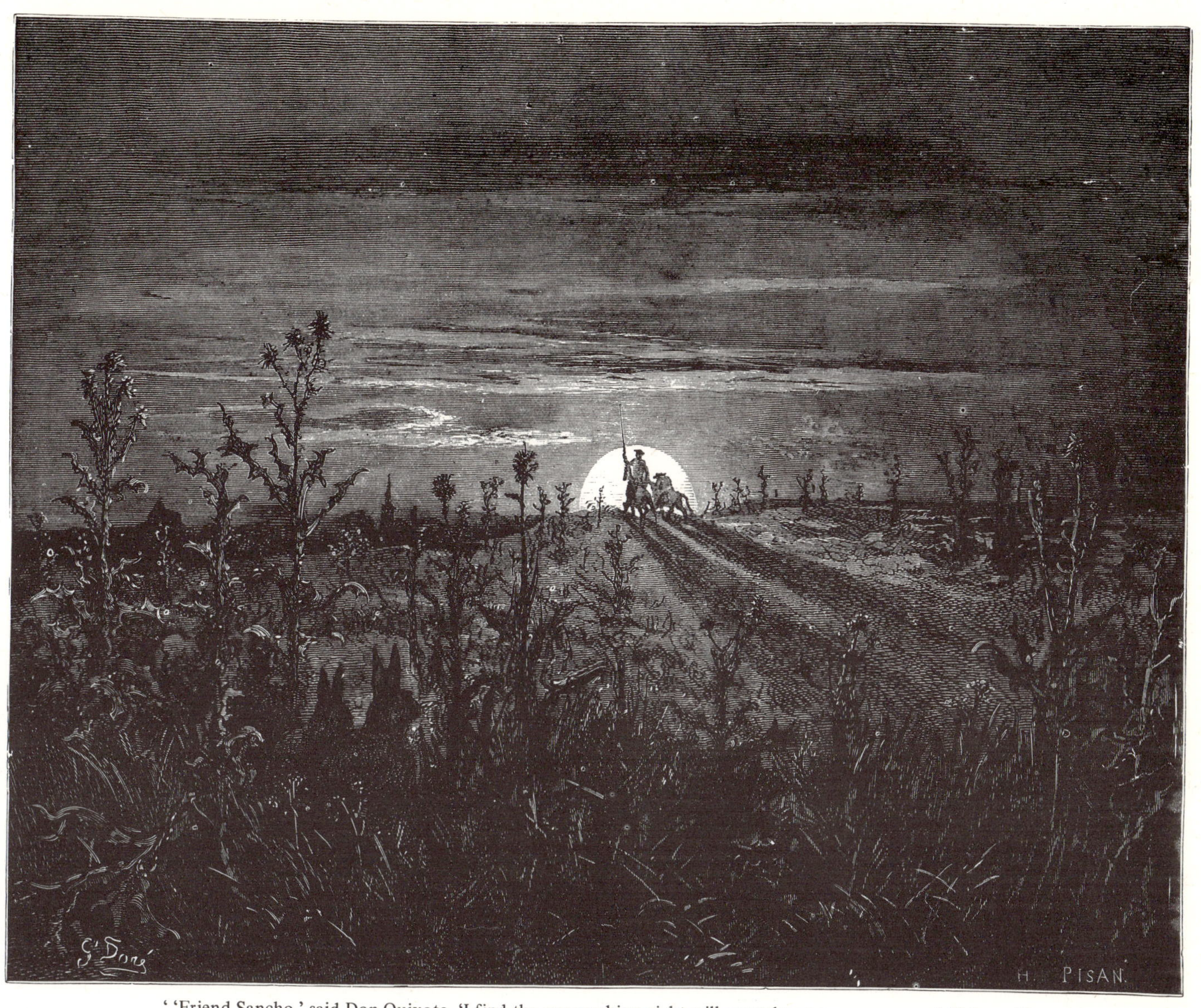

' 'Friend Sancho,' said Don Quixote, 'I find the approaching night will overtake us ere we can reach Toboso.' '

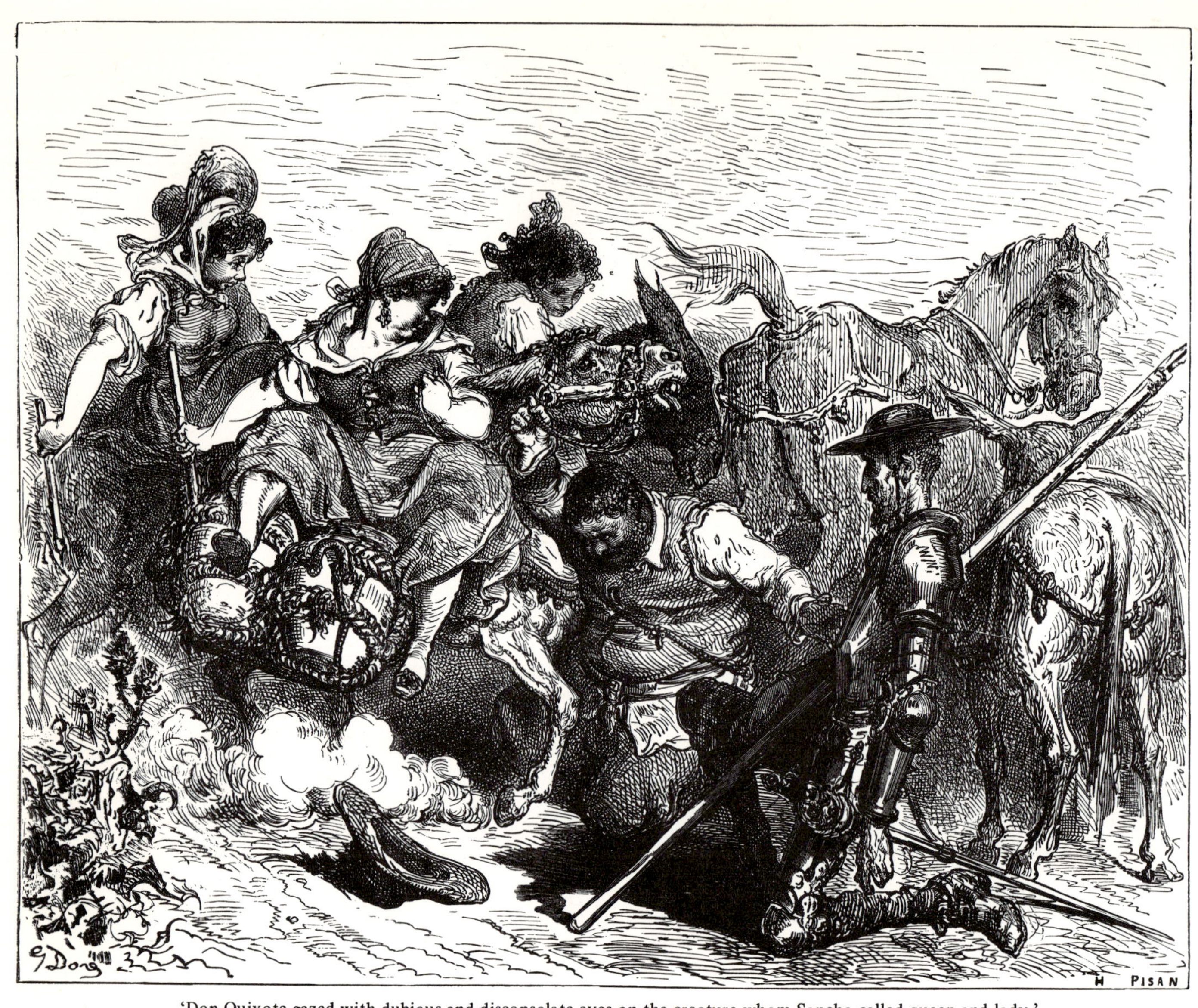

'Don Quixote gazed with dubious and disconsolate eyes on the creature whom Sancho called queen and lady.'

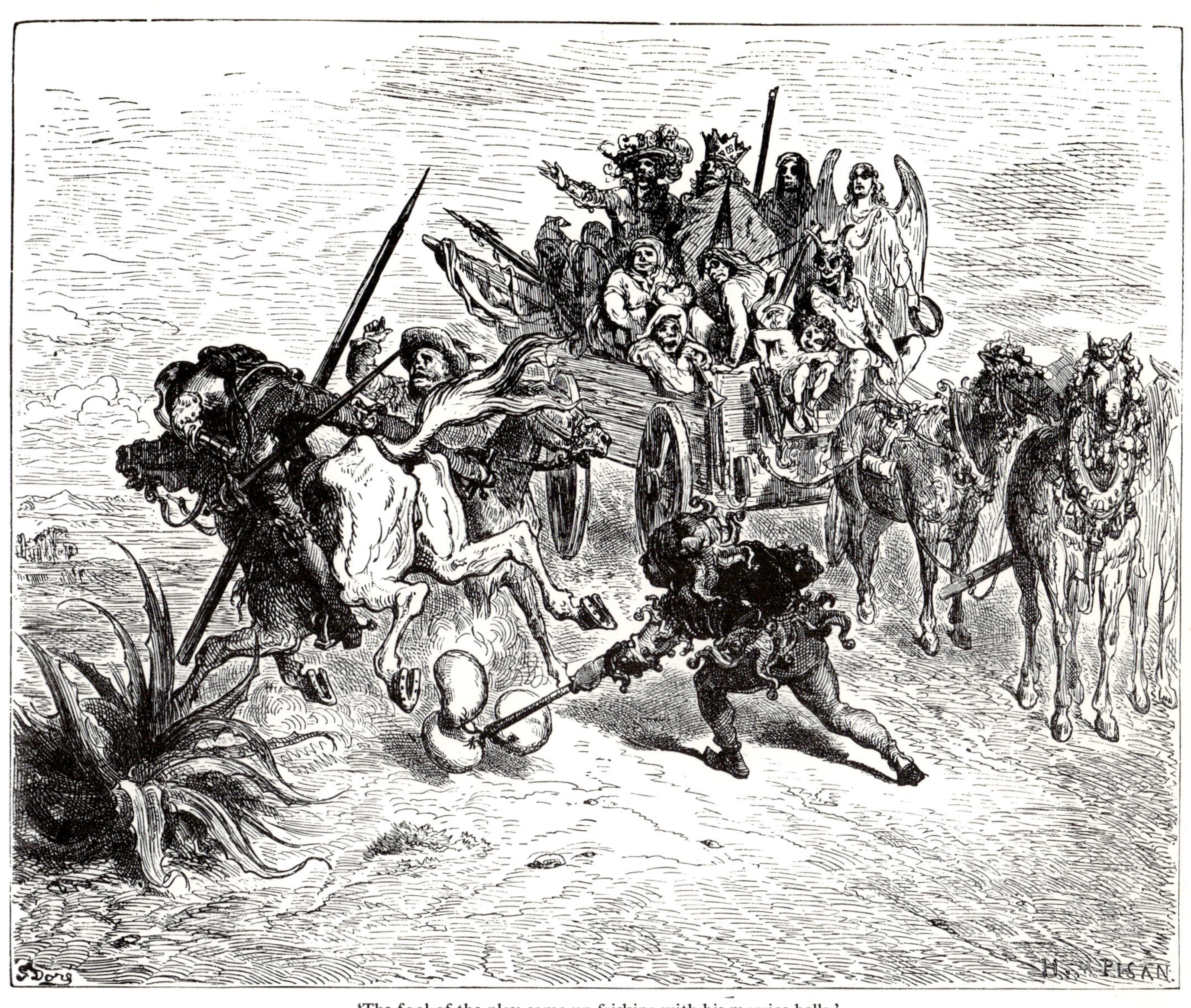

'The fool of the play came up frisking with his morrice bells.'

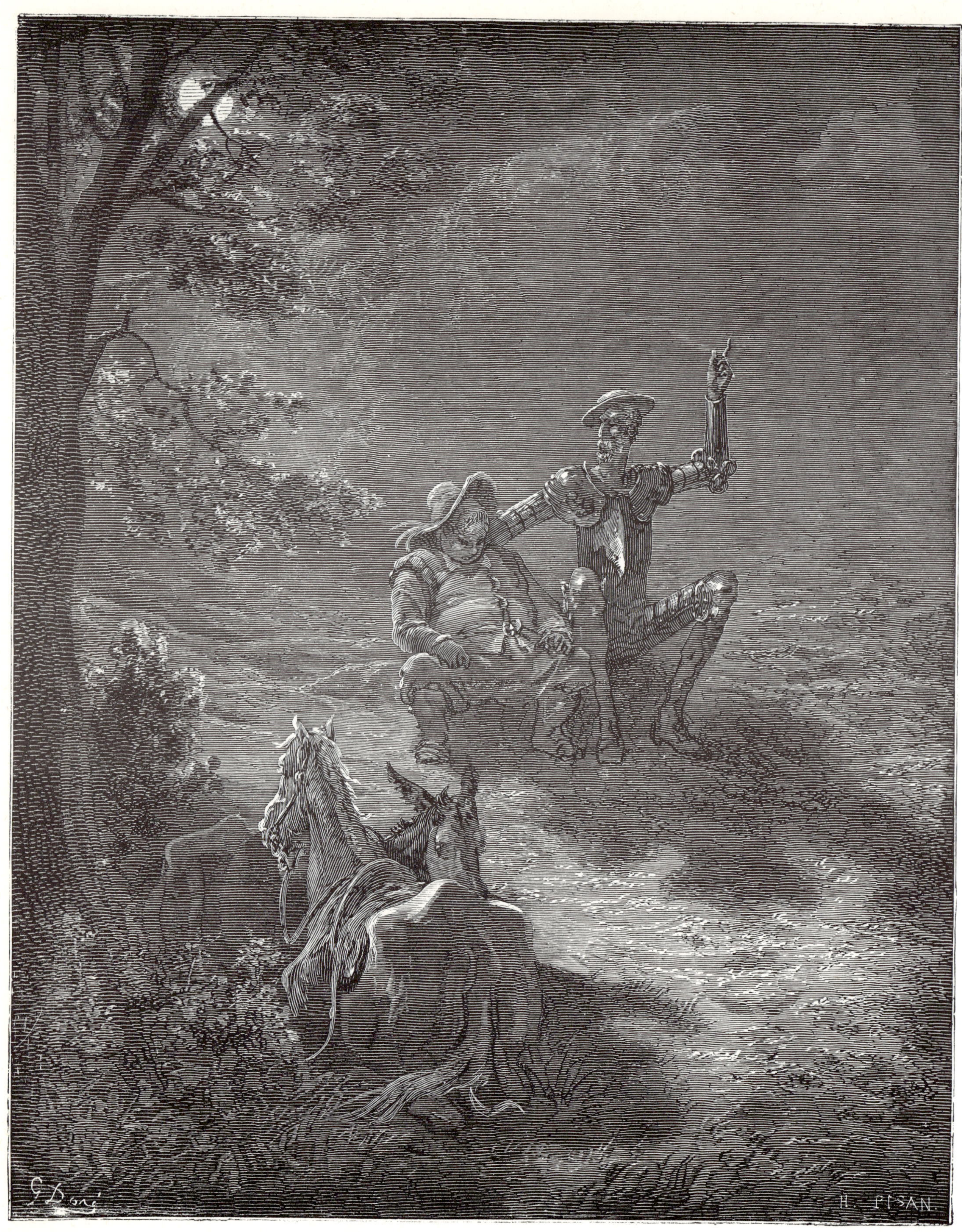

'In such discourses they passed a great part of the night.'

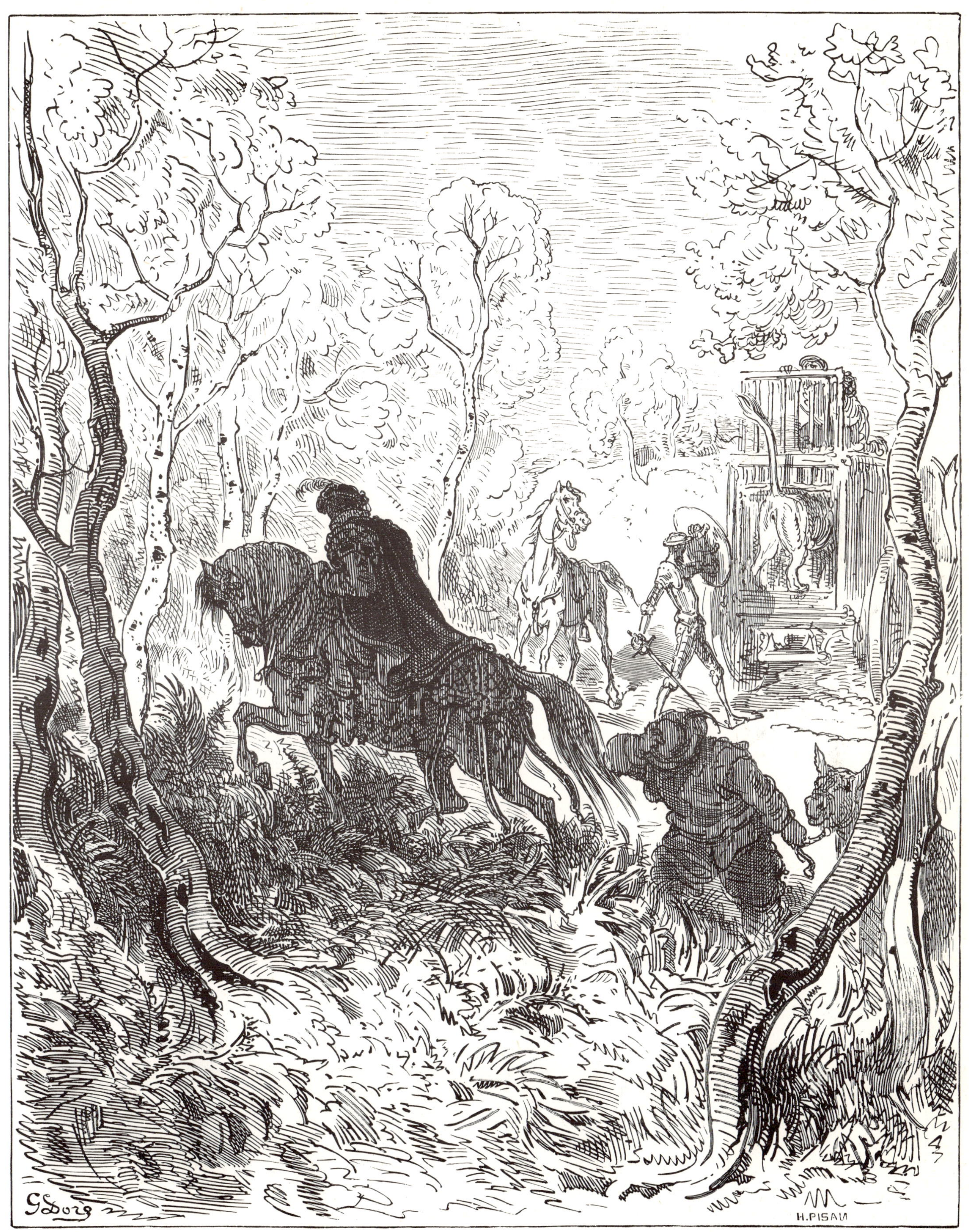

'He posted himself just before the door of the cage.'

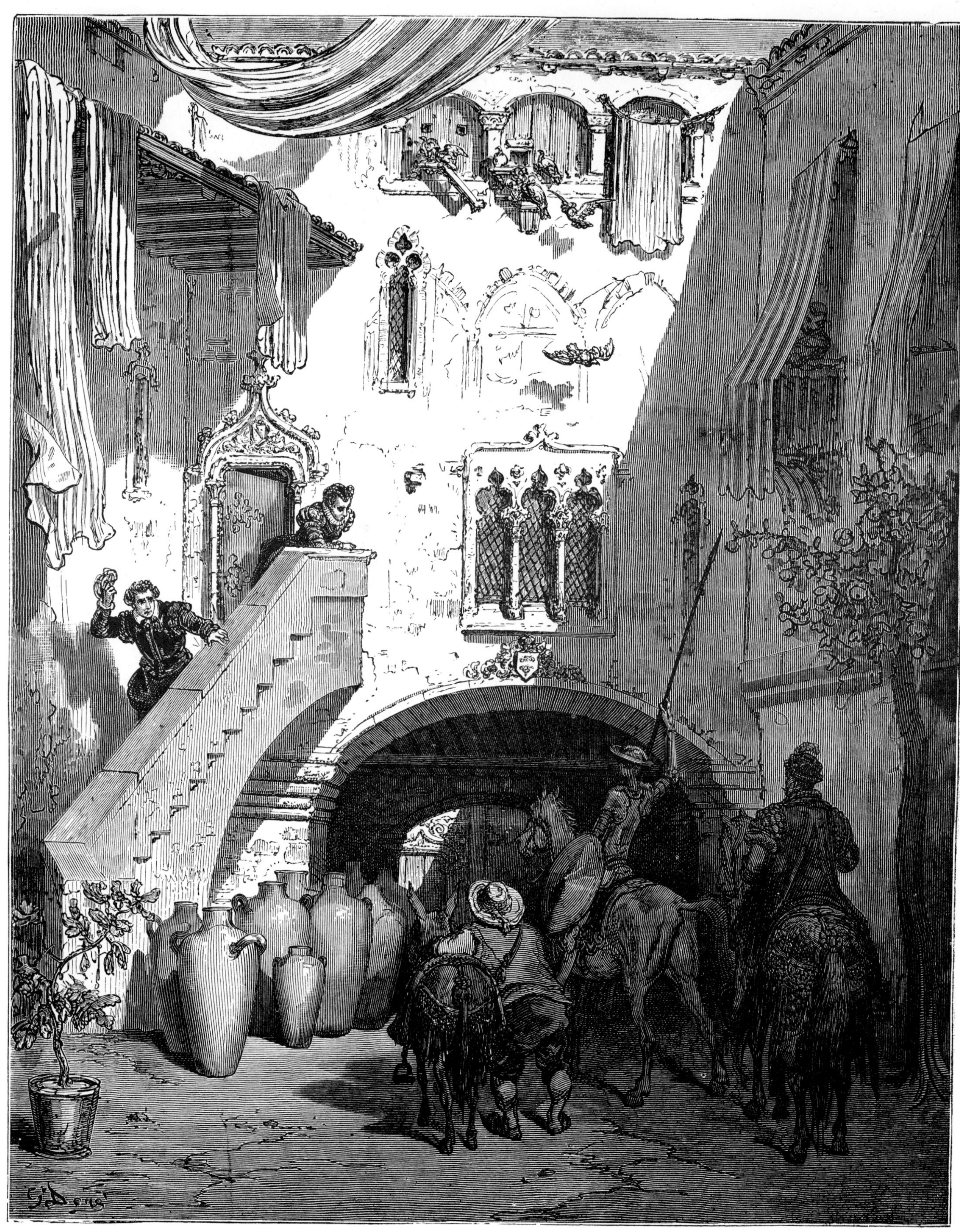

'Oh, ye Tobosian urns! that awaken in my mind the thoughts of the sweet pledge of my most bitter sorrows!'

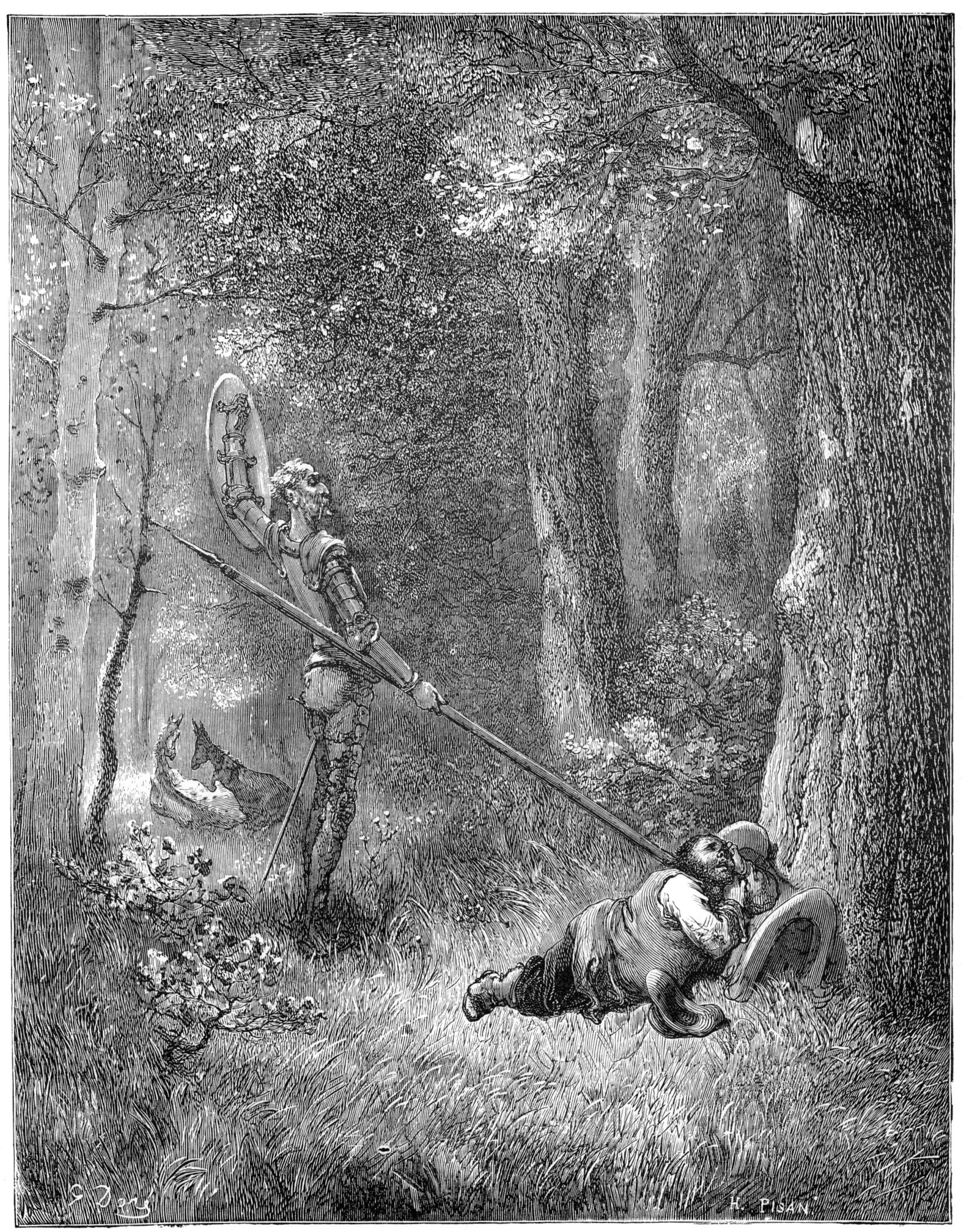

'To all this fine expostulation Sancho answered not a word.'

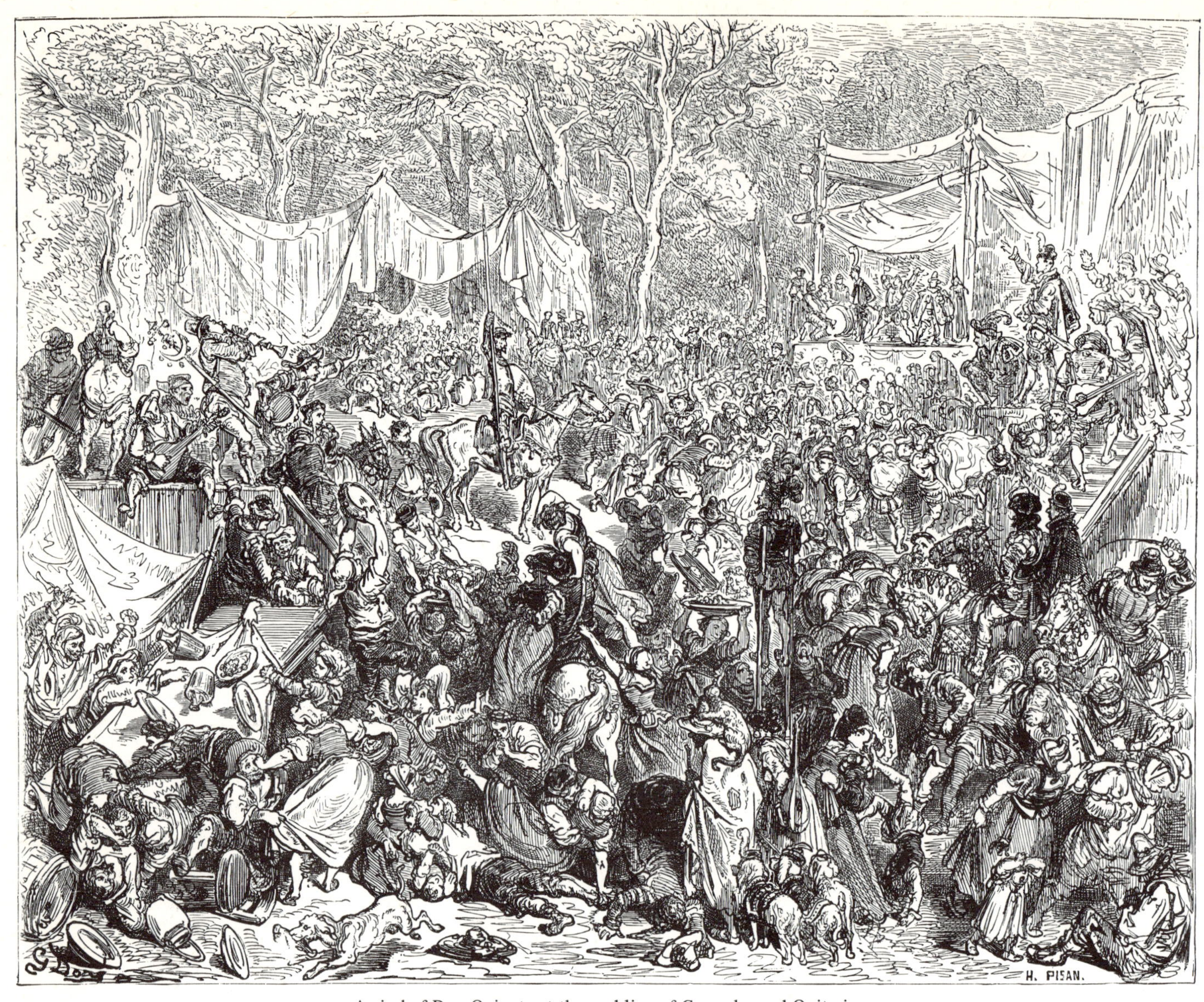

Arrival of Don Quixote at the wedding of Camacho and Quiteria.

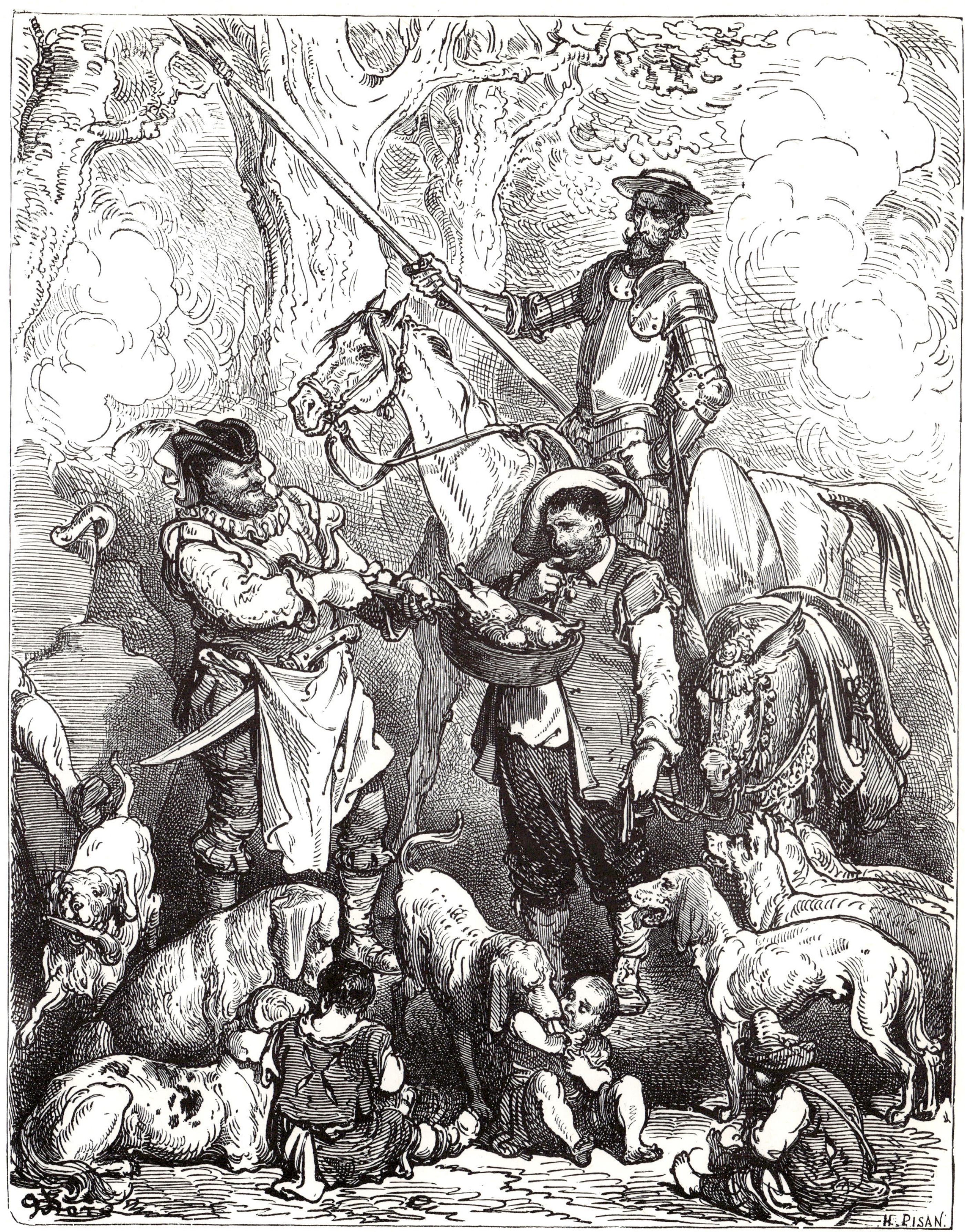

'Make shift to stay your stomach with that till dinner be ready.'

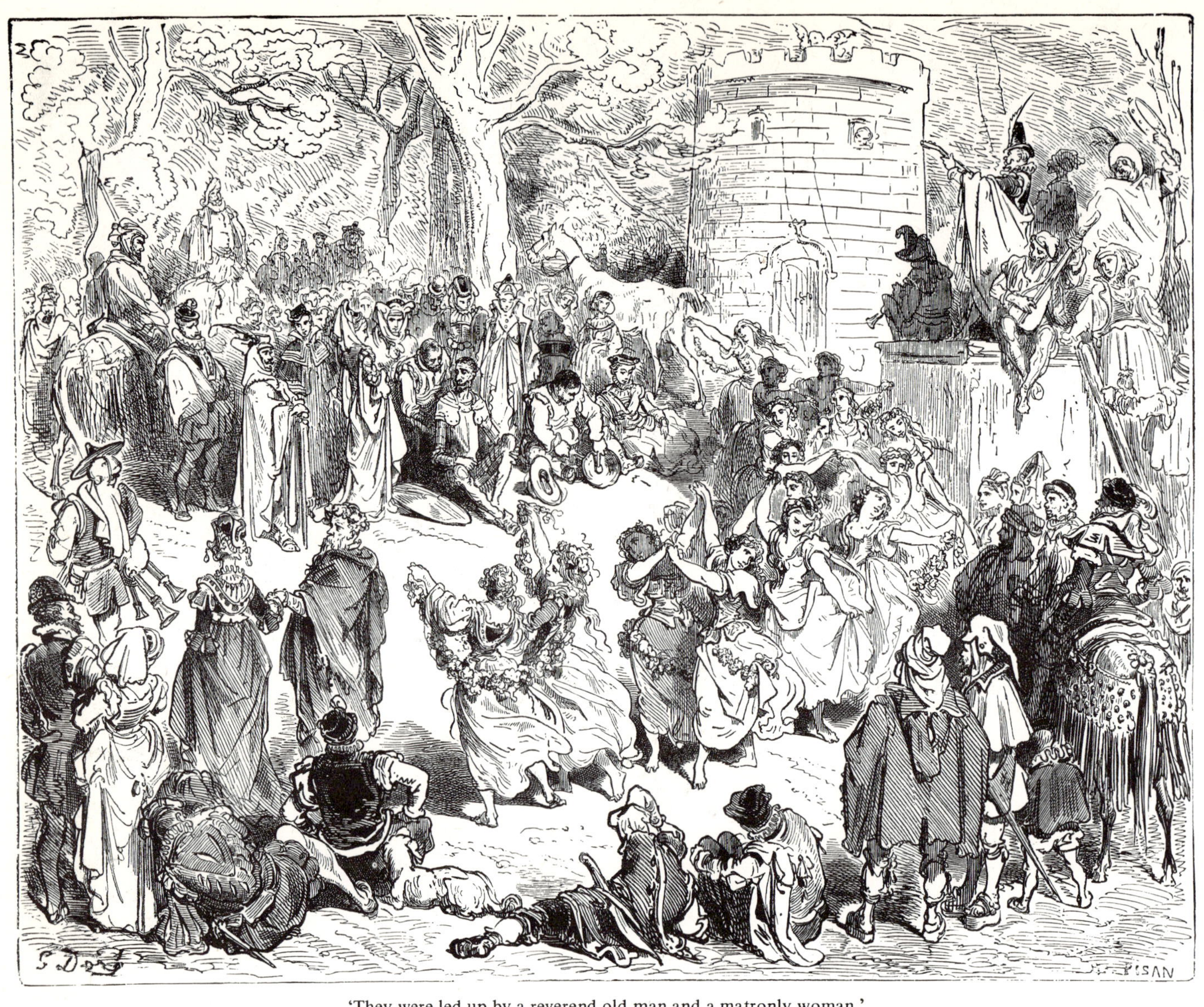

'They were led up by a reverend old man and a matronly woman.'

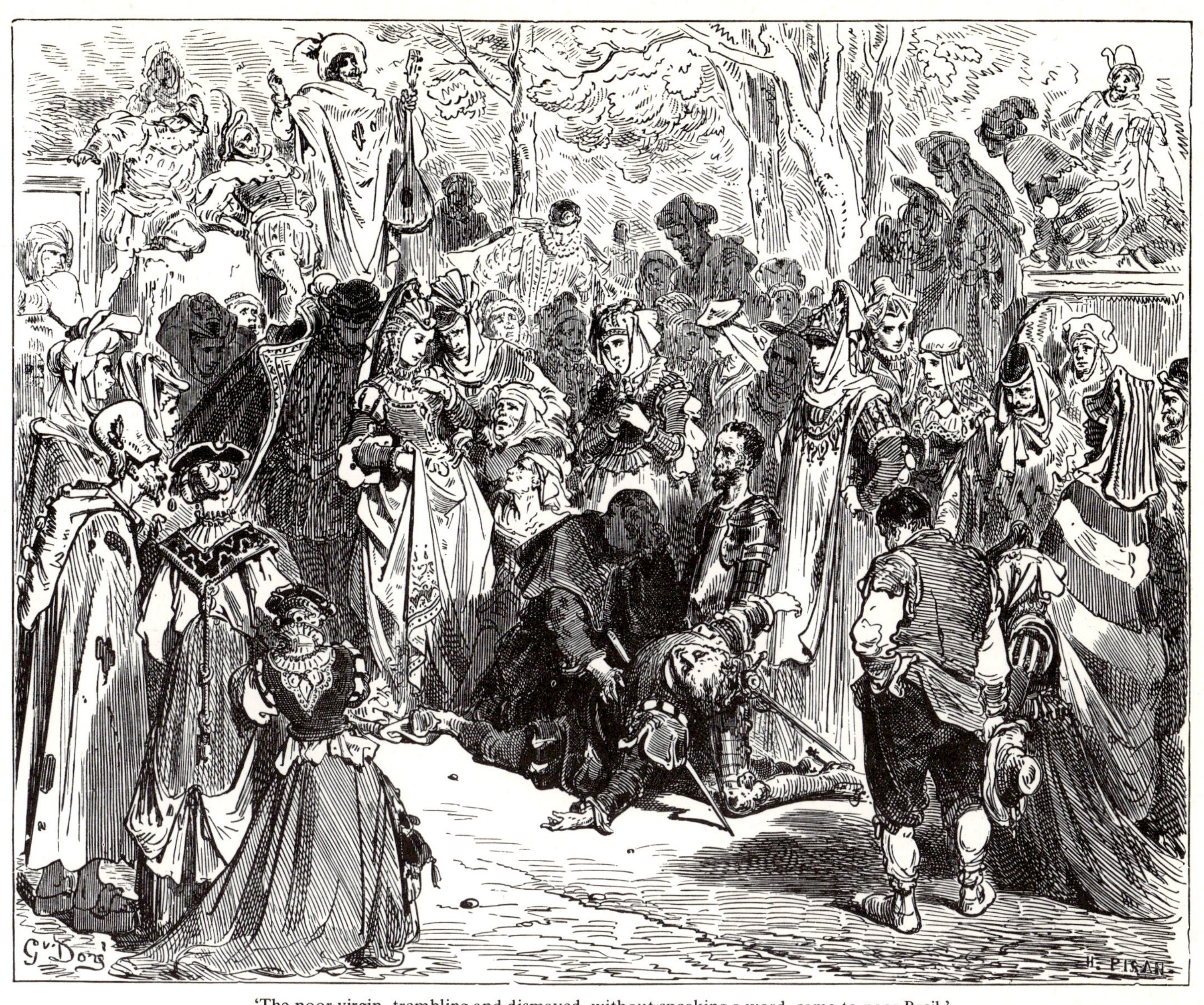

'The poor virgin, trembling and dismayed, without speaking a word, came to poor Basil.'

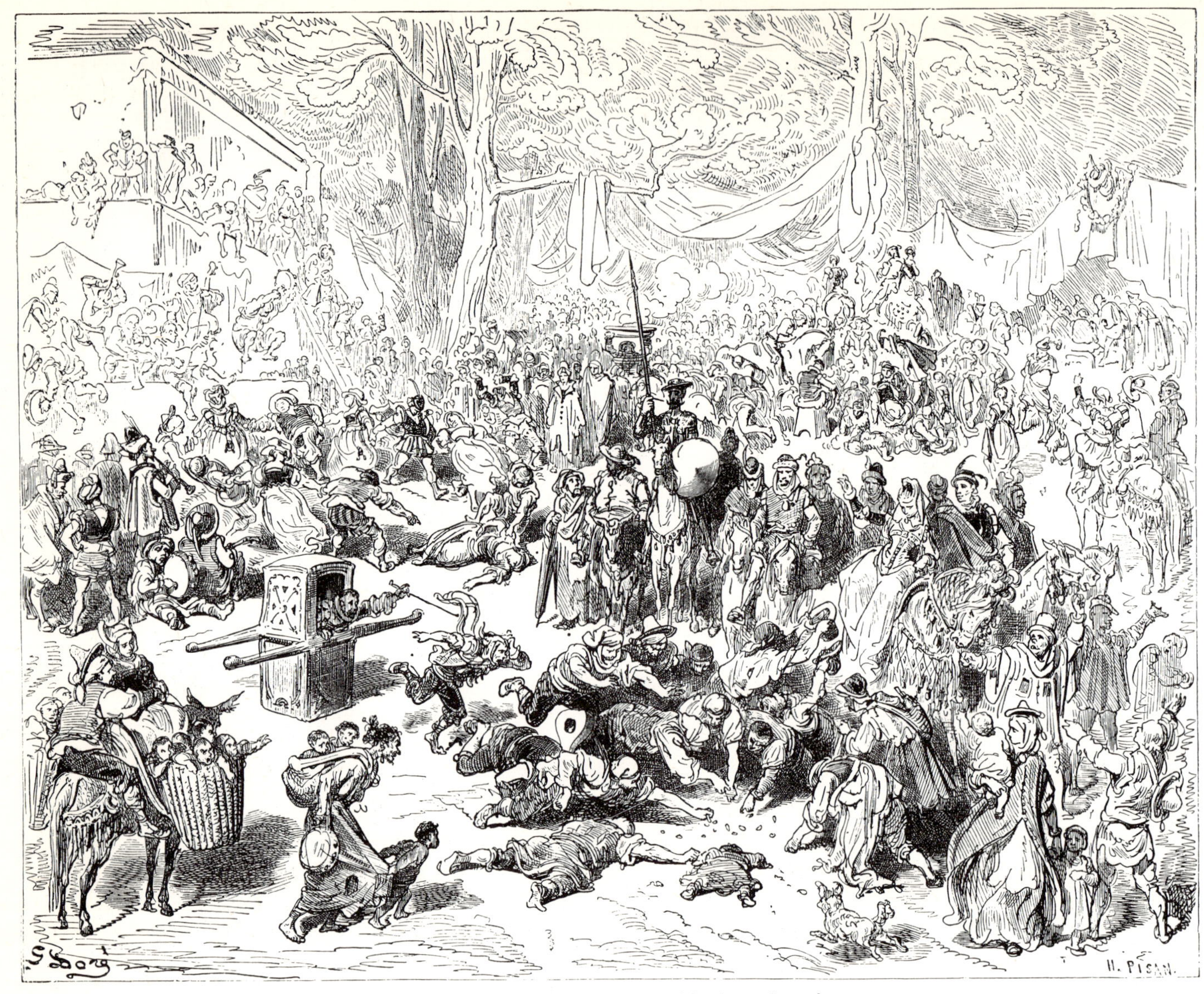

'Poor Sancho followed his master with a heavy heart.'

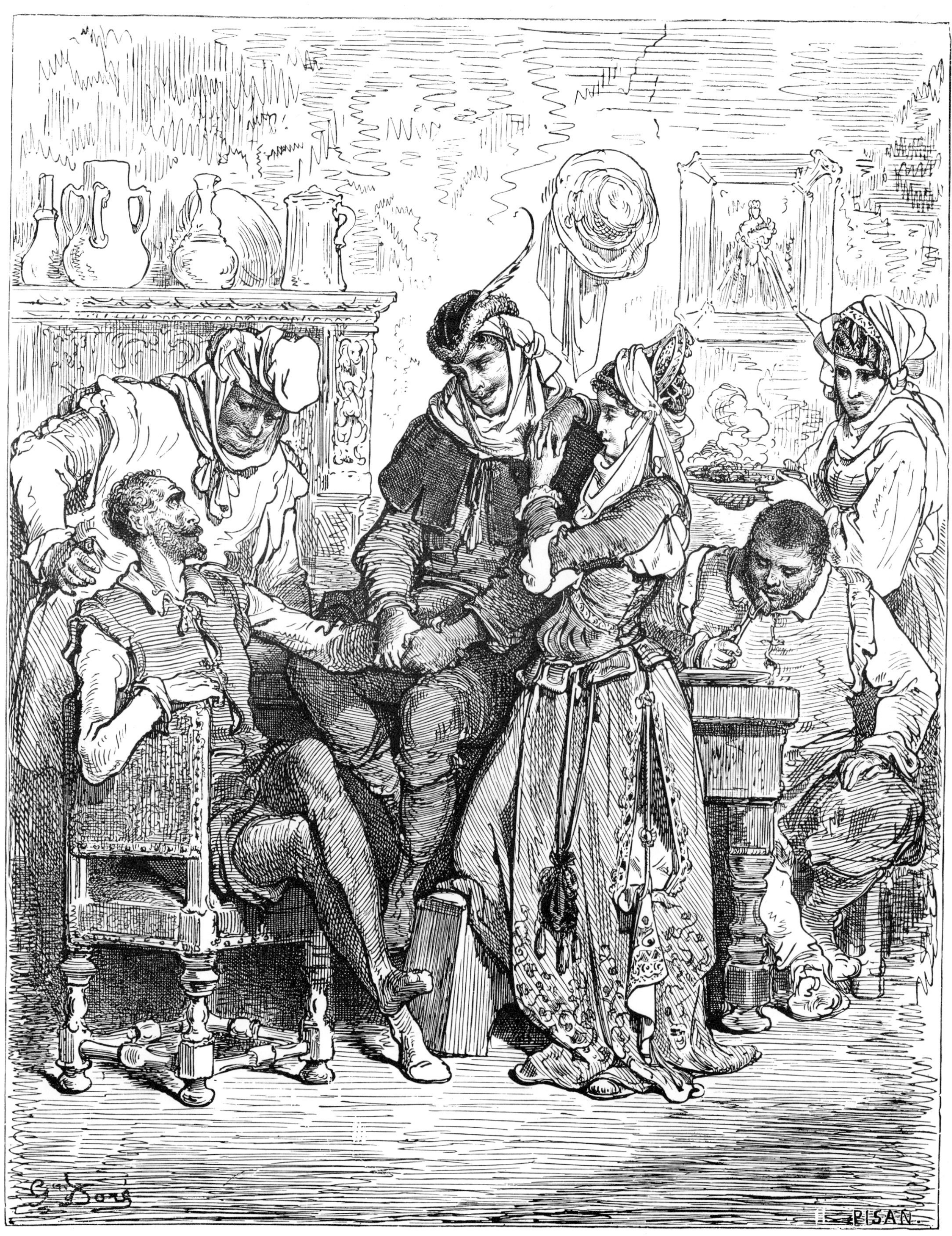

'Sancho and his master tarried three days with the young couple, and were entertained like princes.'

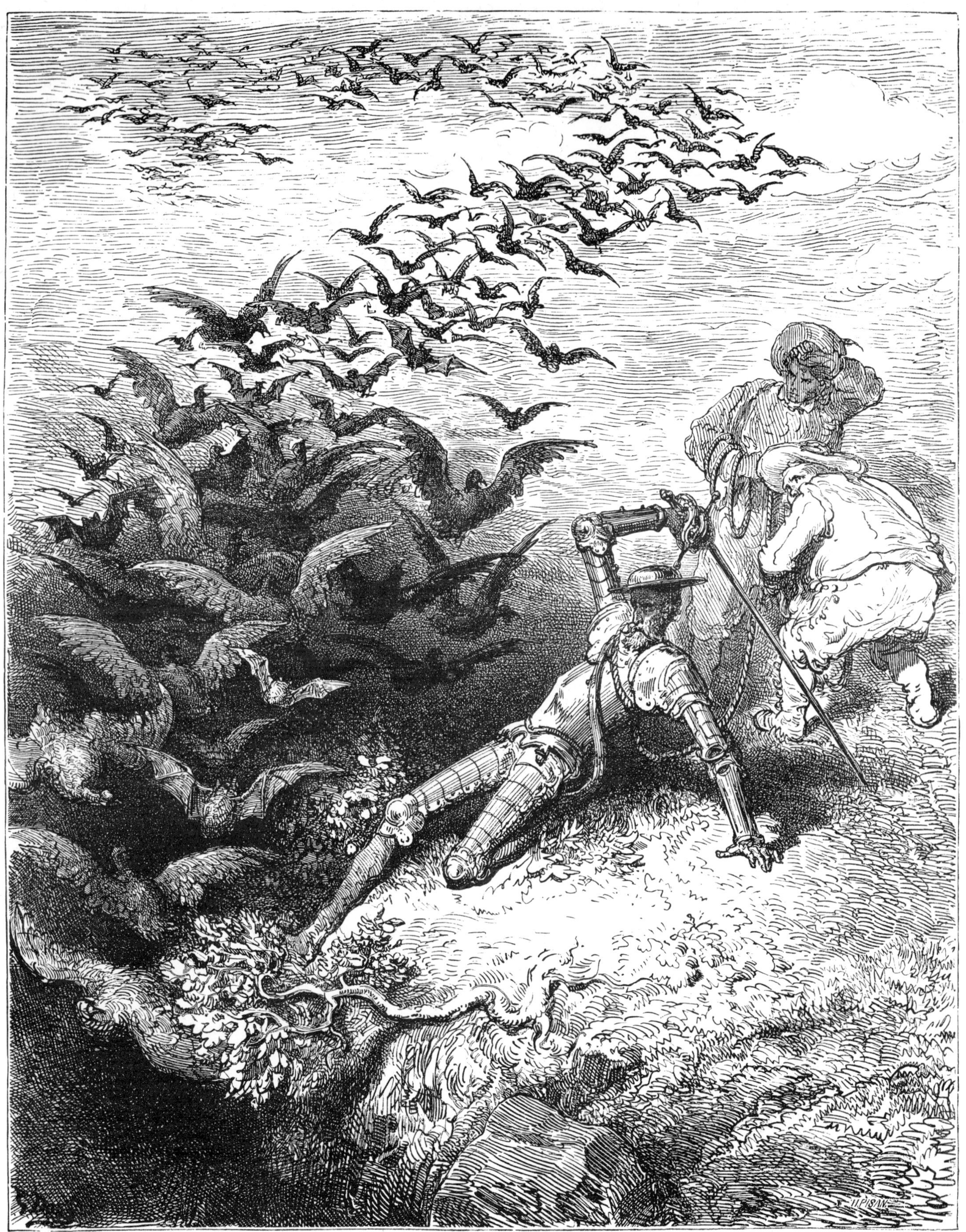

'An infinite number of overgrown crows and daws came rushing and fluttering out of the cave.'

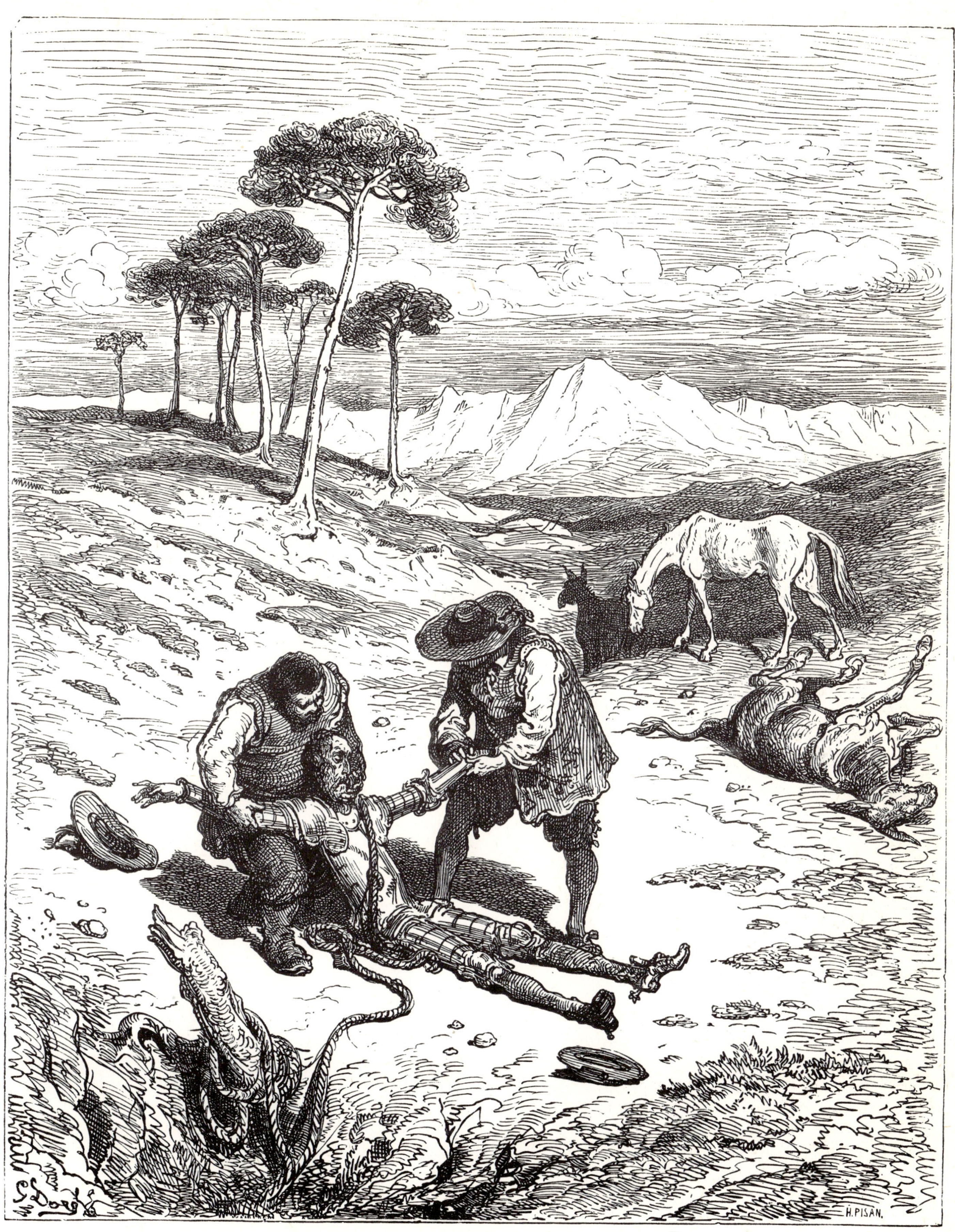

'They found that his eyes were closed, as if he had been fast asleep.'

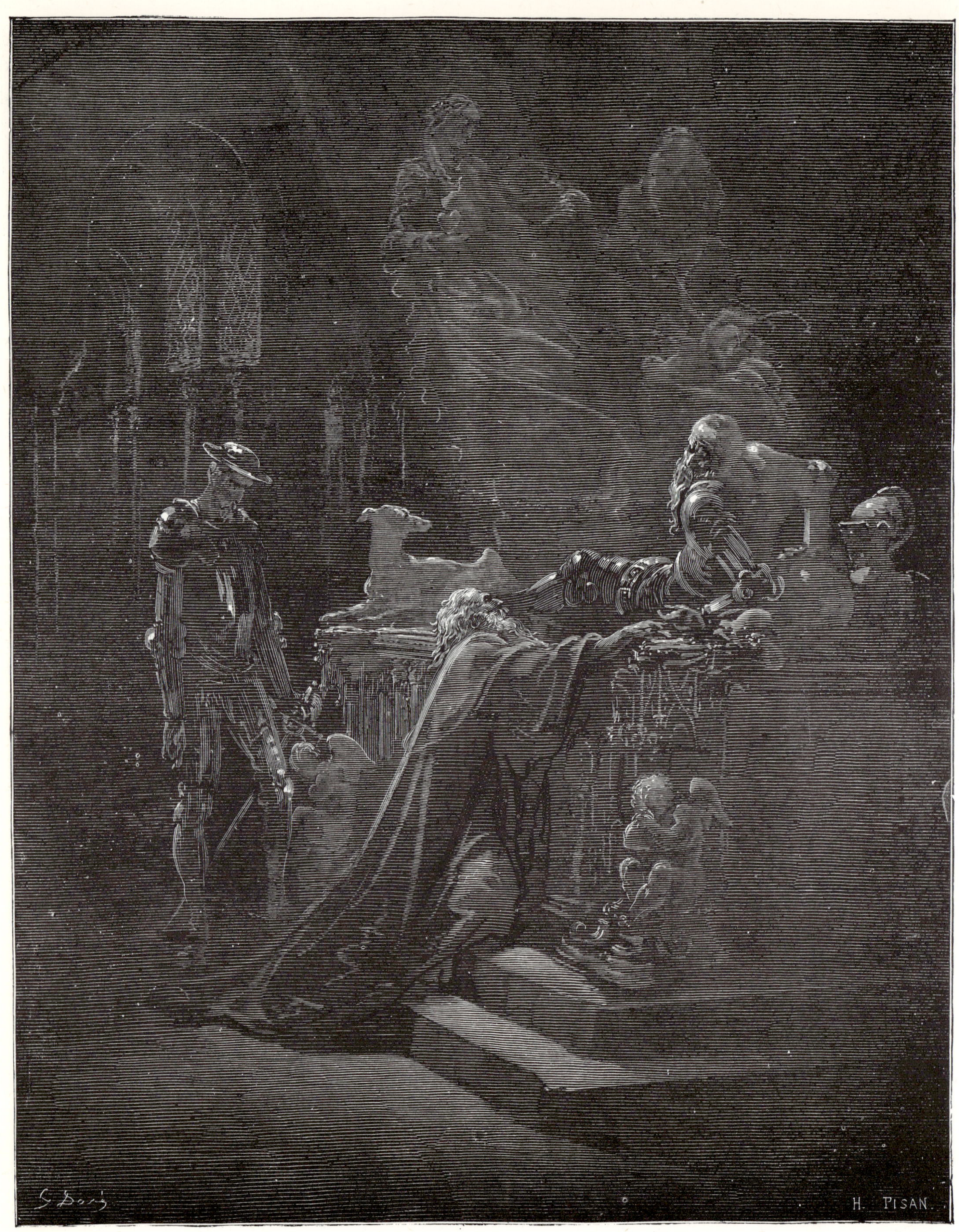

'The venerable Montesinos fell on his knees before the afflicted knight.'

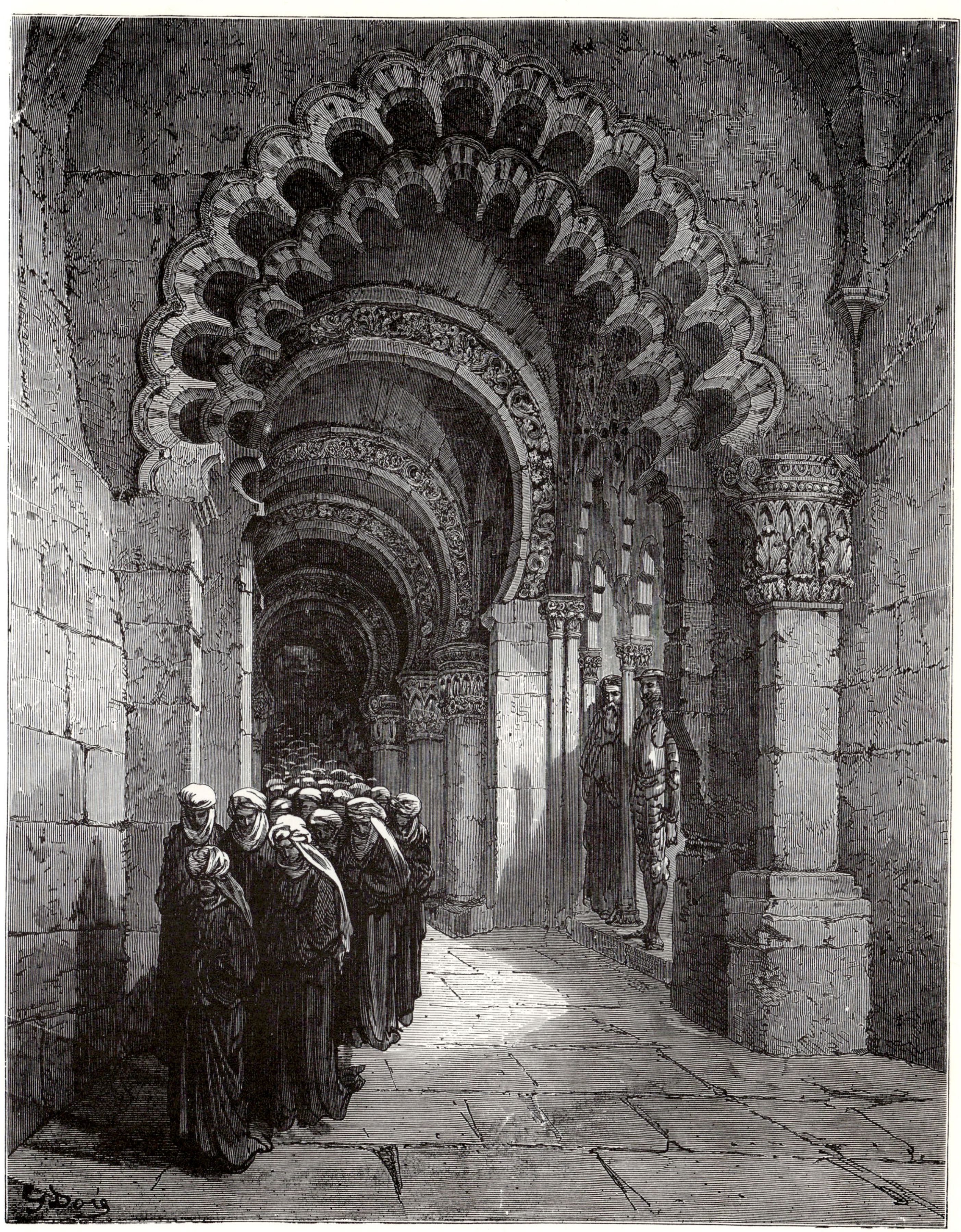

'I saw a mournful procession of most beautiful damsels, all in black.'

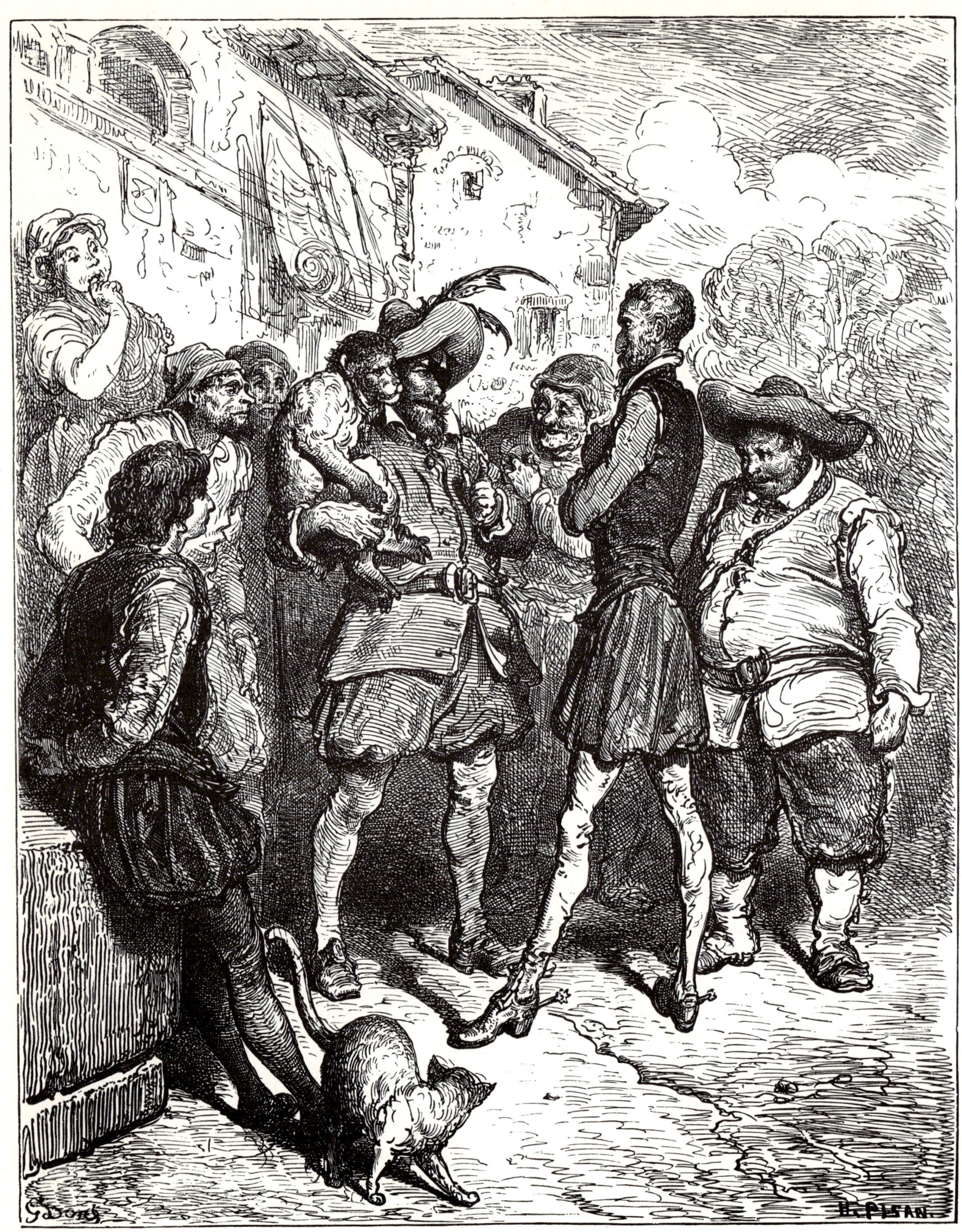

'At these words Don Quixote stood amazed.'

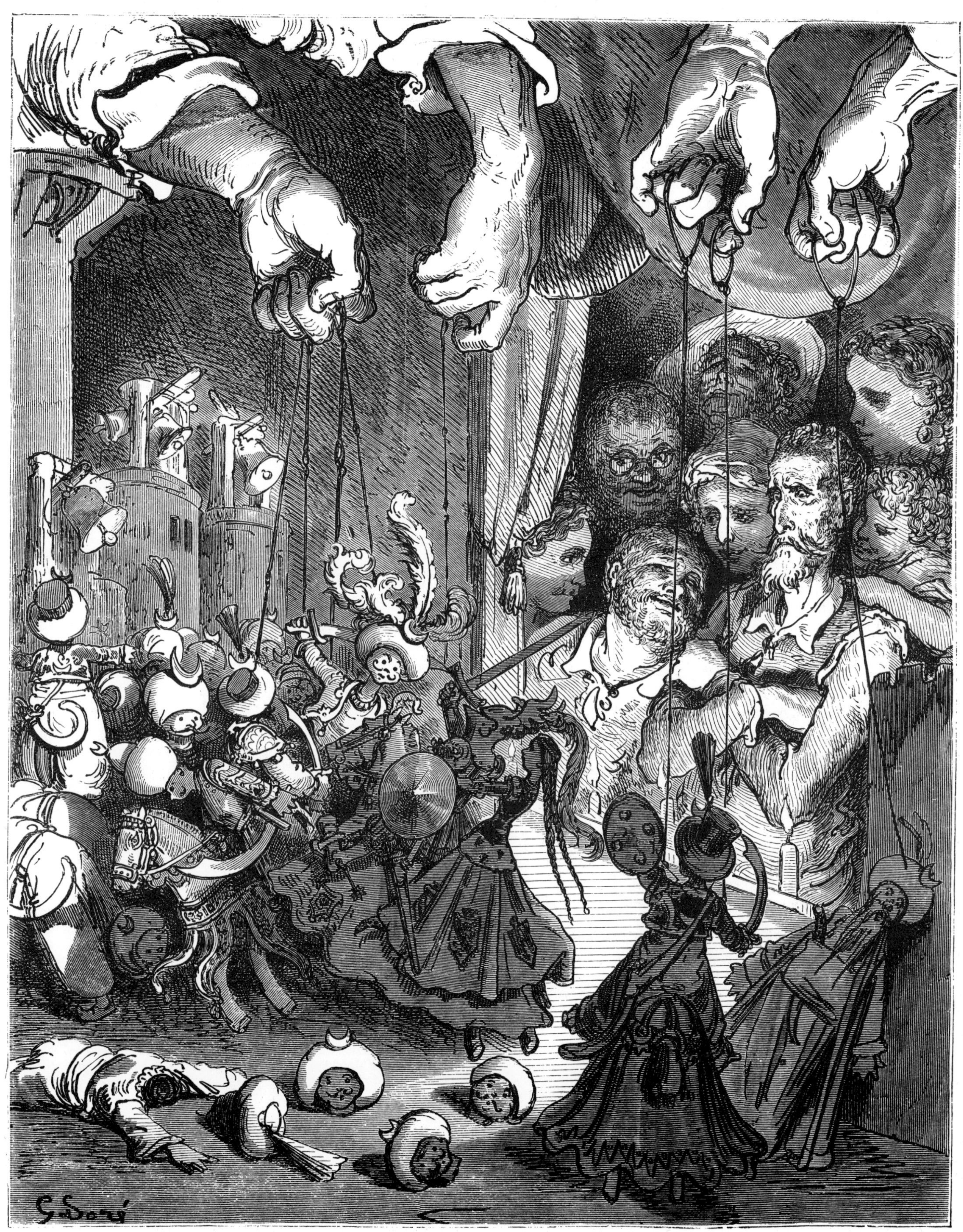

'Observe what a vast company of glittering horse comes pouring out of the city, in pursuit of the Christian lovers.'

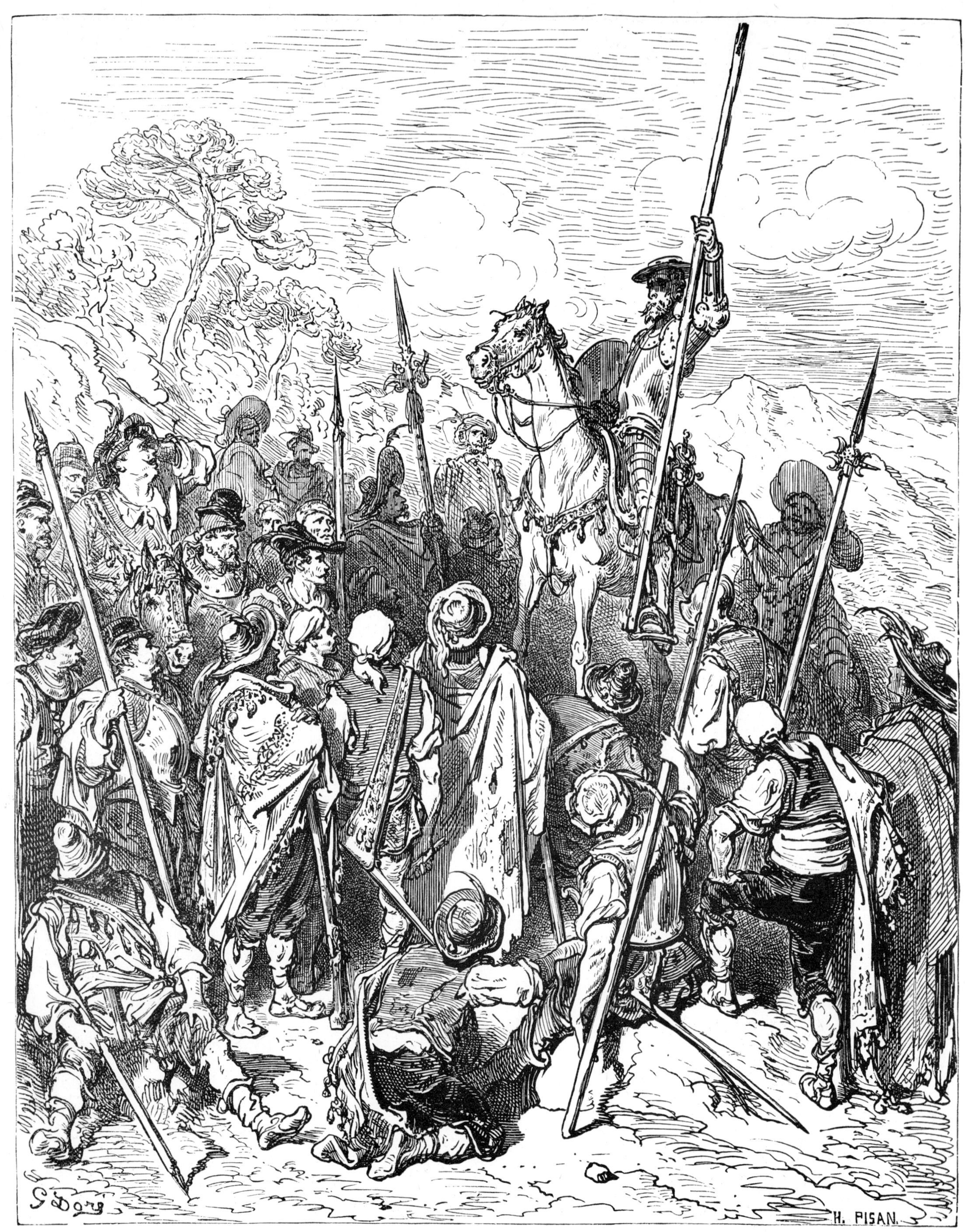

'According to the laws of arms, you really injure yourselves, in thinking yourselves affronted.'

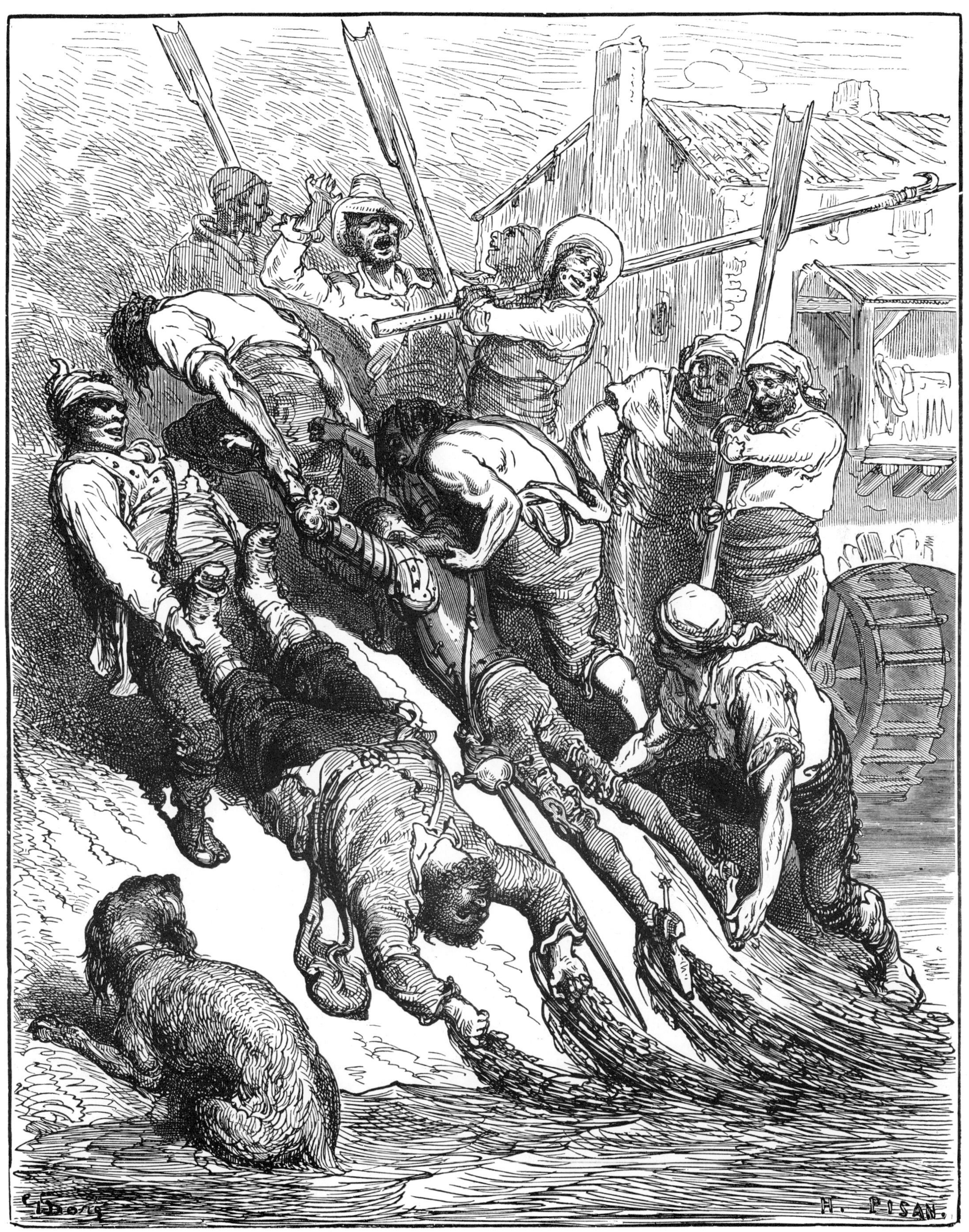

'They were both hauled ashore, more over-drenched than thirsty.'

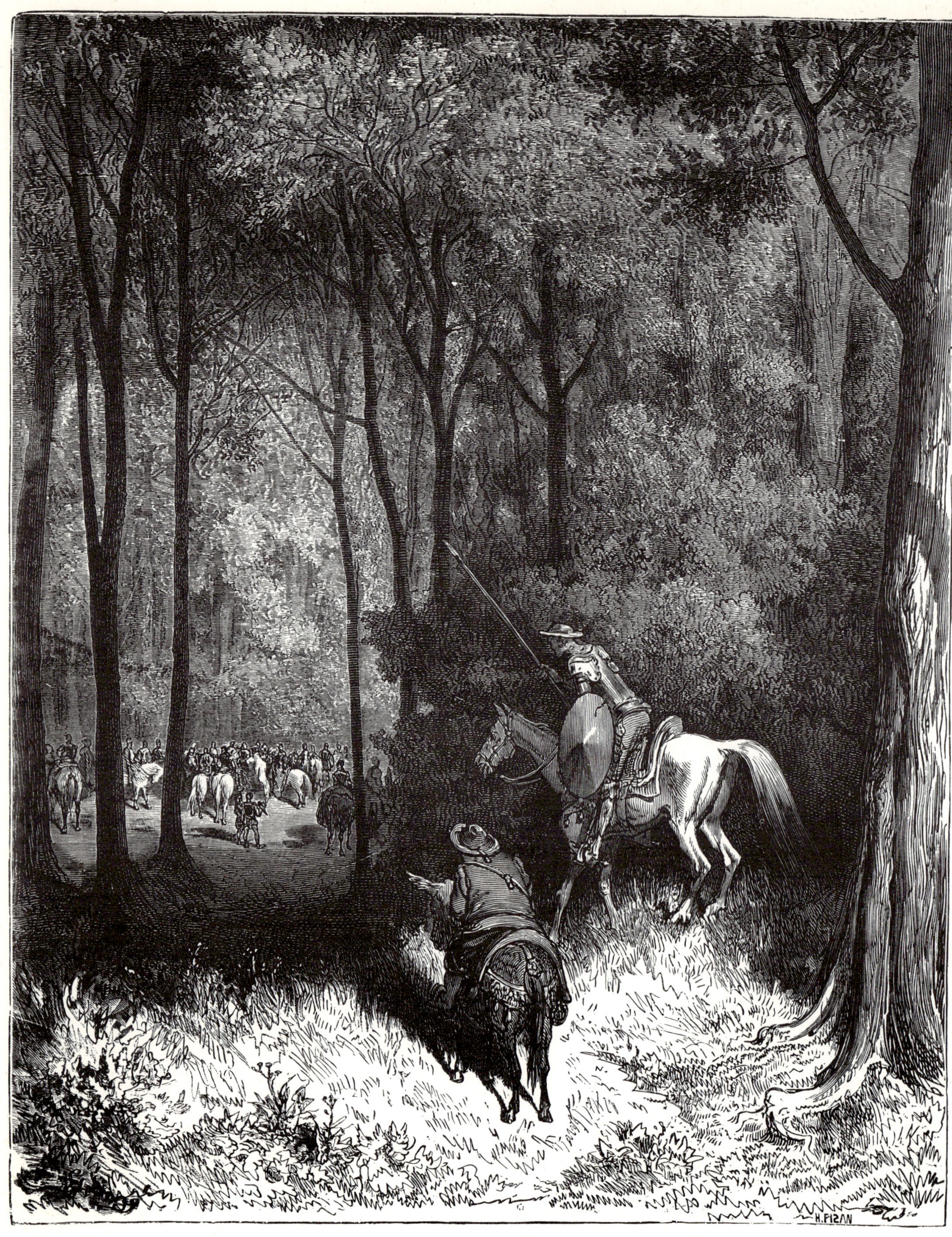

'Don Quixote descried a company, whom, upon a nearer view, he judged to be persons of quality.'

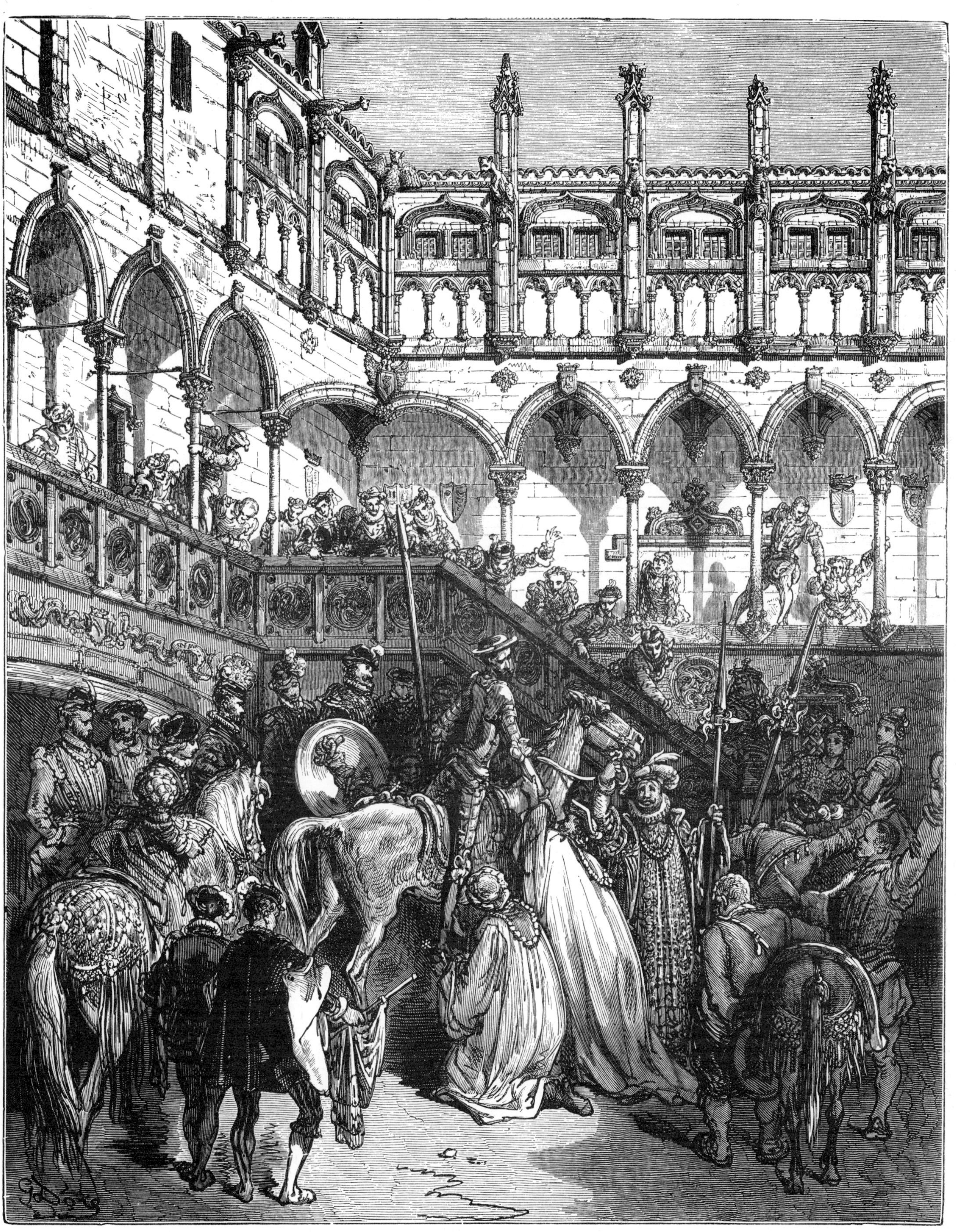

''Go, great and mighty sir,' said they, 'and help my lady duchess down.''

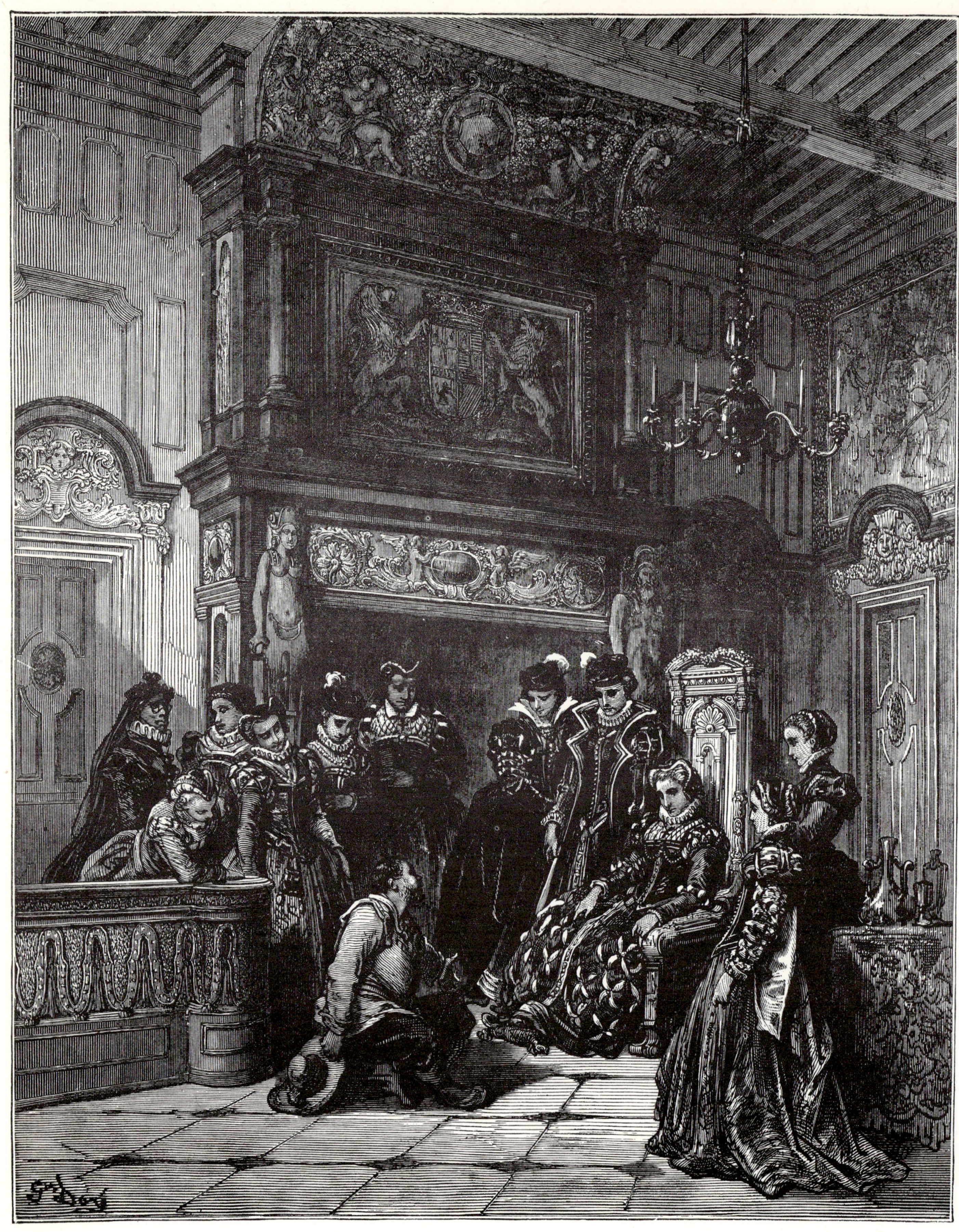

'At the duchess's request, he related the whole passage of the late pretended enchantment very faithfully.'

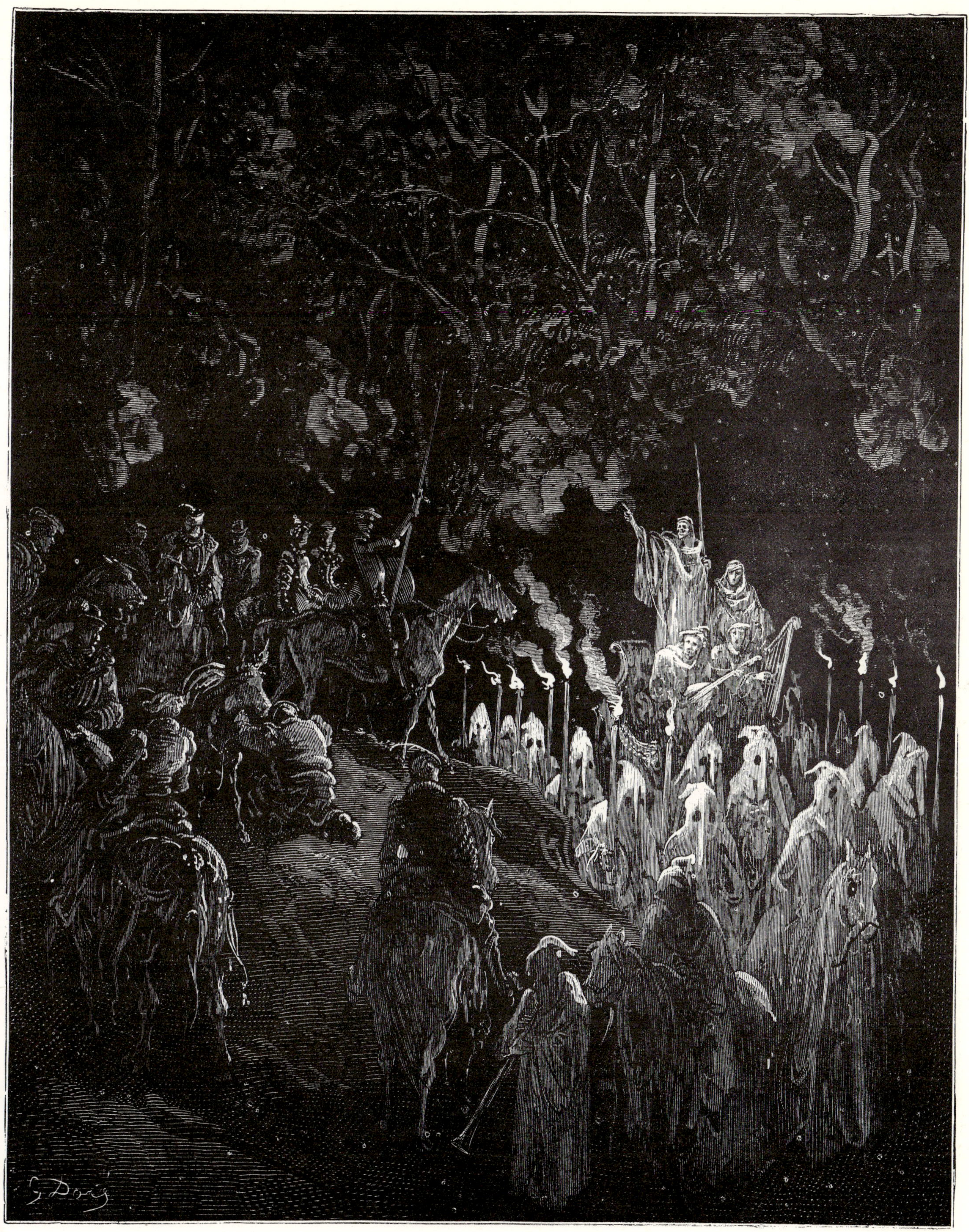

'The figure in the gown stood up.'

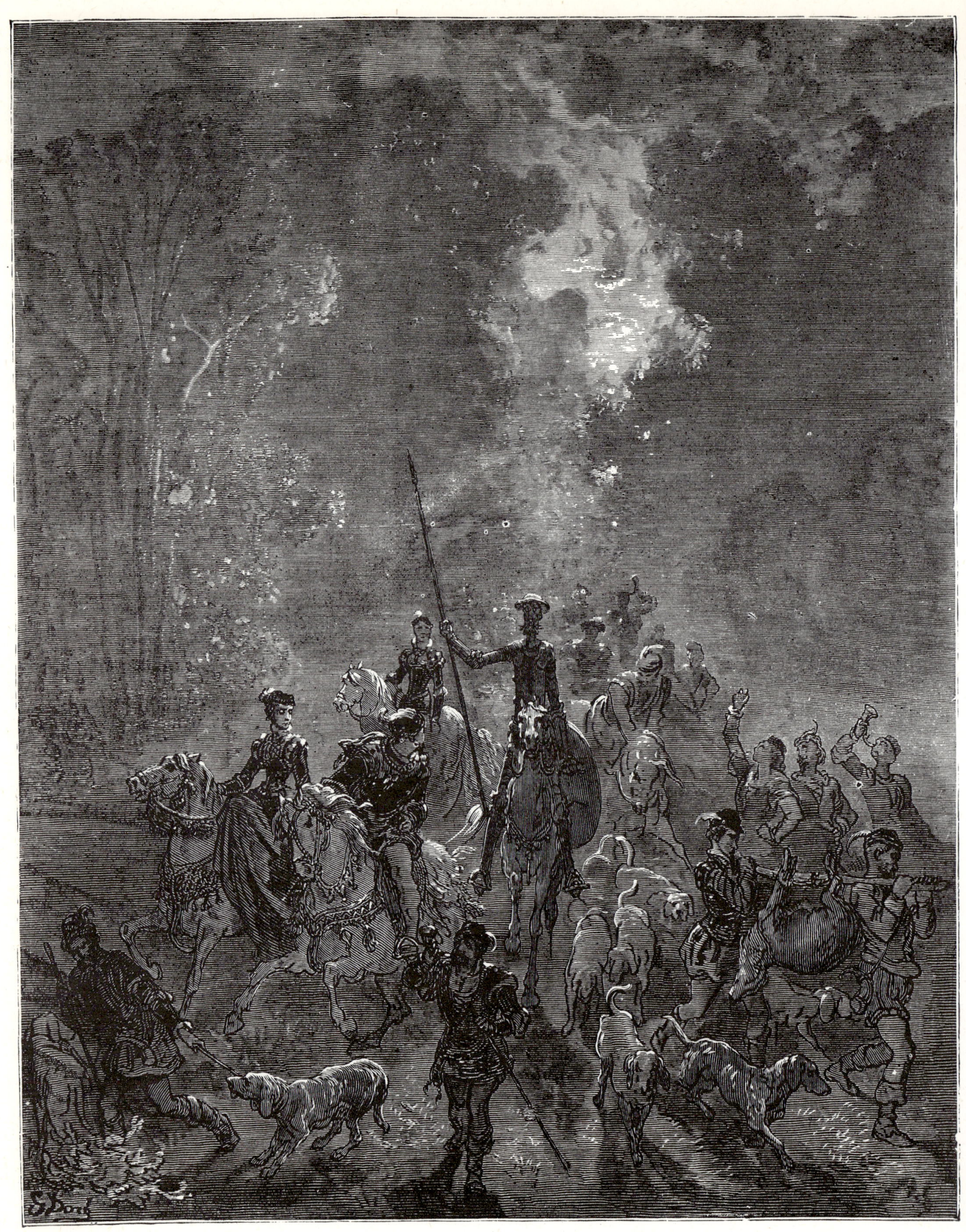

'The morn began to spread her smiling looks in the eastern quarter of the skies.'

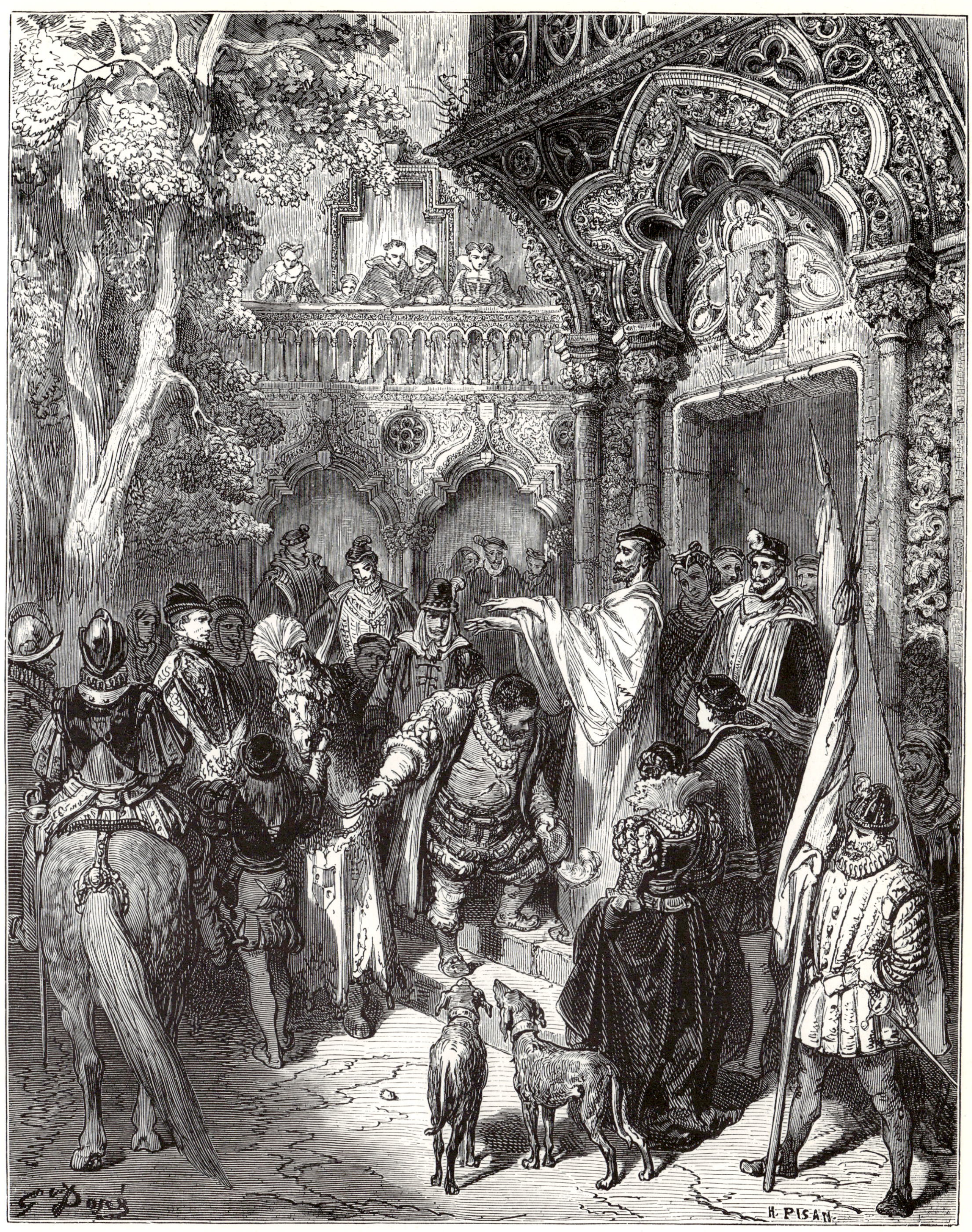

'He kissed the duke and duchess's hand at parting, and received his master's benediction.'

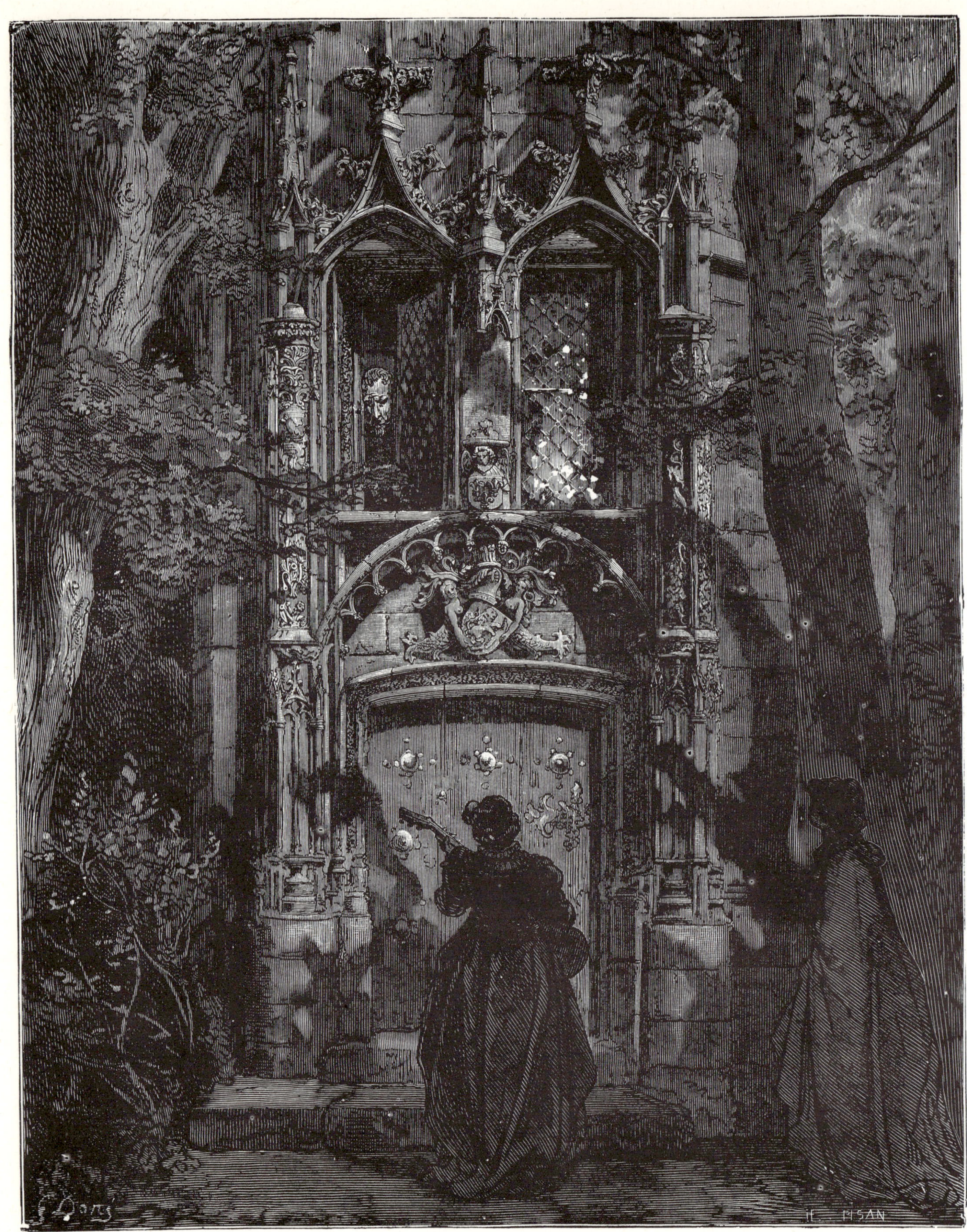

'Here the courting damsel ended her song.'

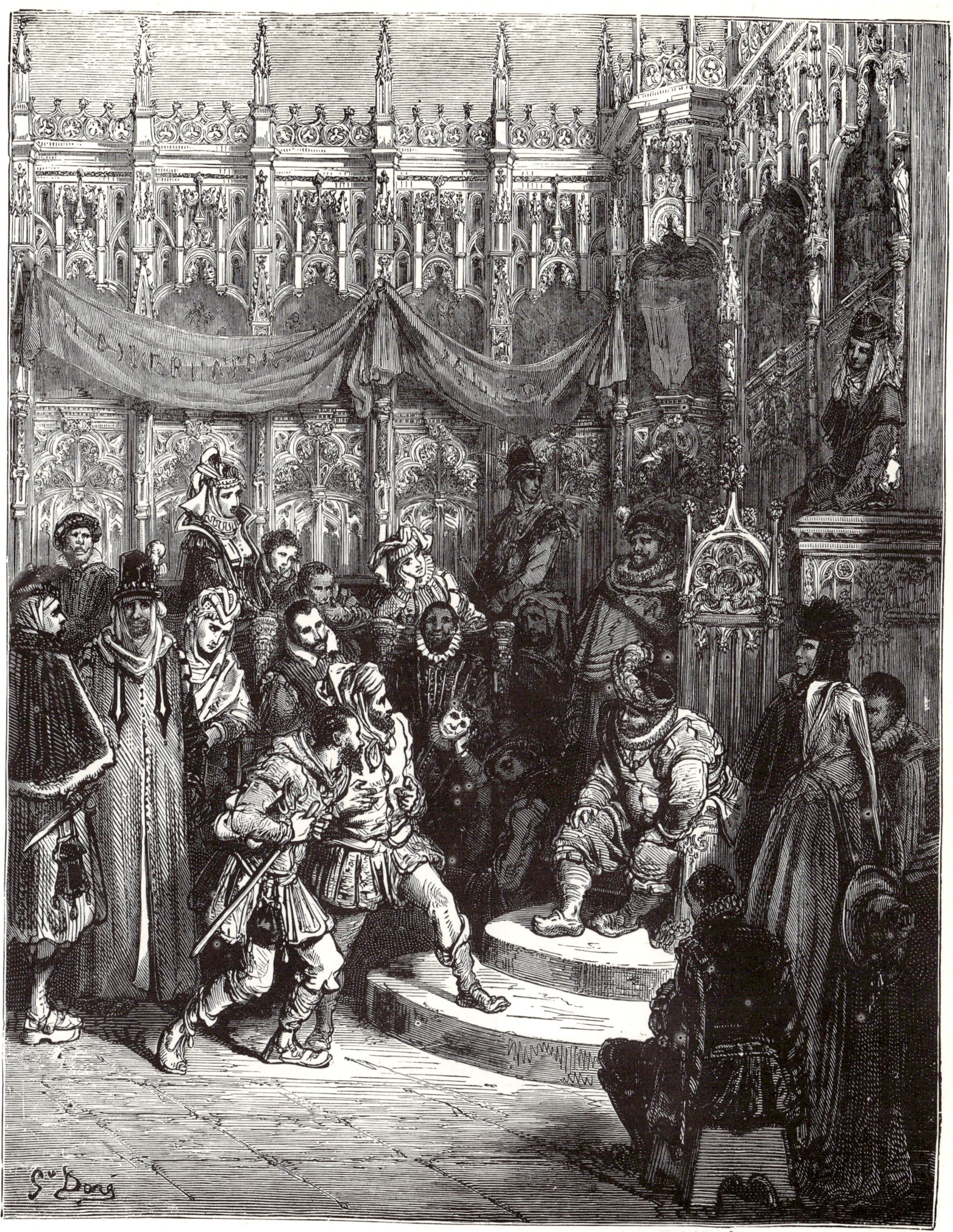
The lord governor Sancho Panza administering justice.

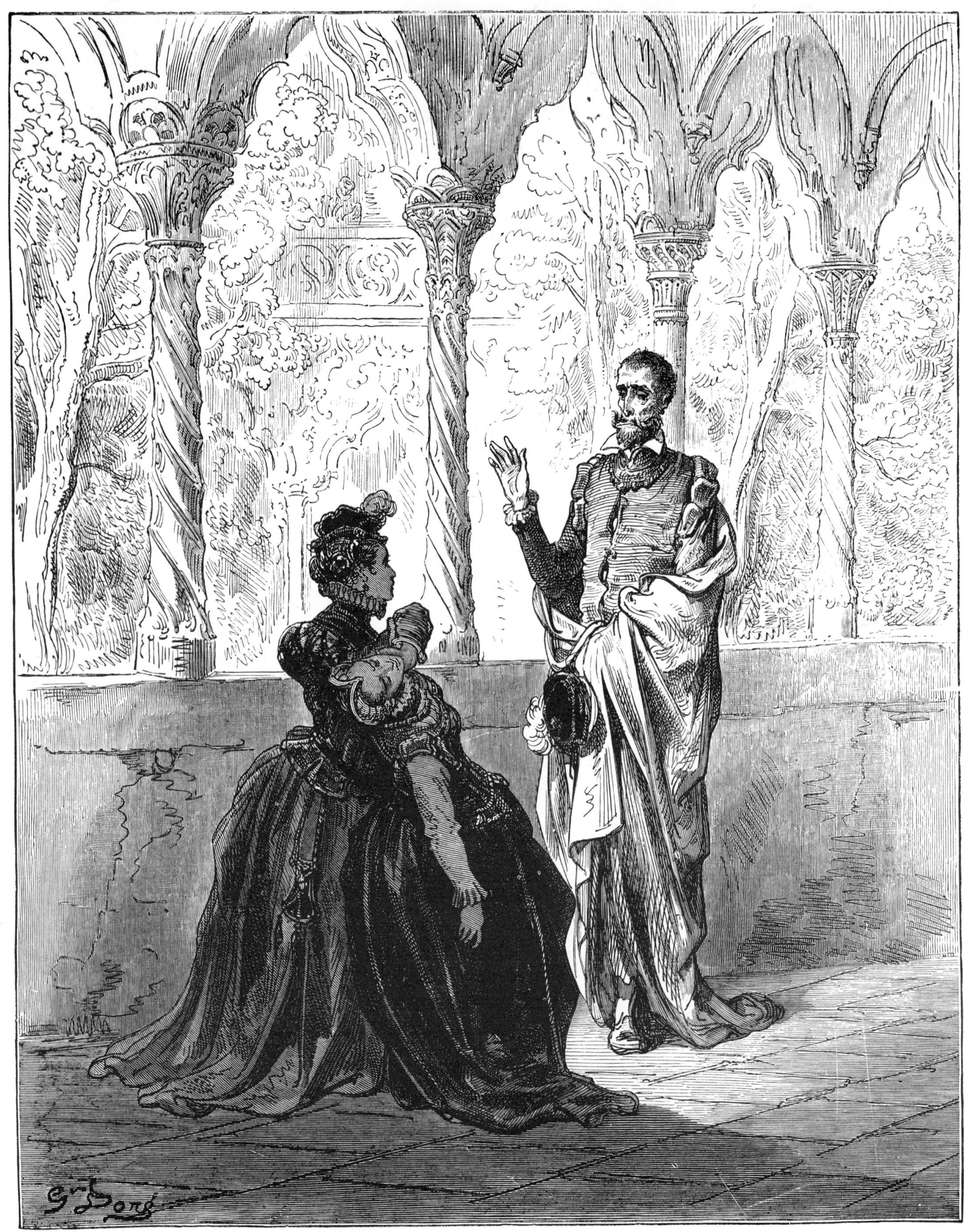

'Pray my lord Don Quixote, retire, for this poor young creature will not come to herself while you are by.'

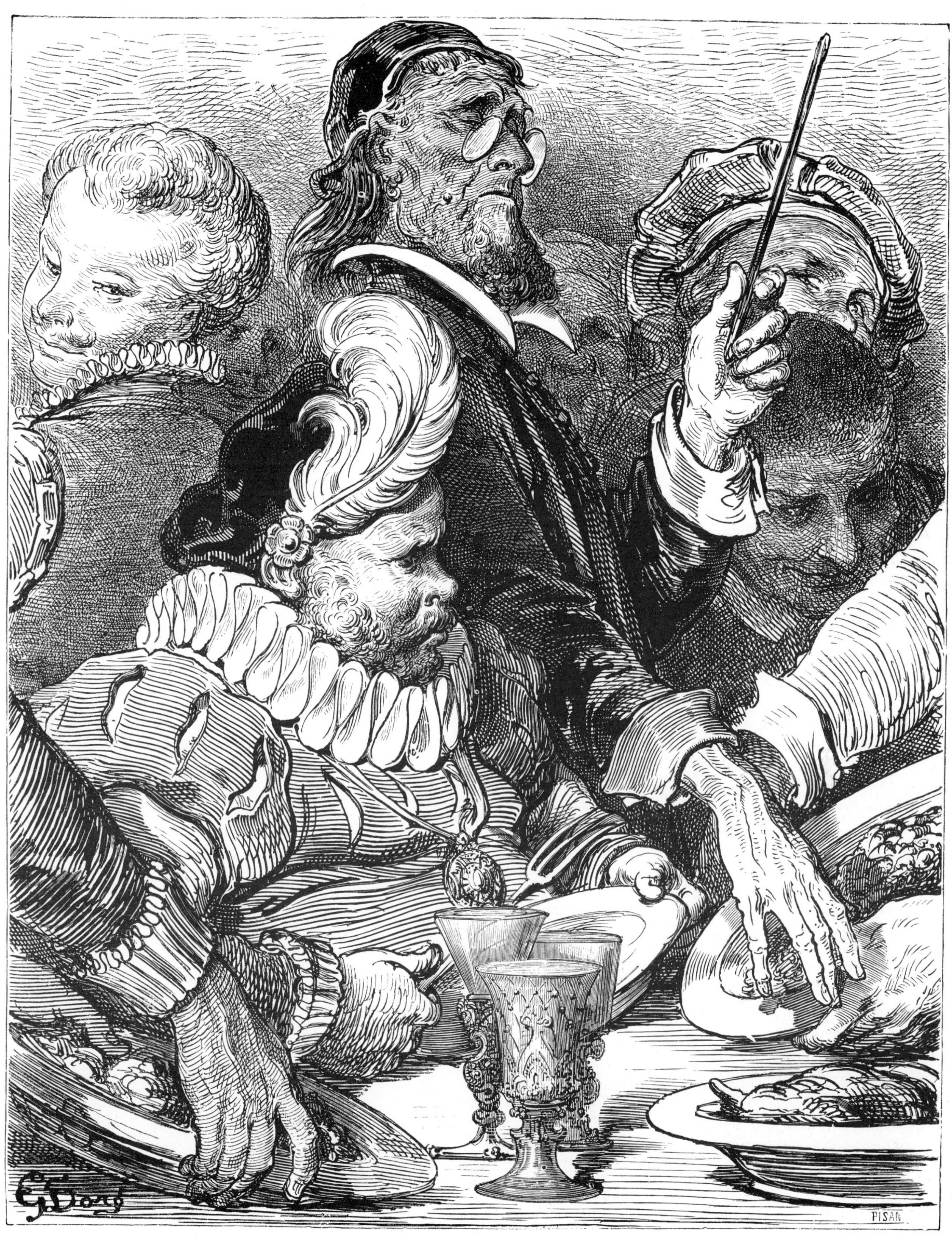

''Absit!' cried the doctor.'

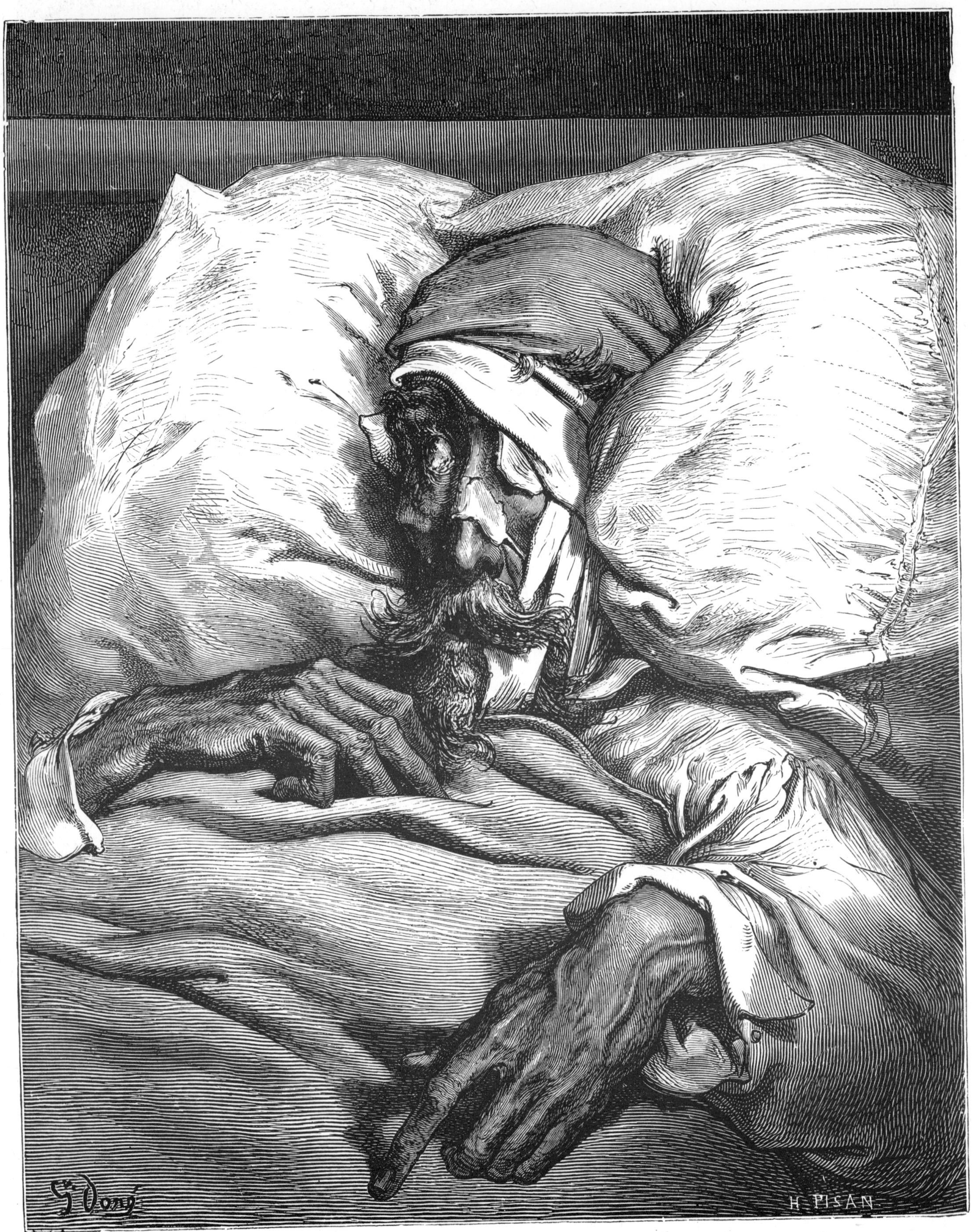

'Don Quixote, thus unhappily hurt, was extremely sullen and melancholy.'

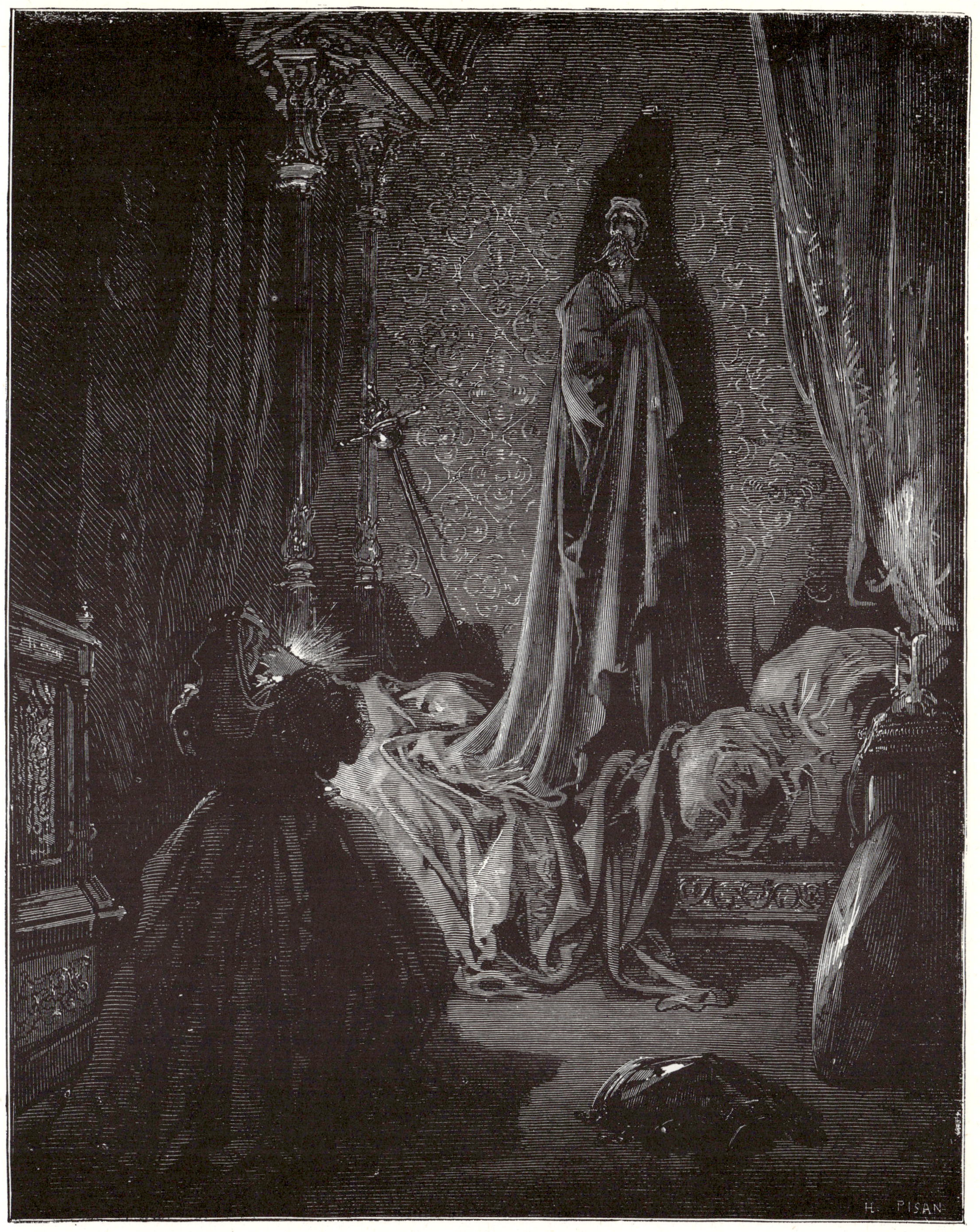

' 'Bless me!' cried she, 'what is this?' '

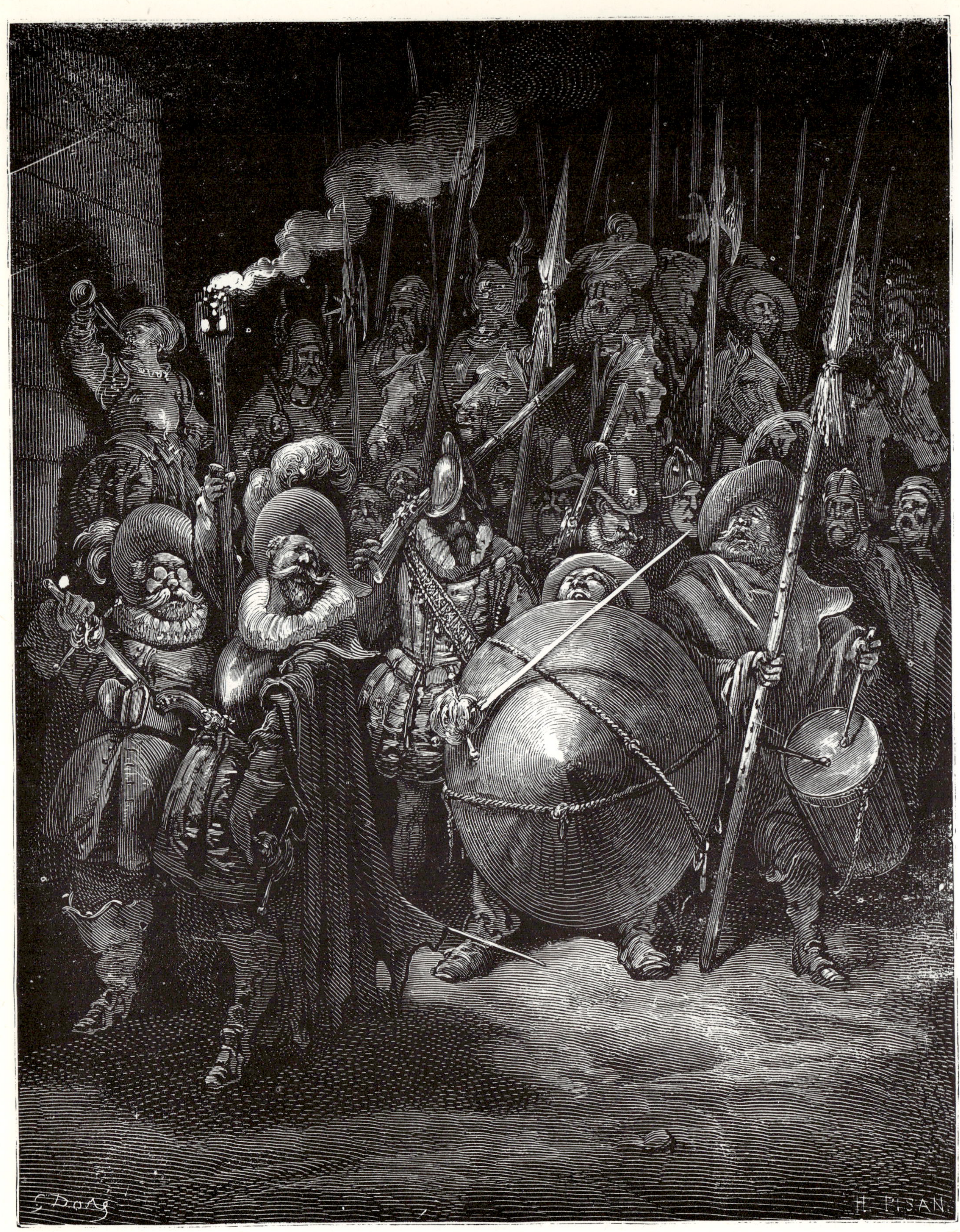

‘ ‘March!’ quoth Sancho. ‘How do you think I am able to do it?’ ’

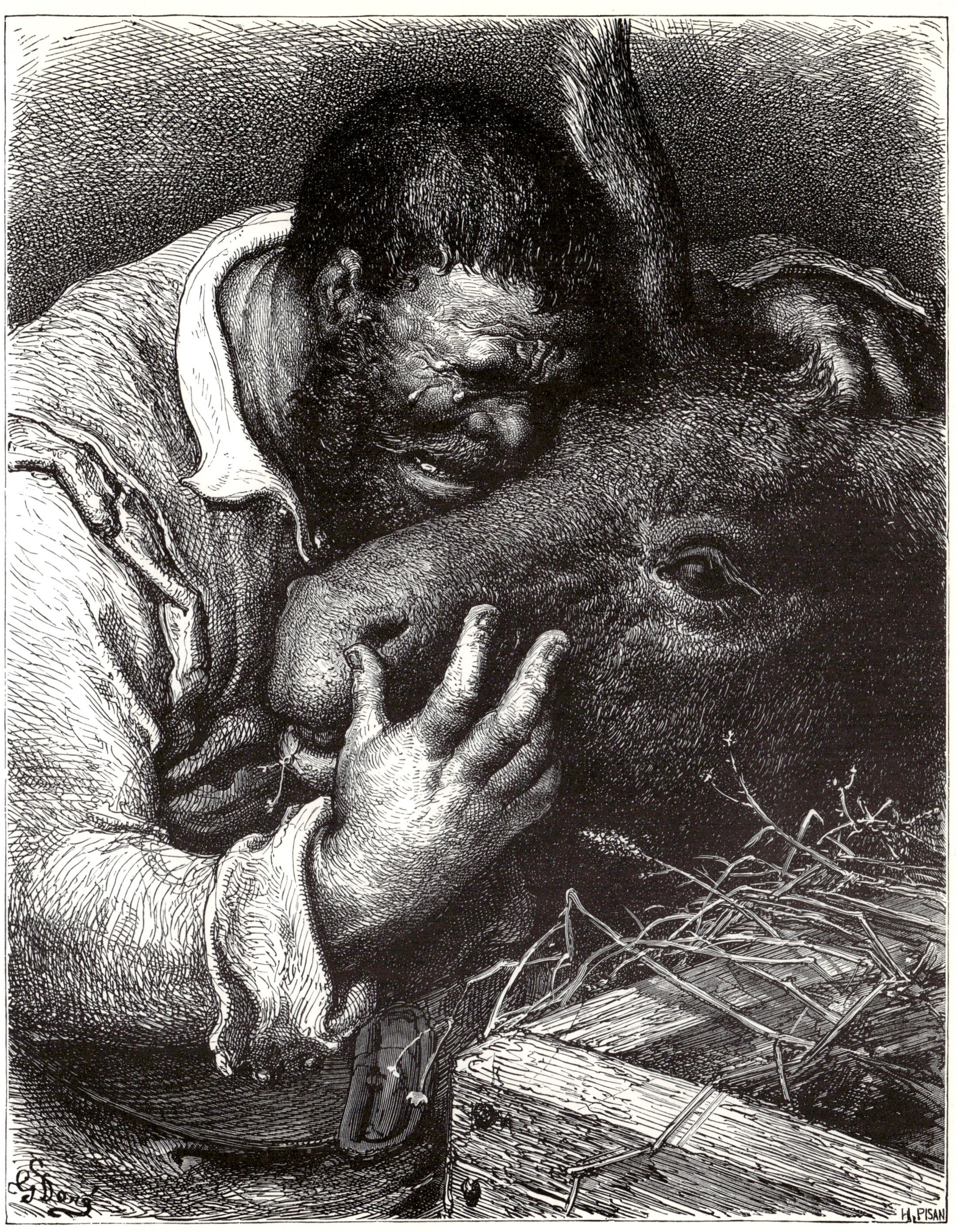

''Come hither,' said he, 'my friend; thou faithful companion and fellow-sharer in all my travels and miseries.''

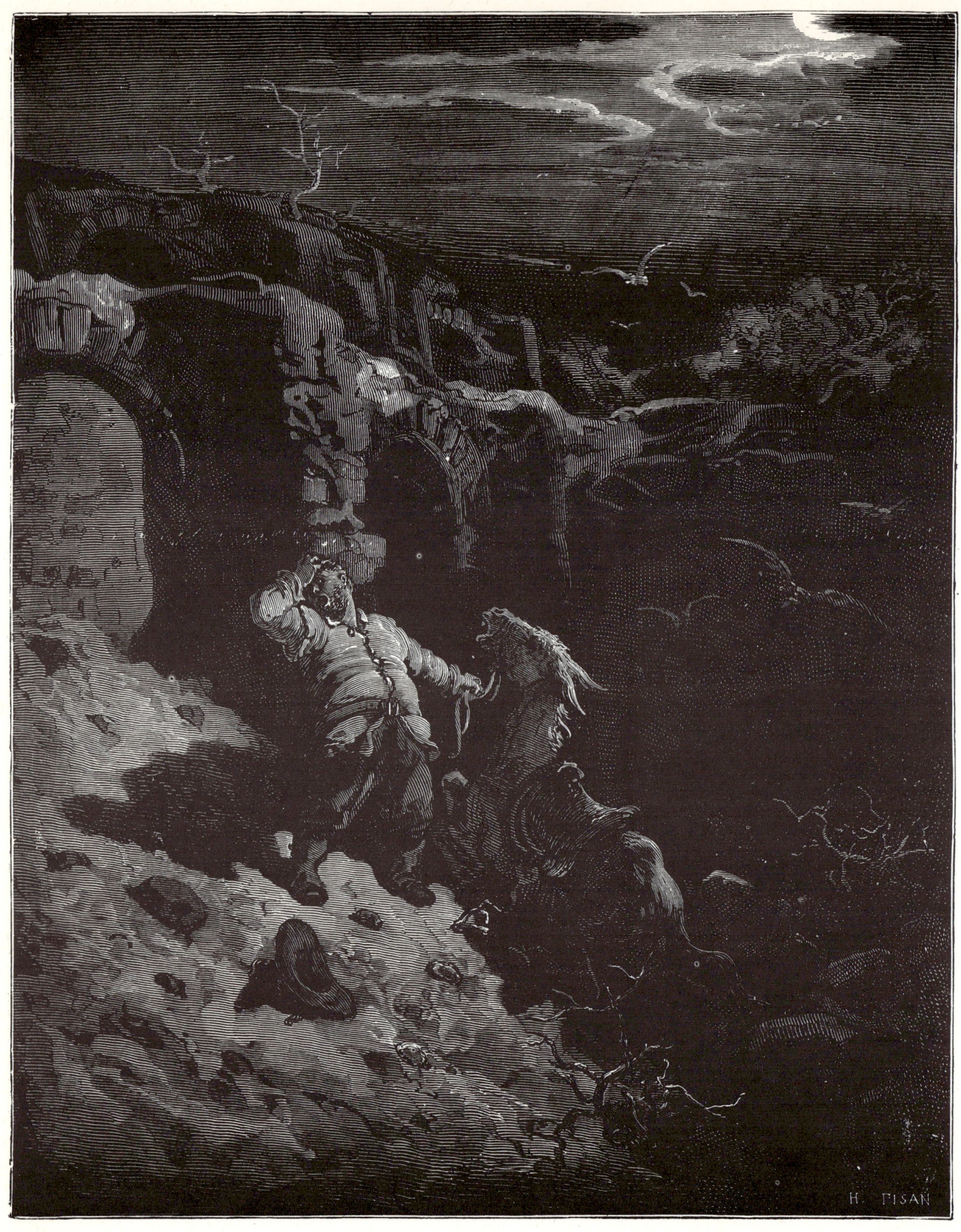

‘ ‘Oh! my dear companion and friend,’ said he to his ass, ‘how ill have I requited thy faithful services!’ ’

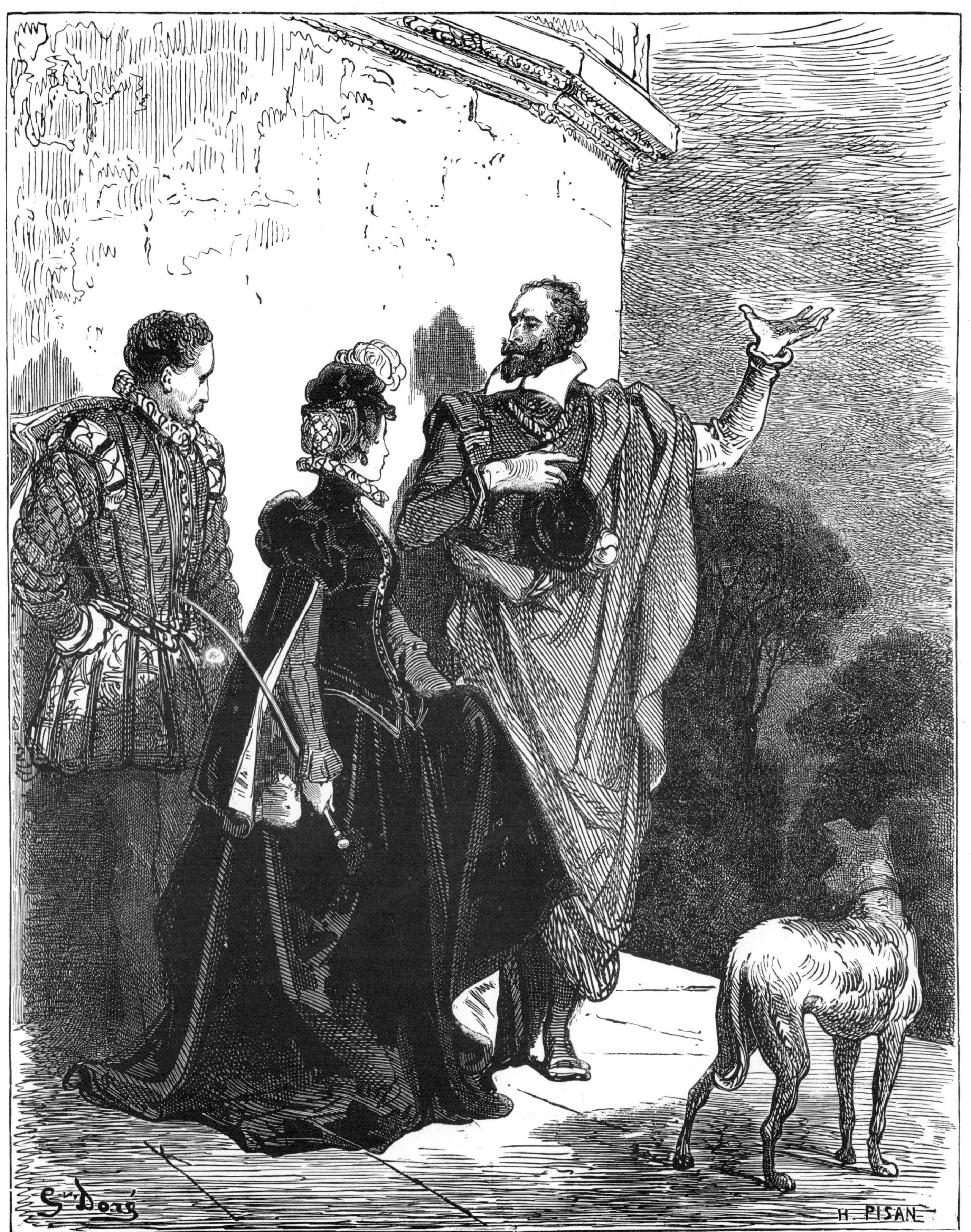

'He acquainted the duke and duchess with his sentiments, and begged their leave to depart.'

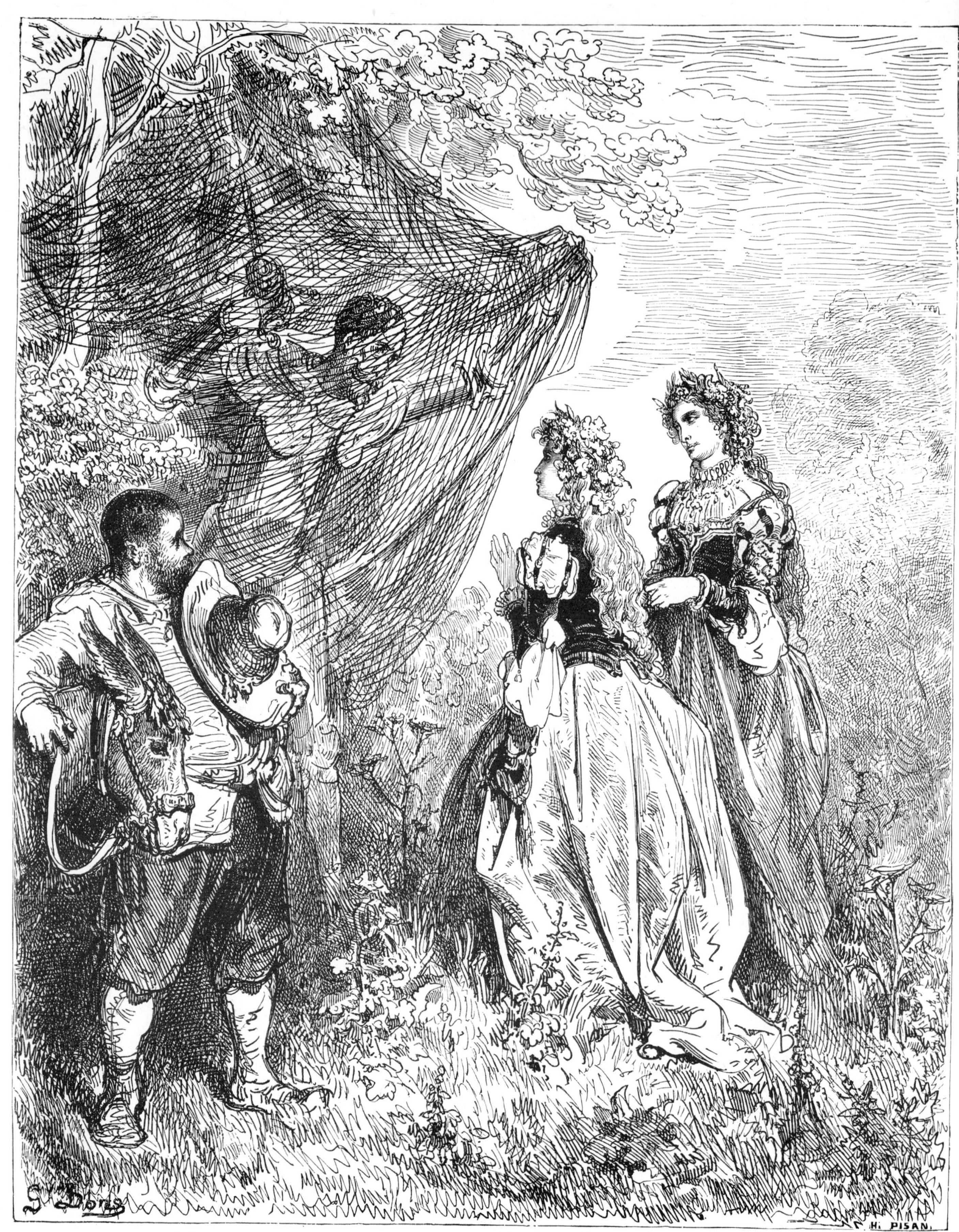

'Now, sir, if you please to afford us your company, you shall be made very welcome.'

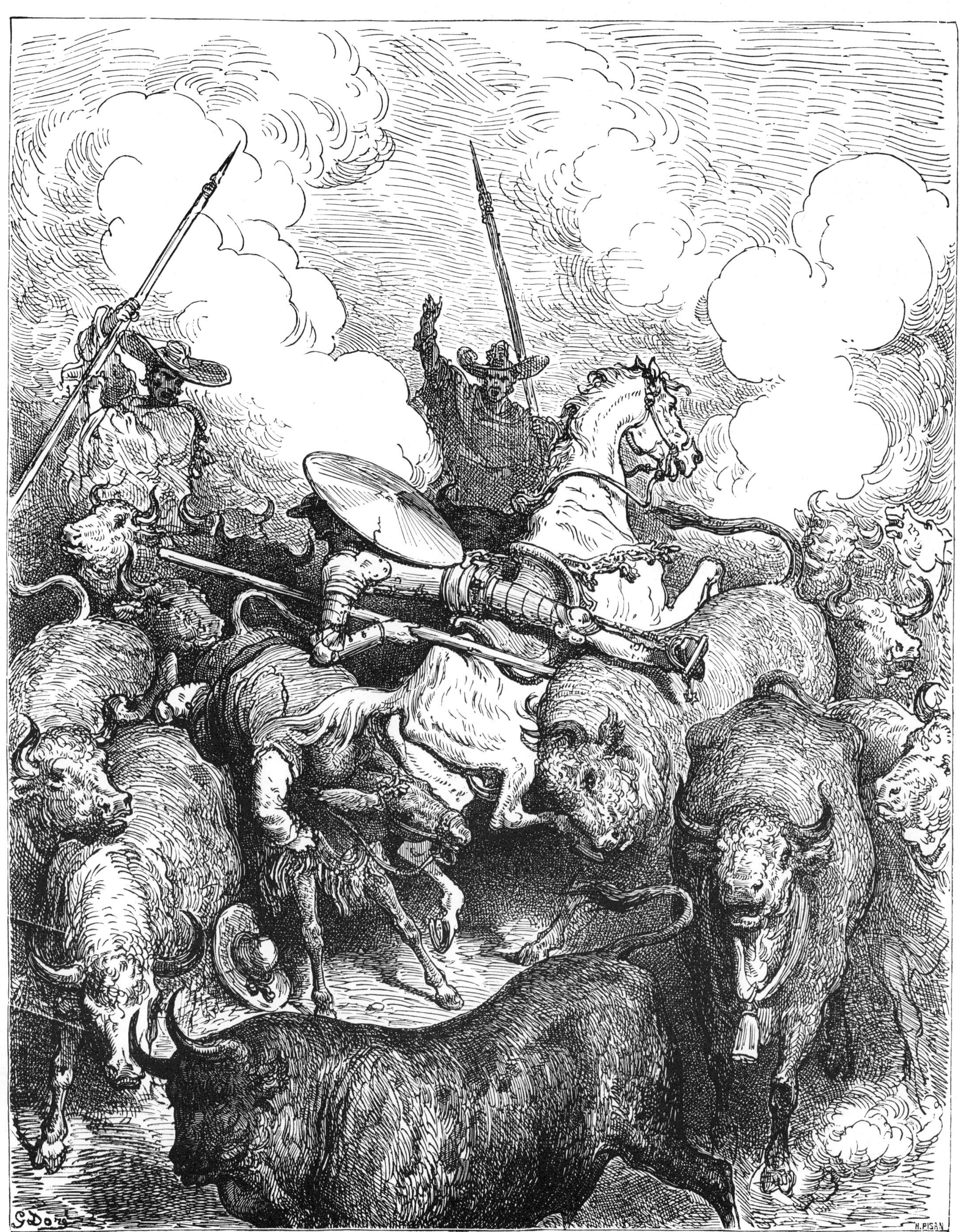

'They trampled them under foot at an unmerciful rate.'

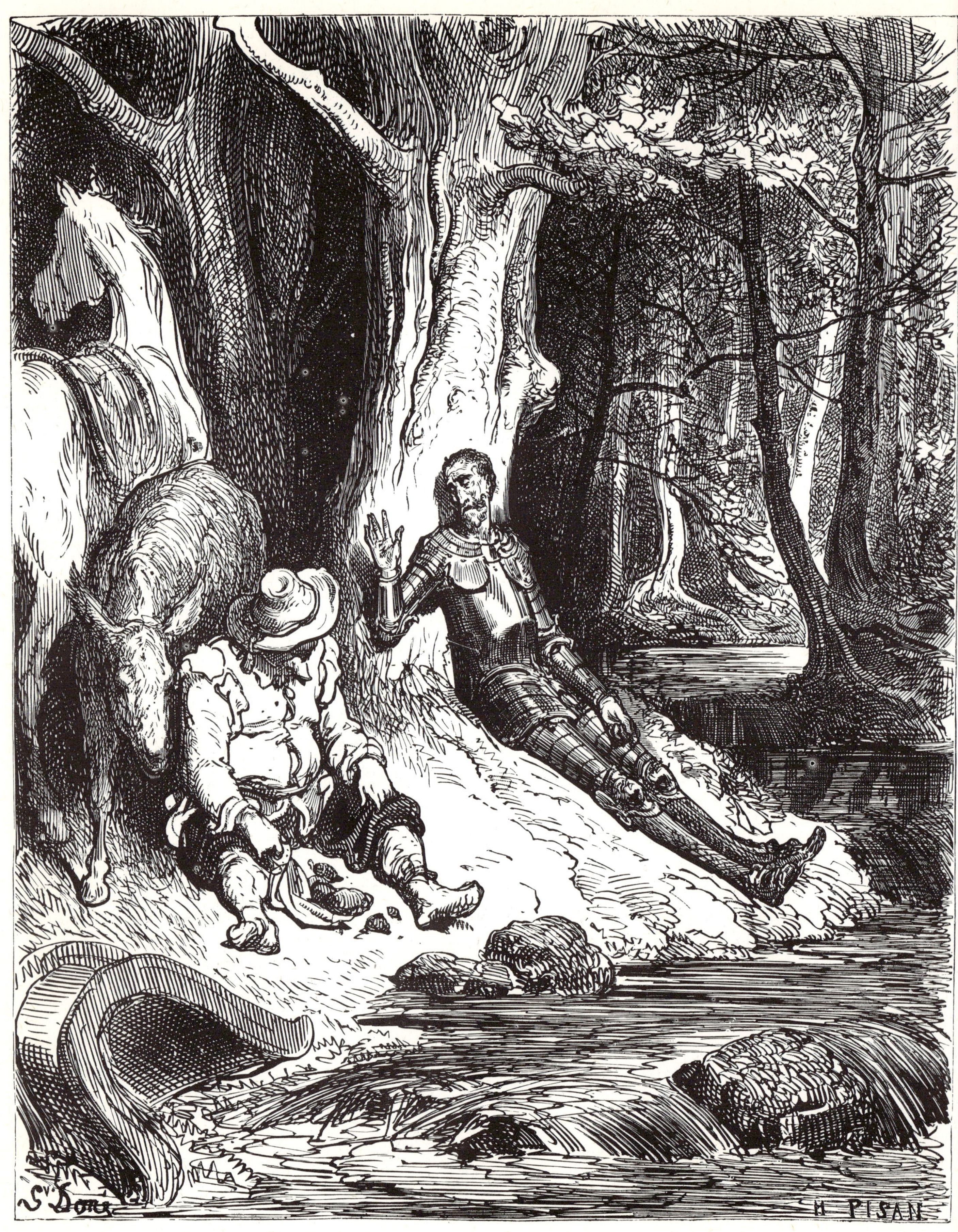

'A clear fountain, which Don Quixote and Sancho found among some verdant trees, served to refresh them.'

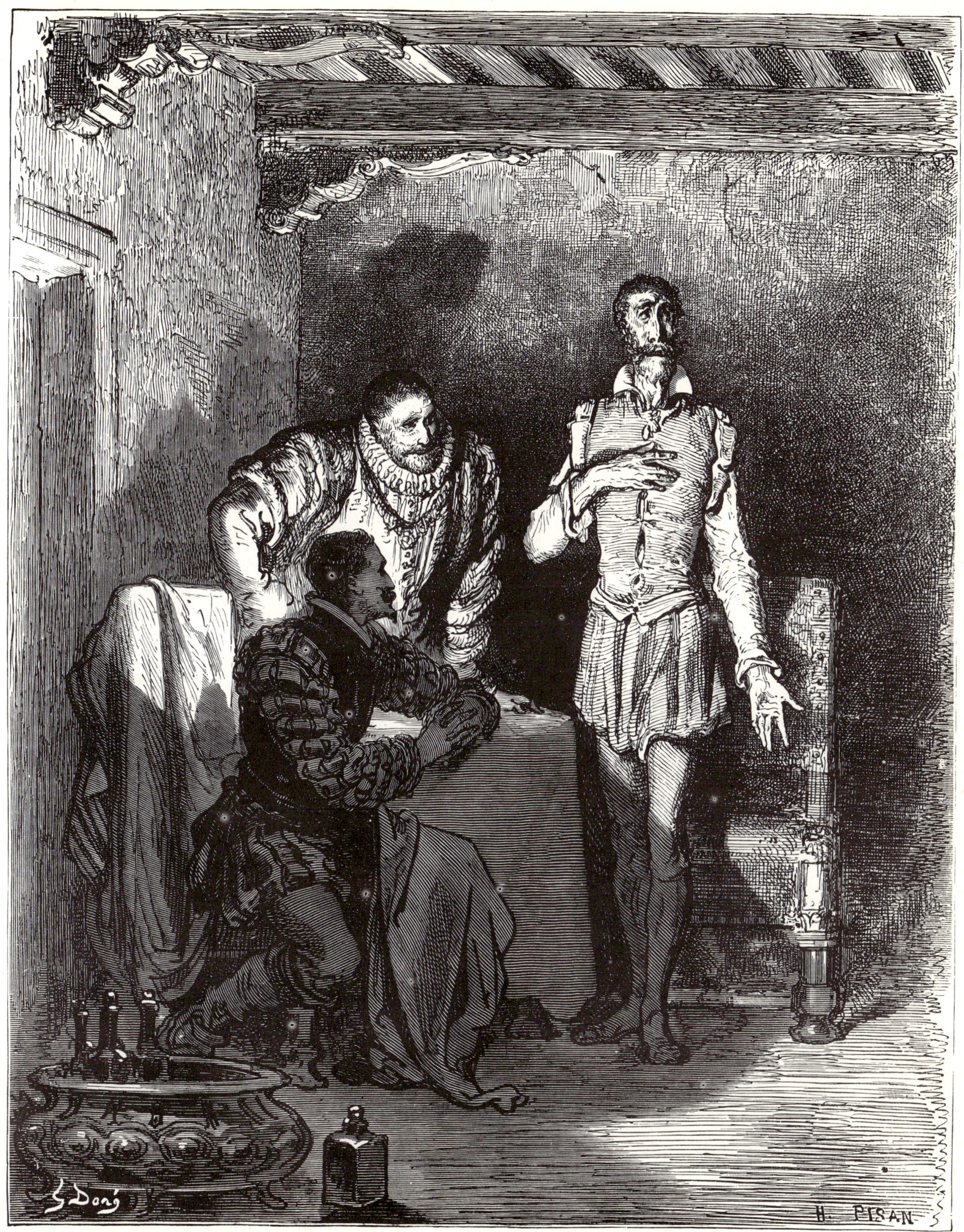

'He told the gentlemen the whole story of her being enchanted.'

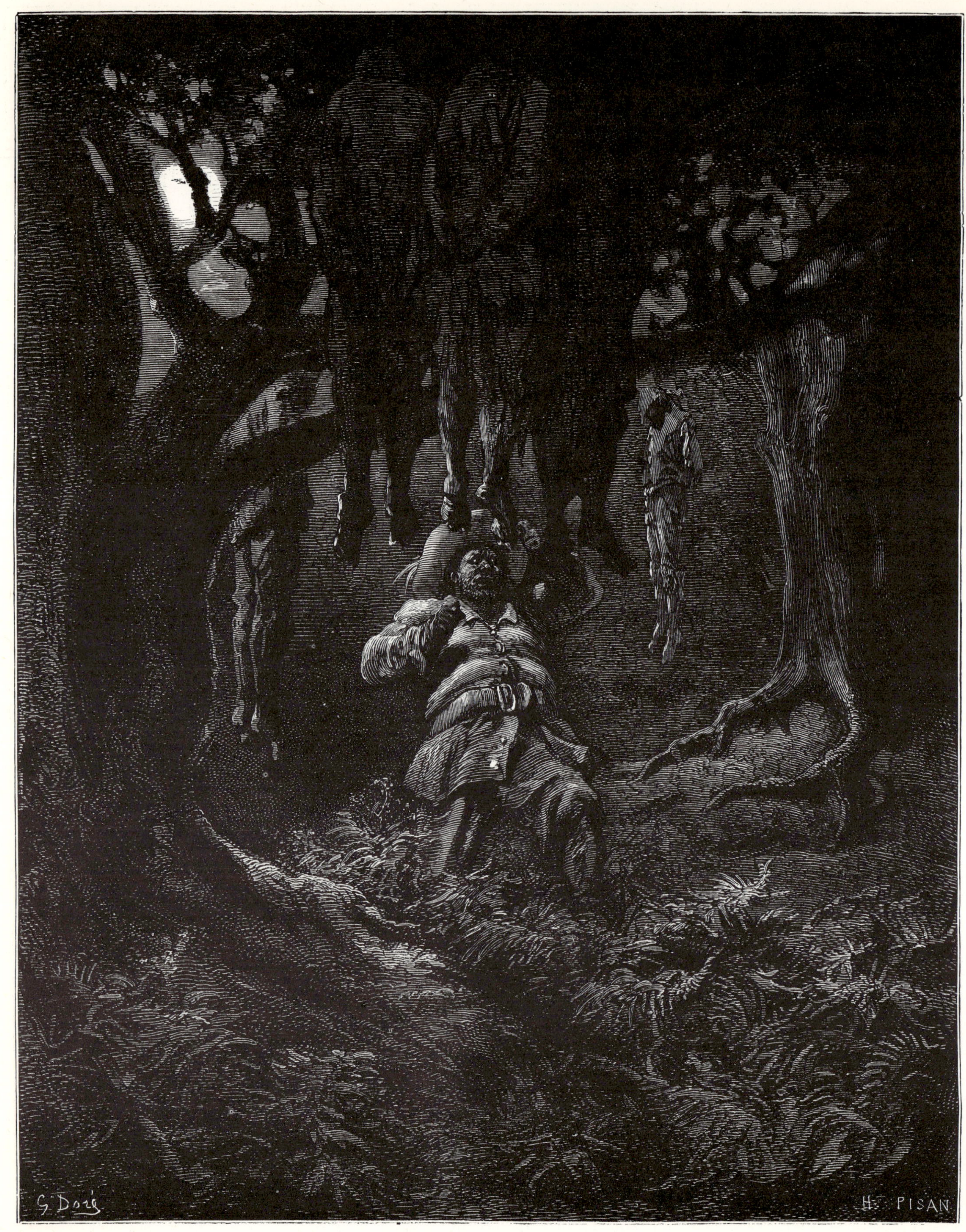

'He called out to Don Quixote for help.'

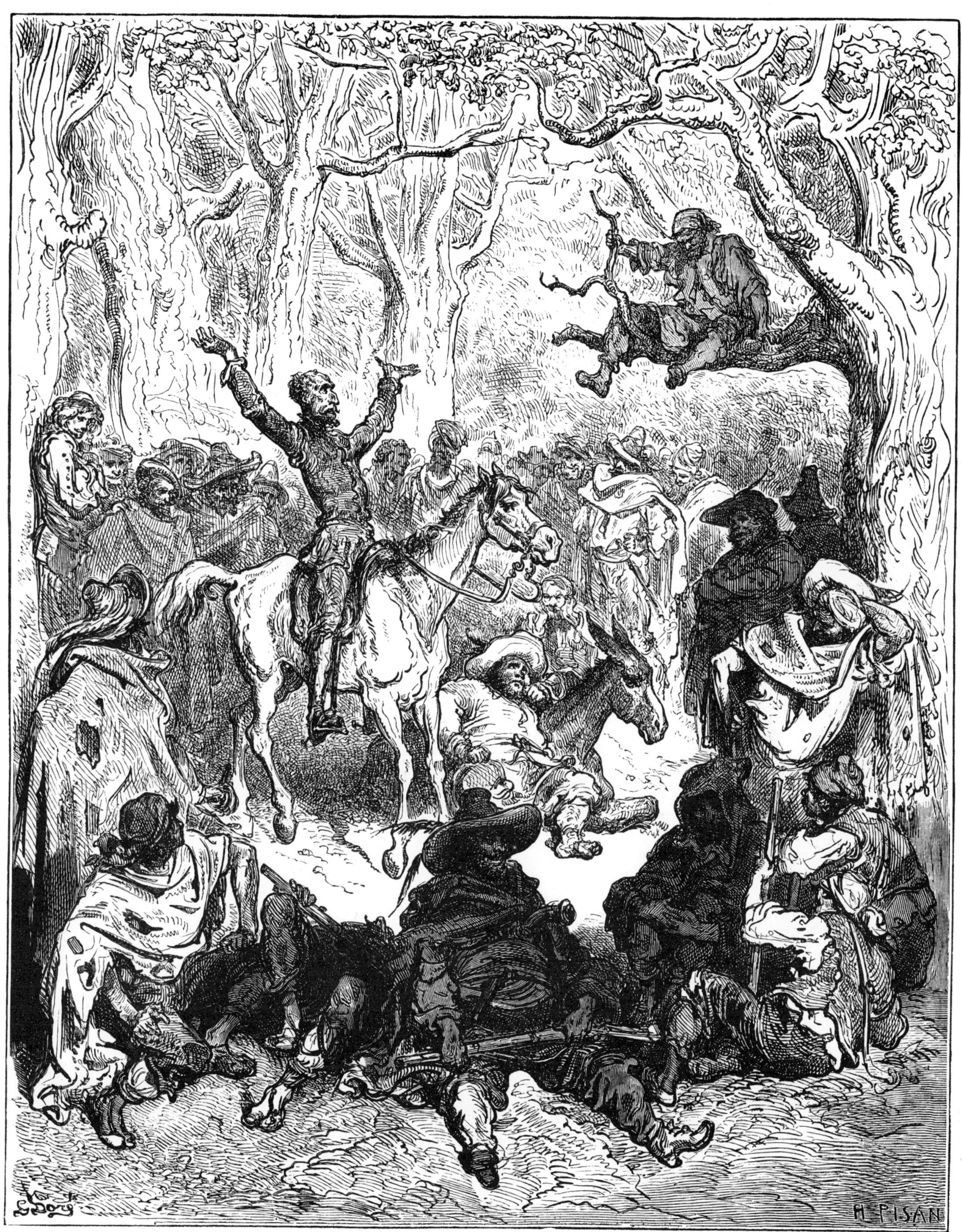

‘Don Quixote, mounted on Rozinante, declaiming very copiously against their way of living.’

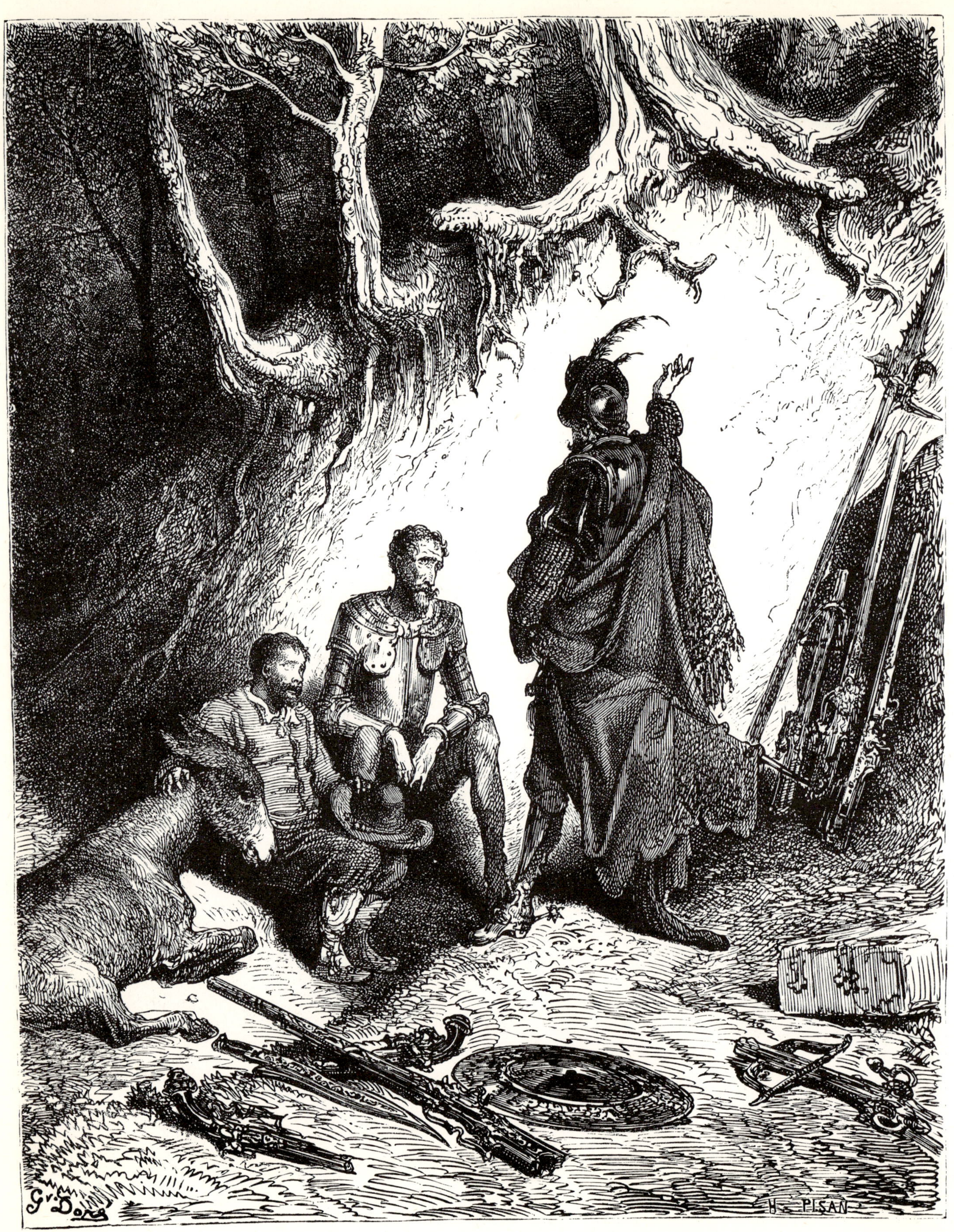

'The squires left Don Quixote, Roque, and Sancho to wait their return.'

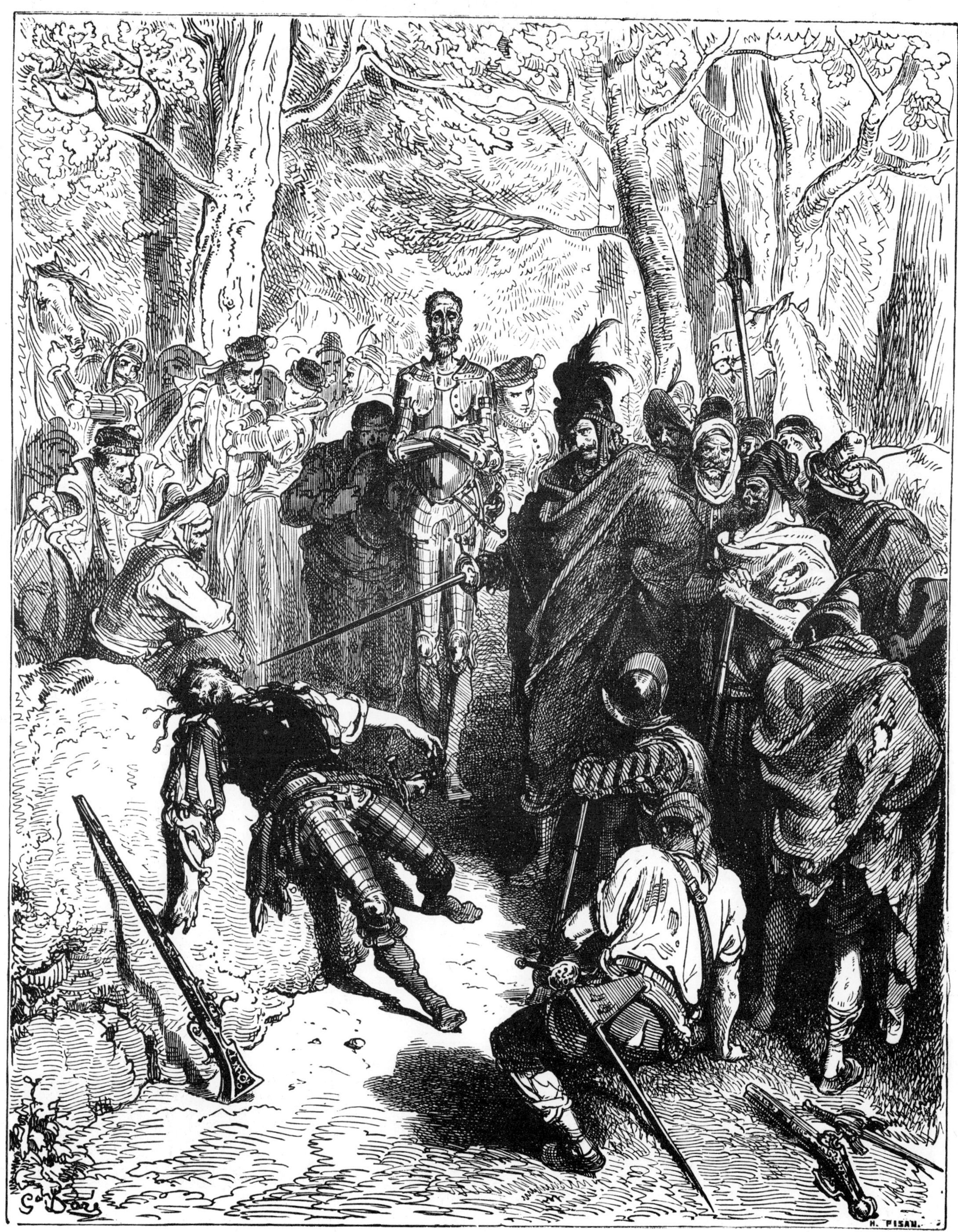

' 'Thus it is I punish mutiny,' said he.'

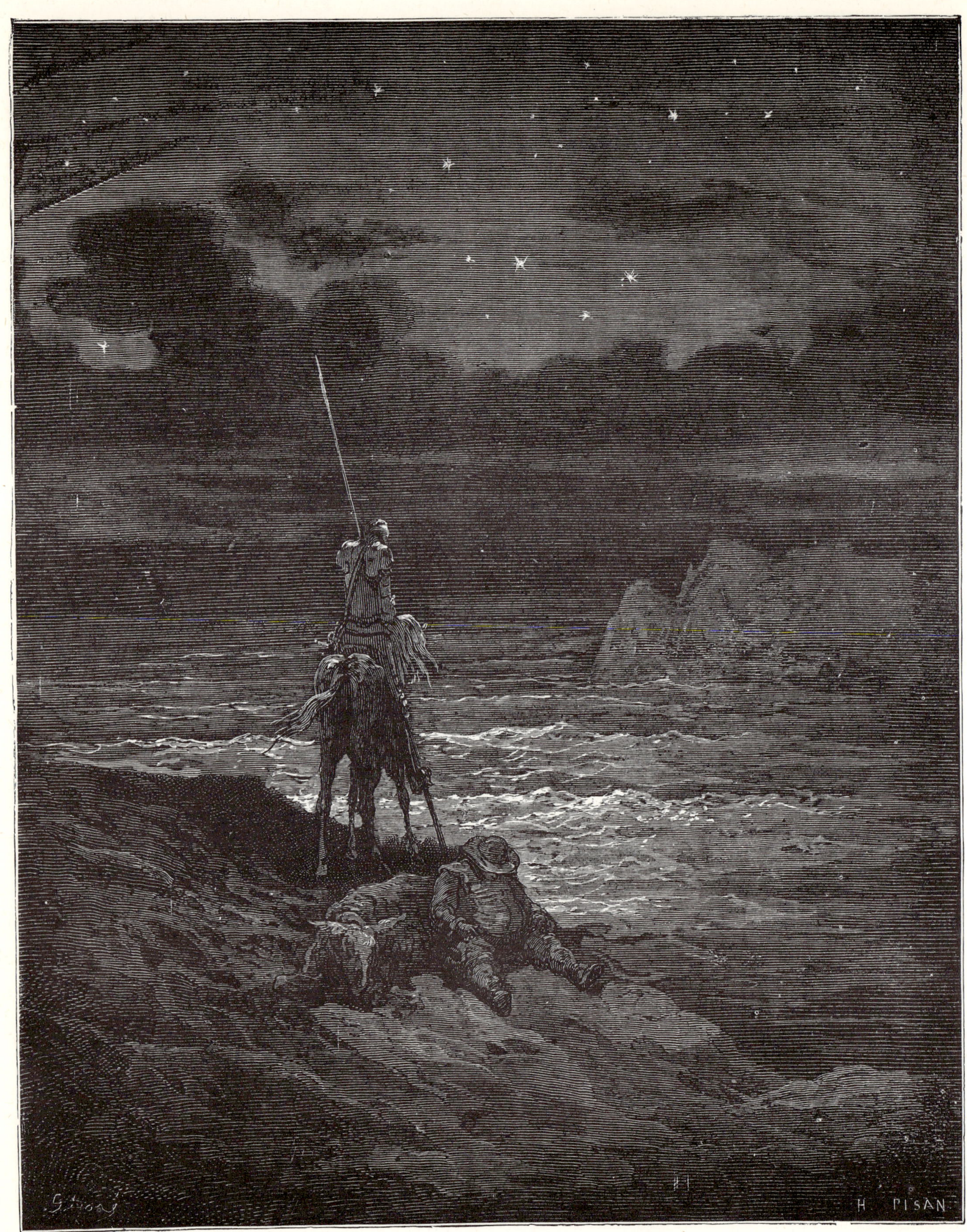

'Don Quixote stayed there, waiting the approach of day.'

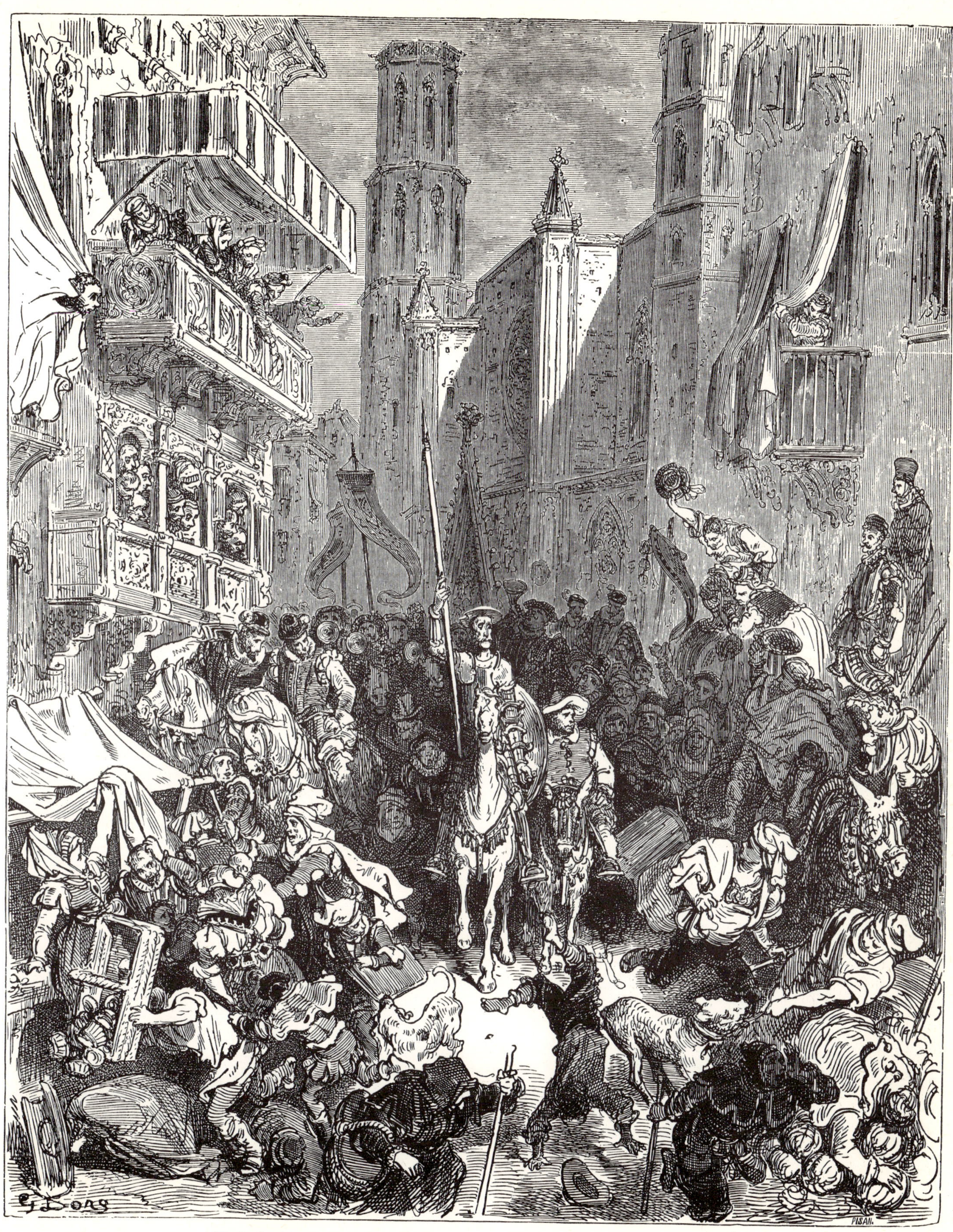

'Enclosing him in the middle of their brigade, they conducted him towards the city.'

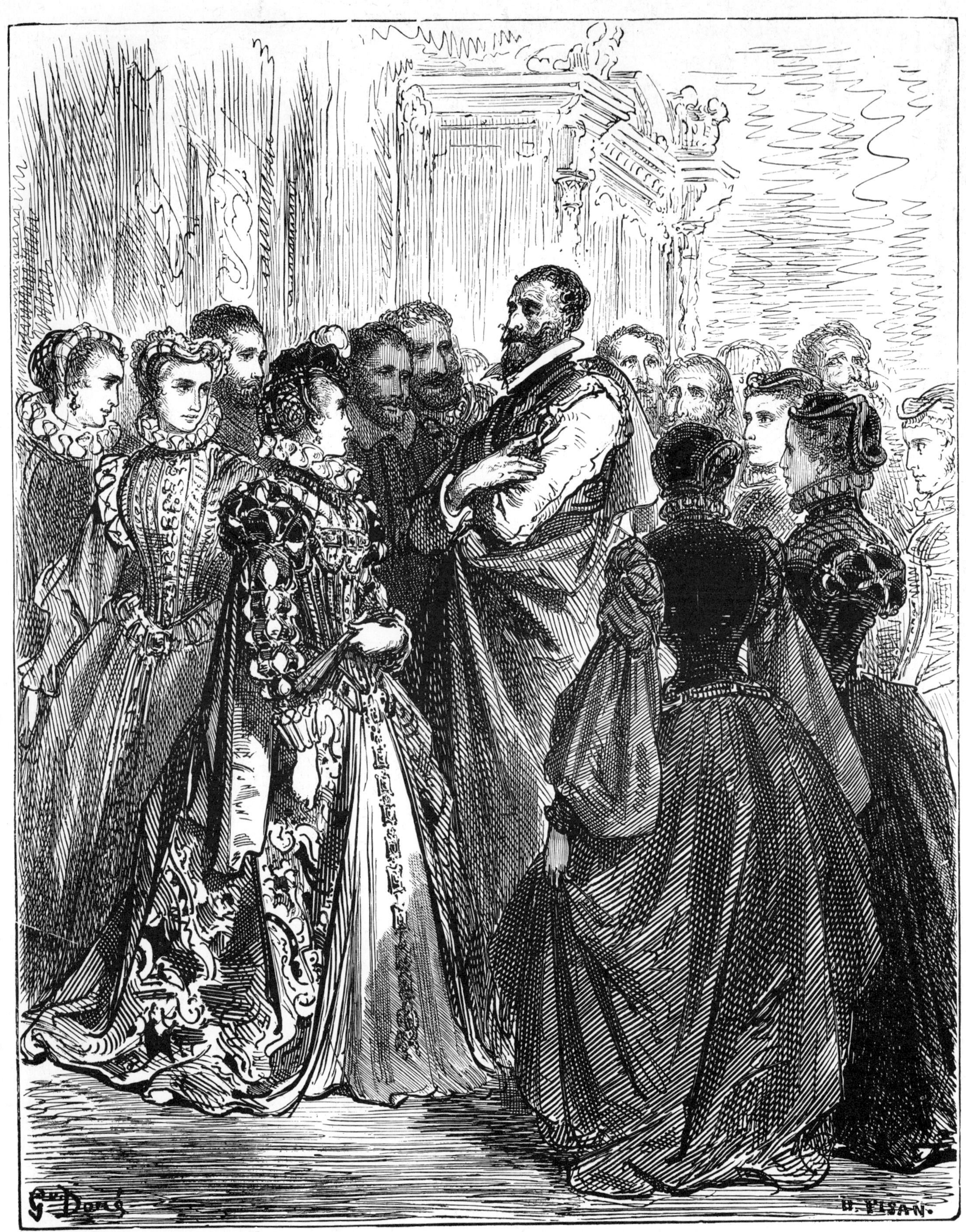

'Don Antonio's wife had invited several of her friends to a ball, to honour her guest.'

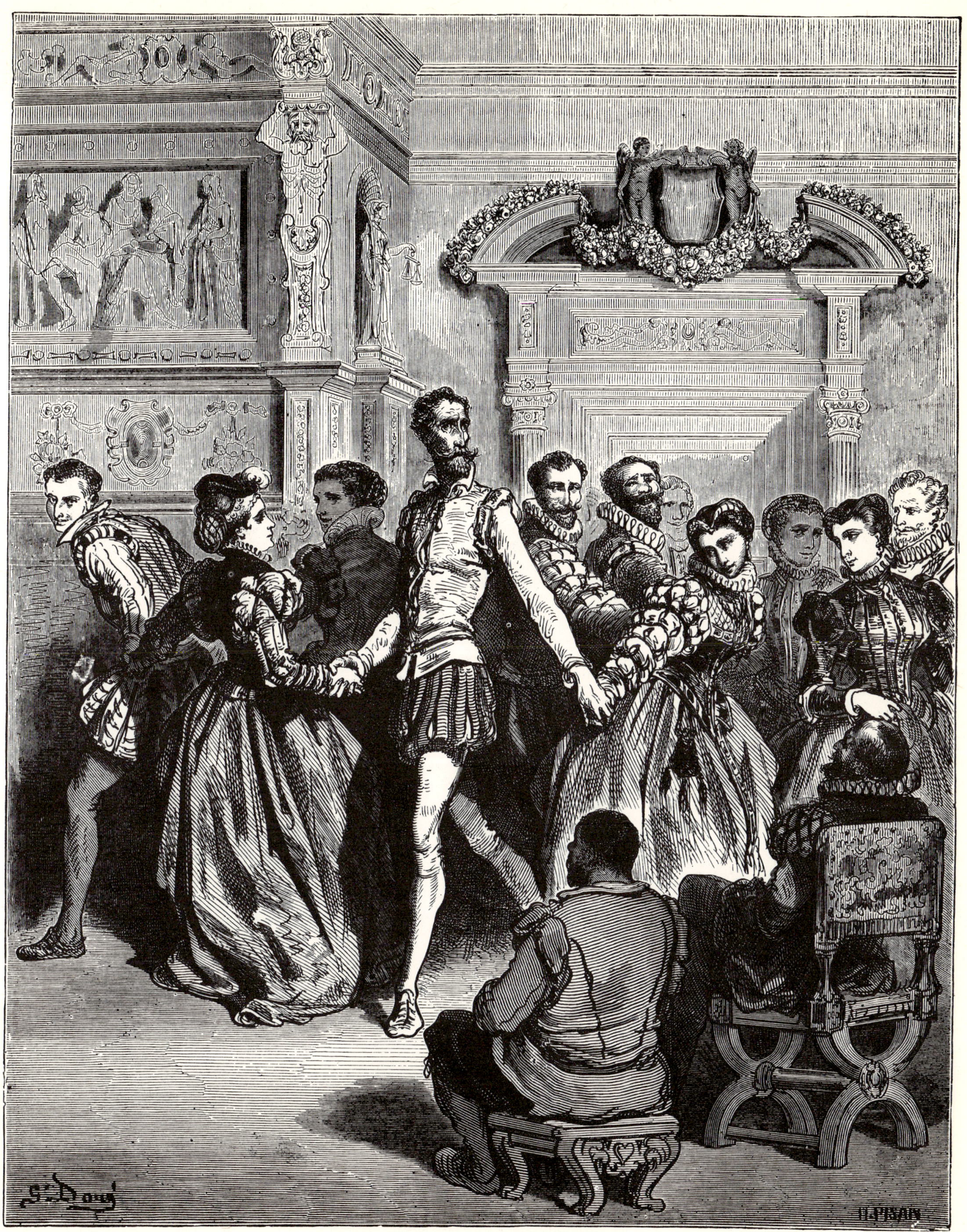

'Two ladies made their court chiefly to Don Quixote.'

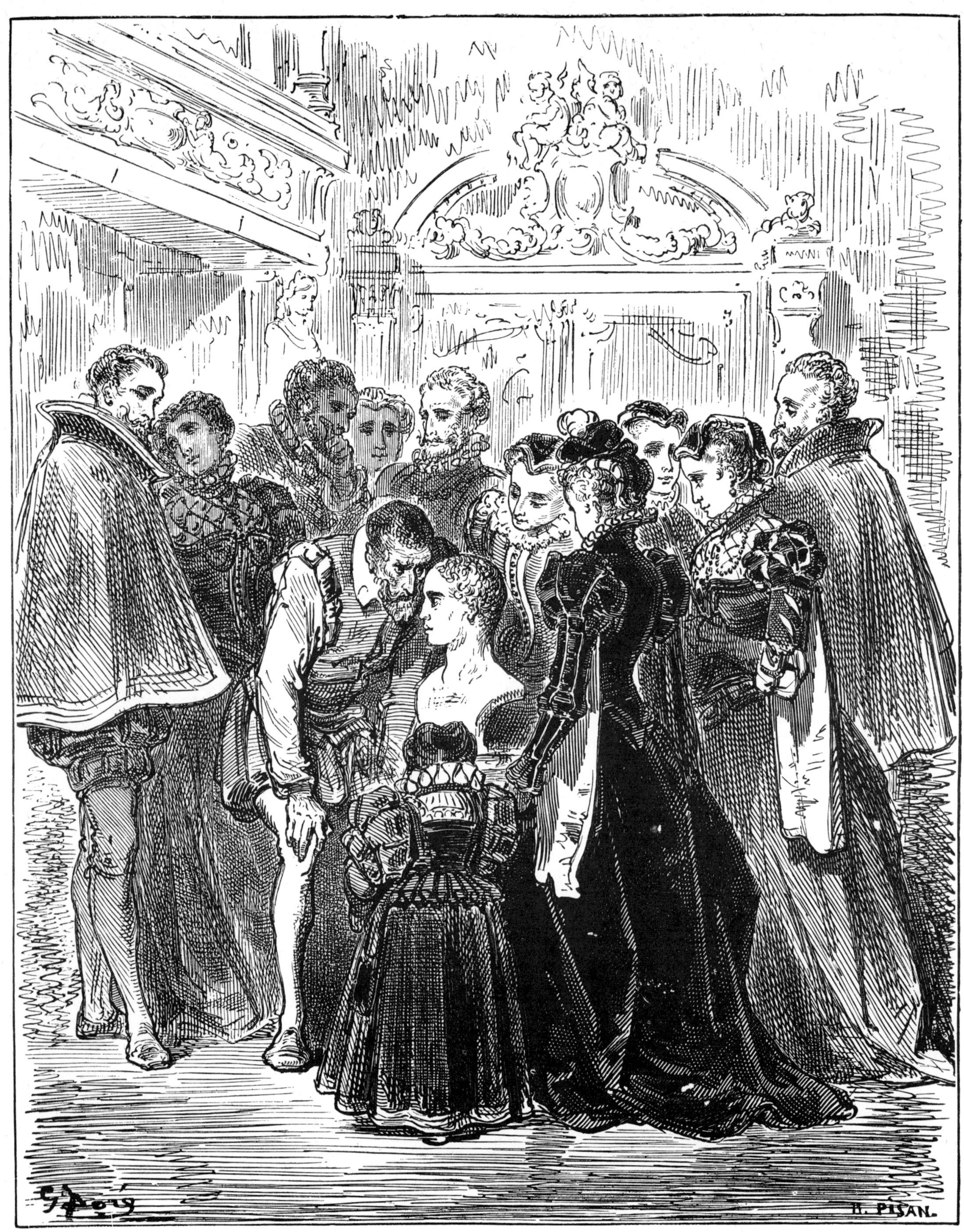

' 'Tell me, thou oracle,' said he, 'was what I reported of my adventures in the cave of Montesinos a dream or reality?' '

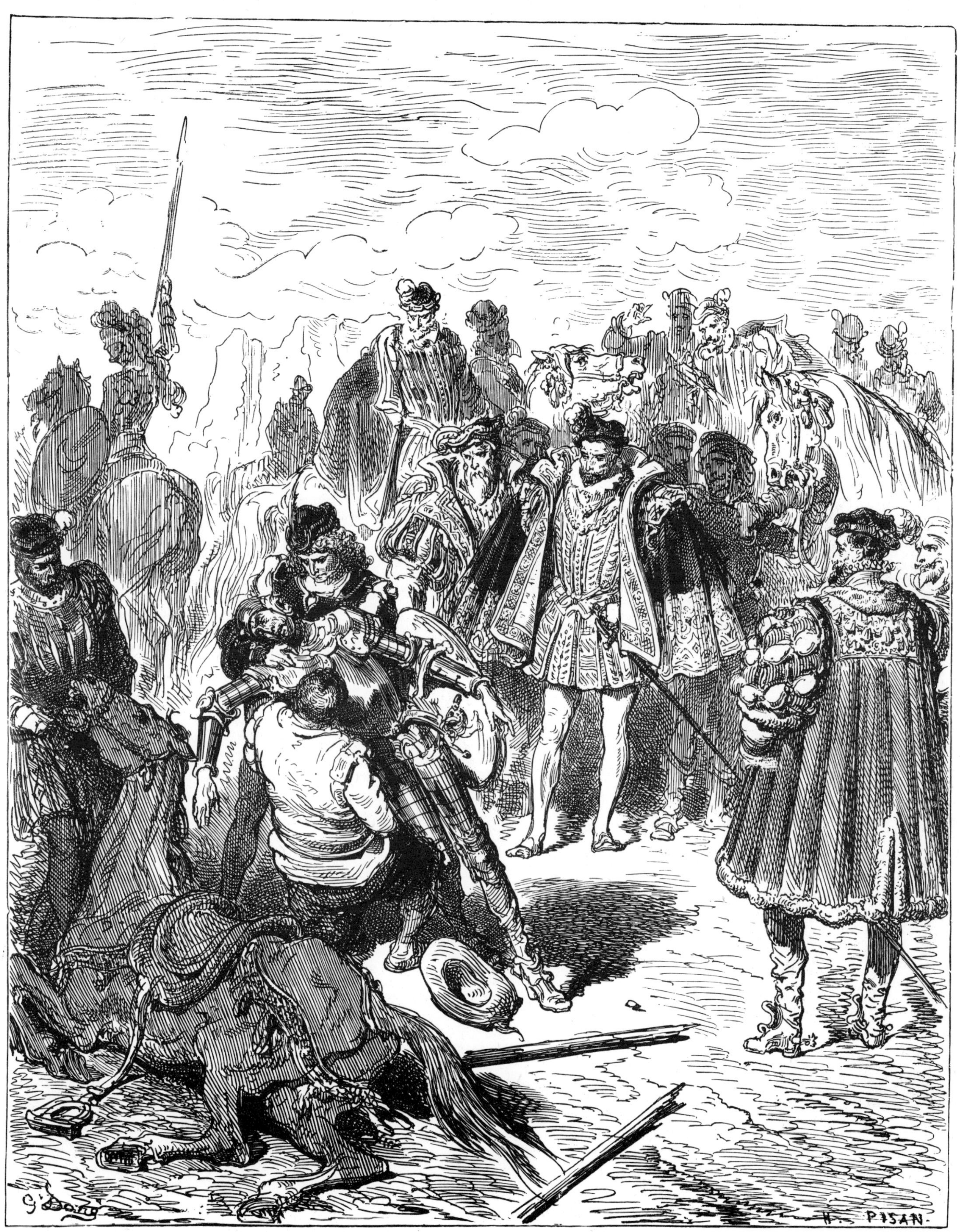

'They found him pale, and in a cold sweat.'

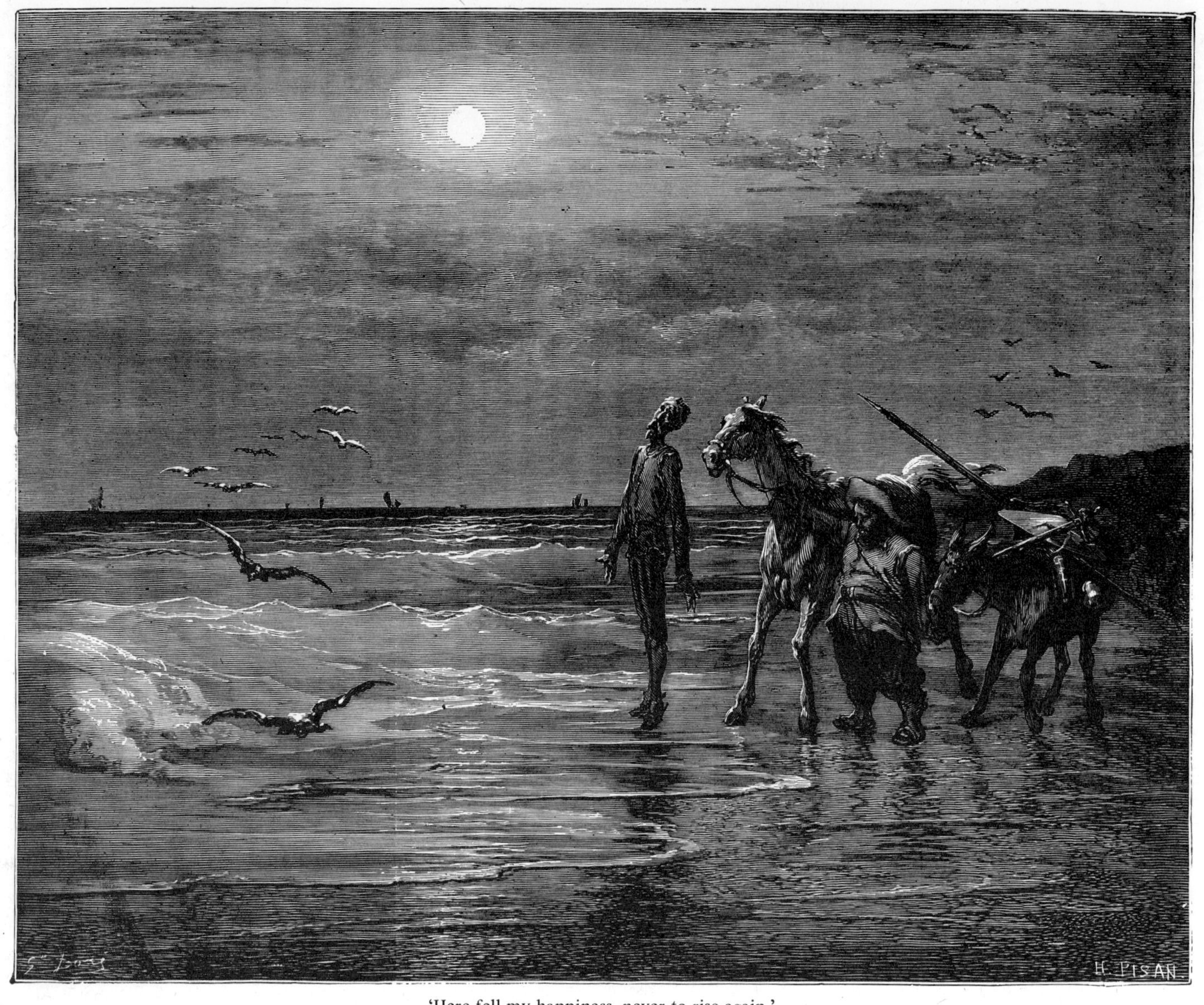

'Here fell my happiness, never to rise again.'

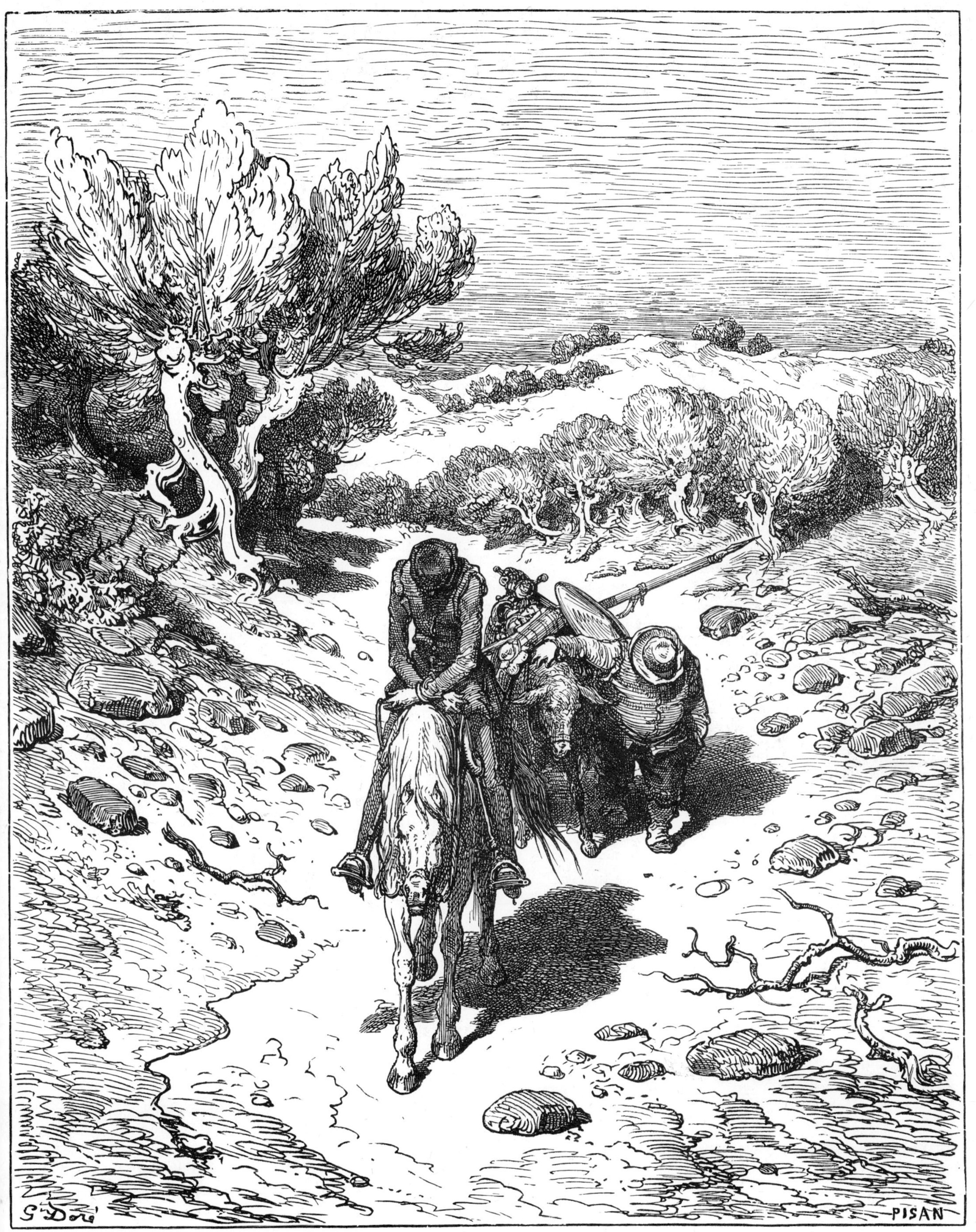

'They passed that day, and four more after that, in such kind of discourse.'

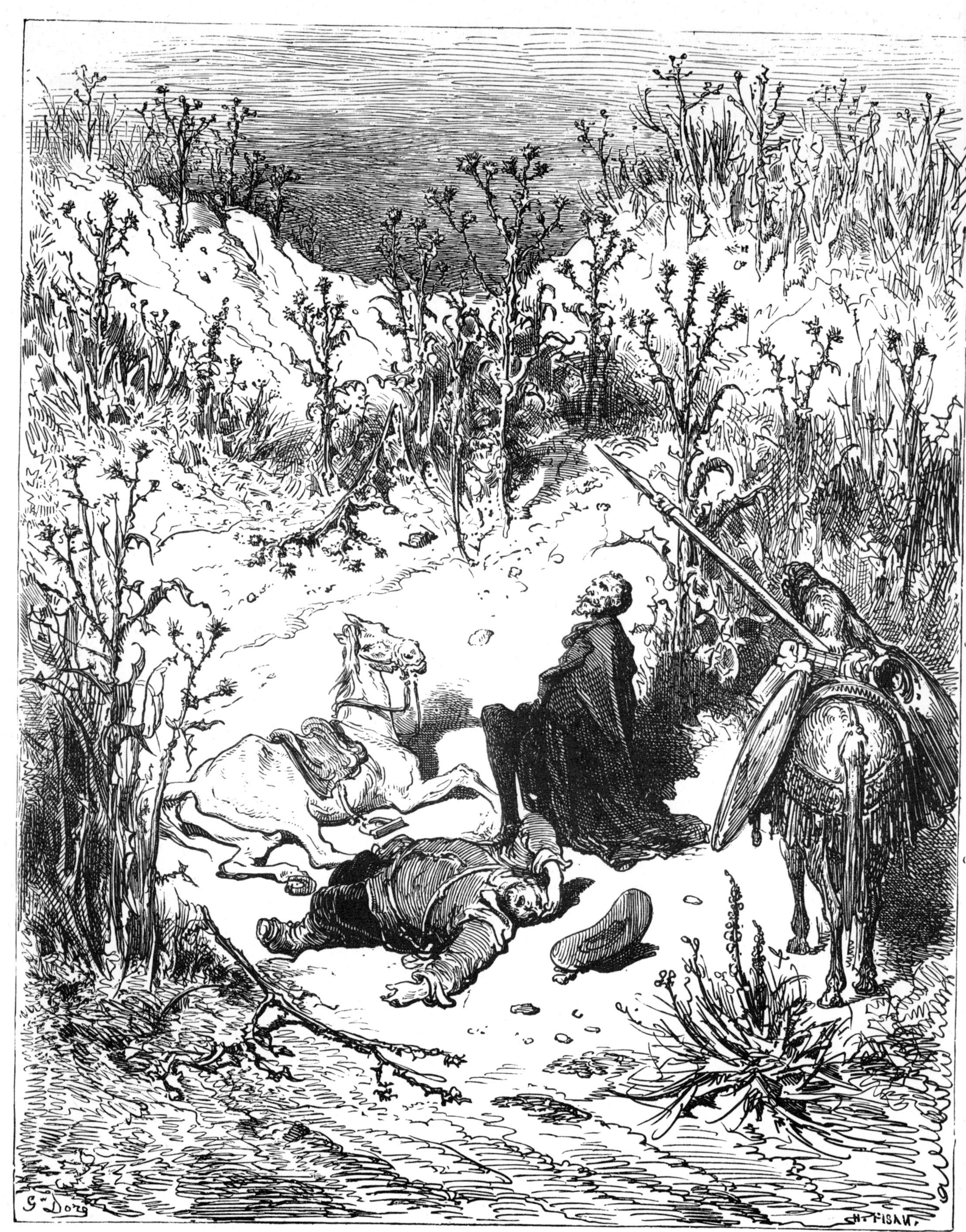

''Sleep, Sancho,' cried Don Quixote; 'sleep, for thou wert born to sleep.''

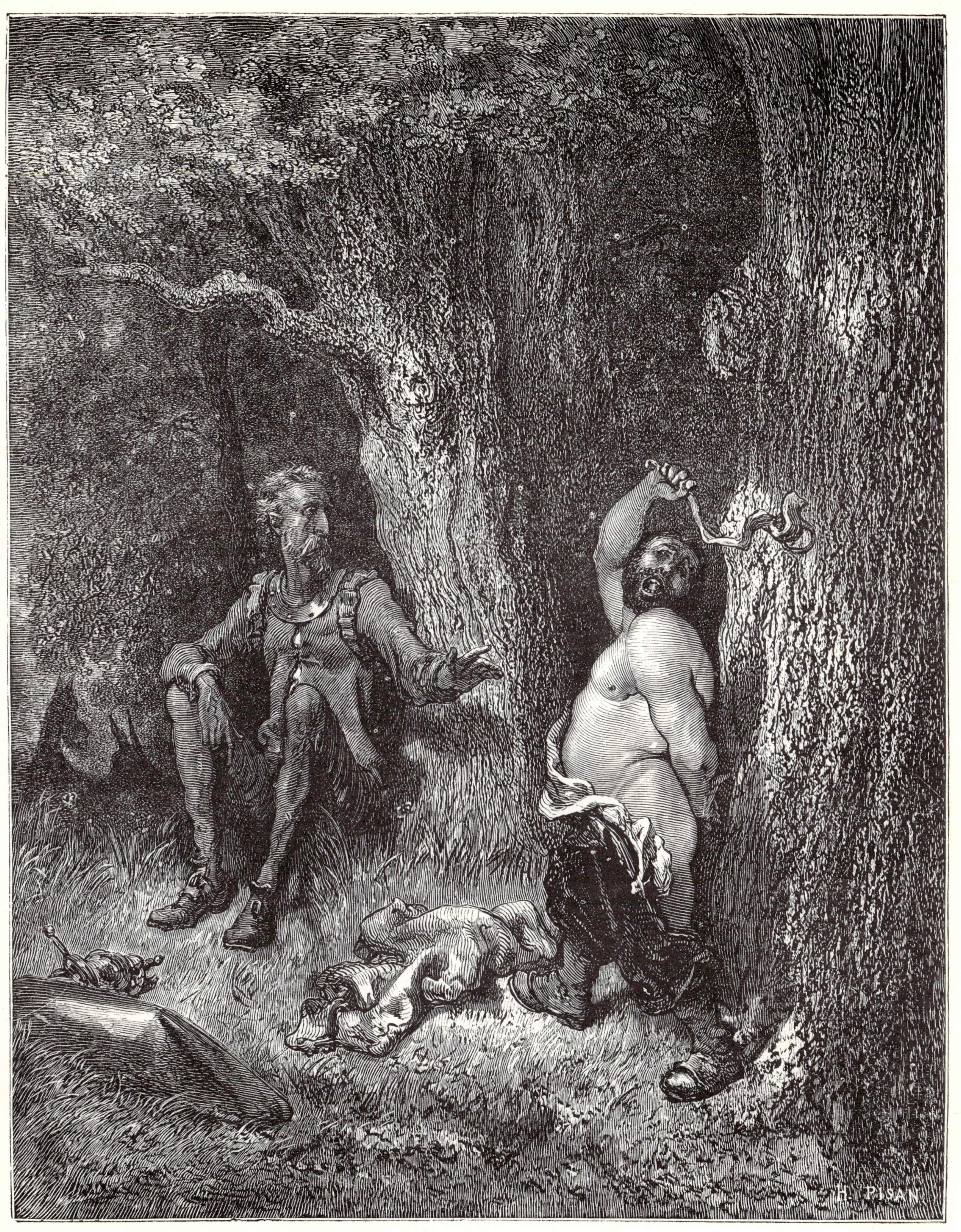

' 'Hold!' cried he; 'friend Sancho, stay the fury of thy arm.' '

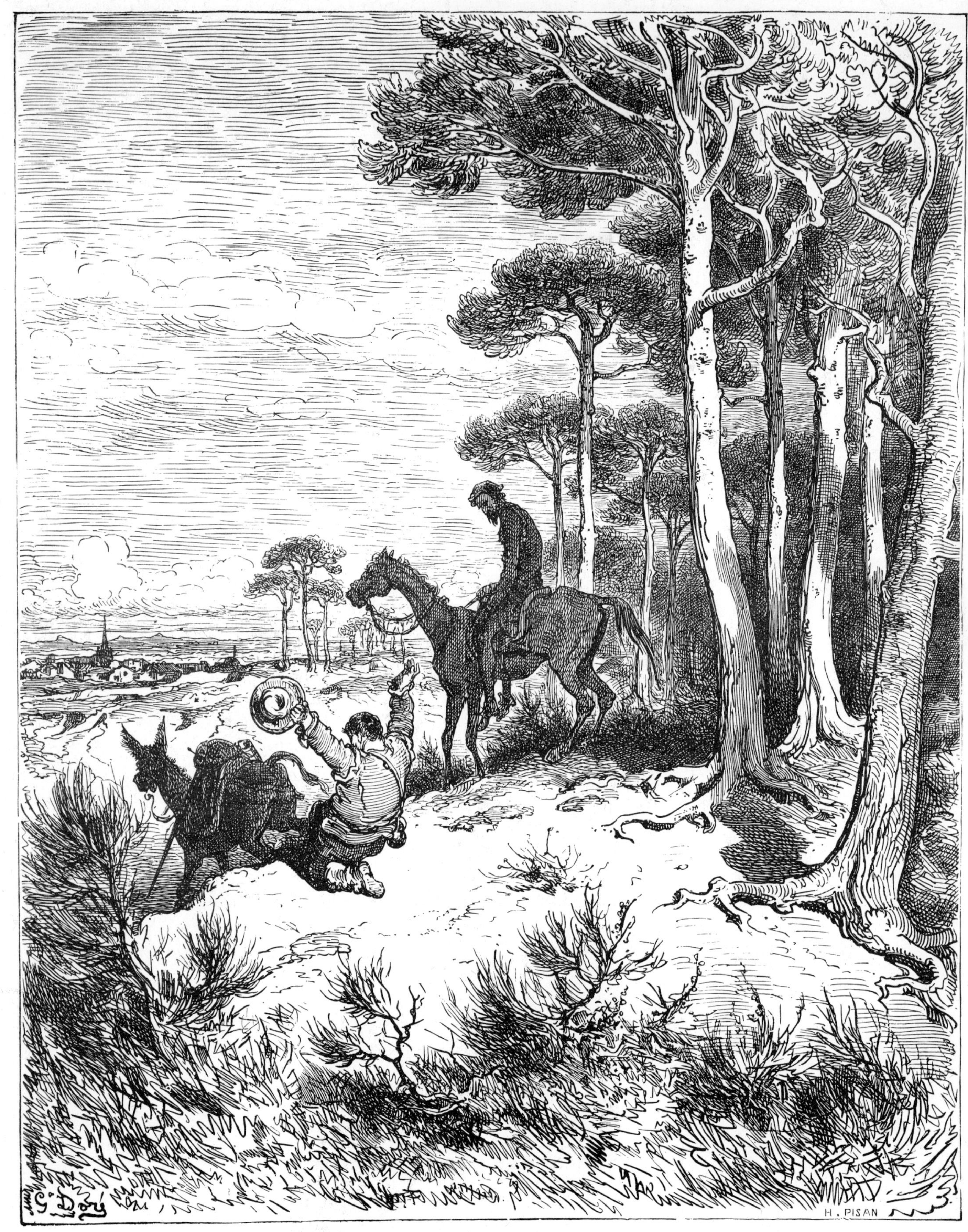

'Oh, my long-wished-for home!'

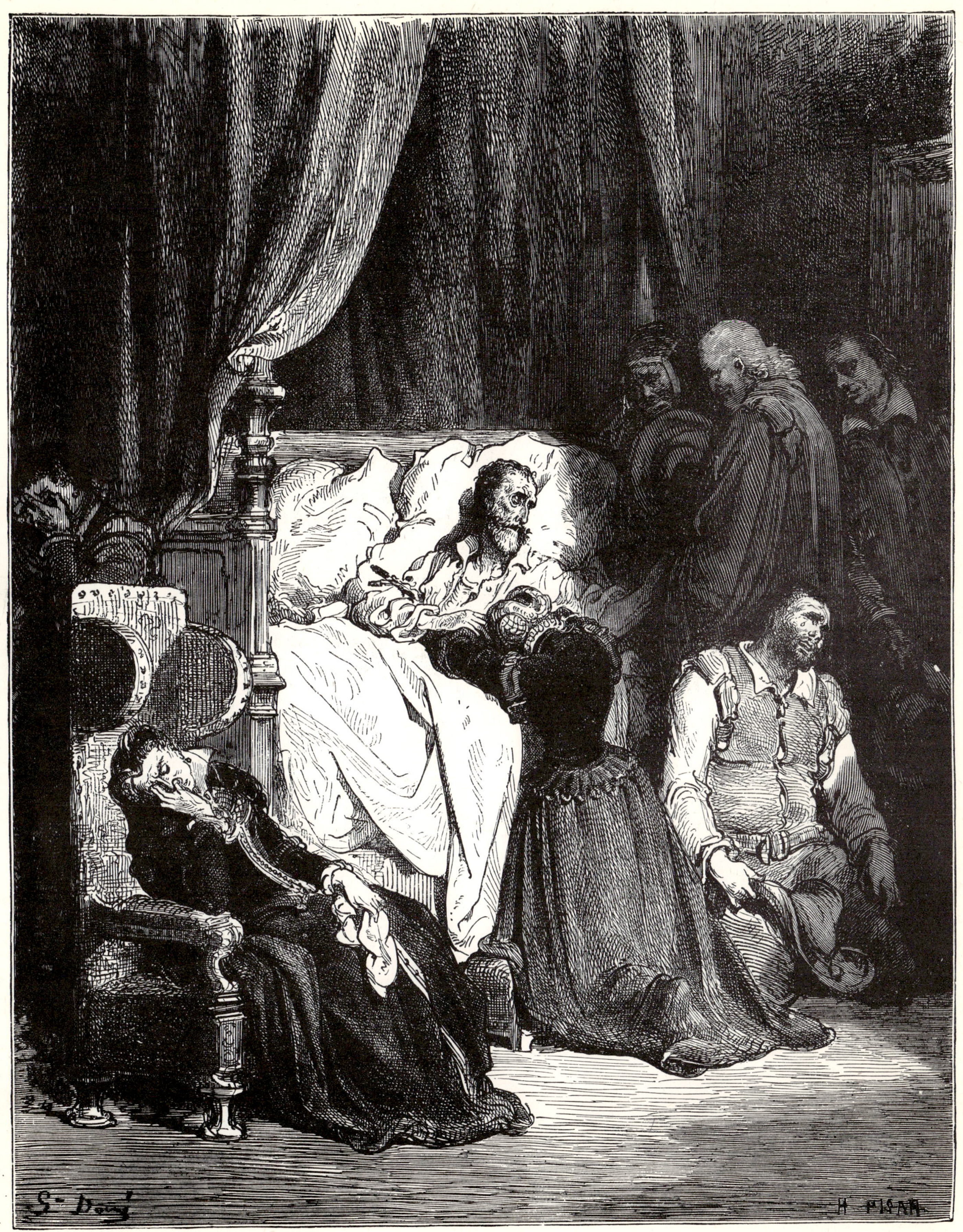

Death of Don Quixote.